Pageant of the Gun

Harold L. Peterson

Pageant of the Gun

A Treasury of
Stories of Firearms:
their romance and lore,
development and use
through ten centuries

Doubleday & Company, Inc.

GARDEN CITY, NEW YORK

1967

The guns on the jacket were furnished Courtesy of the Remington Museum,
Remington Arms Company, Inc., Ilion, N.Y. The revolver is a Remington 1890
Army .44/40 single-action; this specimen is a presentation gun, with pearl grips
and elegant engraving. The rifle is a half-stocked .32-caliber percussion lock with
set triggers, made in about 1830 at Eliphalet Remington's first plant in Ilion, N.Y.
Photograph by Leonard Heicklen.

Foreword

The history of arms is a fascinating subject, full of odd and surprising facts, interesting characters and dramatic incidents; it should be fun to read and study. Unfortunately, most books on the subject quickly become bogged down in statistics and detailed descriptions that are of more value to scholars than to the general public. I have written some such volumes myself, and they have their place. We need to know these details for proper identification of given specimens. But they are not the whole story. They leave out so much of the excitement, the humor, and the drama.

In the following chapters I have attempted to write an entirely different kind of arms book. Here are the stories (and observations regarding them) that have appealed to me over the years. Some of them follow the main highway of gun history; others take off on little-explored bypaths. Some deal with arms that had worldwide importance; others treat insignificant failures. In addition to the main content of this book—that is, firearms—I have devoted several chapters to related equipment and devices such as crossbows, bayonets, sabers, and ammunition. The evolution of guns is not, after all, an isolated phenomenon, but is closely related to the development of arms in general. The only criterion for inclusion is that I have found these subjects interesting, amusing or revealing. All of the chapters in this volume first appeared as part of a continuing series in *Guns and Hunting*, a monthly magazine devoted to sportsmen and firearms enthusiasts. In order to appeal to a knowledgeable audience, every article had to combine an accuracy of detail with an infusion of unfamiliar anecdote and some originality of interpretation. It has been the kind of project that makes thorough research most enjoyable.

This is arms history as I like to think of it, a vital account that involved *people* as well as things. The result is a book meant for the bedside table rather than the study—for pleasure and enjoyment rather than work.

Arlington, Virginia   Harold L. Peterson
1966

Contents

Part I

EVOLUTION

German crossbow of the mid-sixteenth century with steel bow and crannequin. Courtesy the Smithsonian Institution.

Chapter 1

The Terrifying Crossbow

"*A weapon hateful to God and unfit for Christians*," declared the Second Lateran Council in 1139. With these words the Church, acting as Europe's moral sovereign, banned the crossbow for military purposes (except, of course, against infidels). Many European leaders, especially the mounted knights who would be its chief targets, agreed, for this was a weapon whose arrows could pierce the finest armor then made. The English Barons who forced King John to sign the epic Magna Carta in 1215 felt this way, too, and they included a proviso banning crossbowmen from coming to their island. Other leaders disagreed. They wanted this terrible weapon for their armies. Richard the Lion-Hearted of England was one who favored it, to his sorrow; he died near Limoges, France, of a wound from a crossbow bolt, or arrow, in 1199. Pope Innocent III again banned the crossbow about 1200, but it was a futile gesture. Like all the dread new weapons of history before or since, it had quickly been accepted as a tool of war.

The arm that aroused all this soul-searching and furor had been developed many centuries before. Probably it had first appeared in the East or Near East. It was known by the Romans, who used large, heavy crossbows as siege weapons. After the fall of the Roman Empire, crossbows seem to have disappeared for a period, finally coming into use again during the tenth century. Almost immediately, they started to attract attention. Their use began to spread throughout Europe, and the frantic efforts to outlaw them had little or no effect on their increasing popularity. The crossbow itself was nothing more than a short, powerful bow mounted crosswise on a stock—or tiller, as it was usually called. In the beginning, these bows were made of wood, then of built-up layers of whalebone or horn, wood, and sinew, and finally, beginning in the 1400s, of steel. When the bow was bent, the string was pulled back and hooked in a notch on a rotating nut which, in turn, was held in position by the upper tip of the trigger. A short arrow called a bolt or quarrel could then be laid in the shallow channel on the top of the tiller, and the bow was ready to fire. Pressure on the trigger freed the nut, which revolved and released the bowstring to propel the bolt on its course.

The average military crossbow, carried by the equivalent of today's infantryman, had a tiller from about 2½ to three feet long and a bow perhaps 2½ to 2¾ feet from tip to tip (when not bent in firing position). Siege crossbows were much larger, of course. Typical infantry arms generally shot a bolt that measured about 12 to 18 inches long—a good bit shorter than the standard longbow arrow. The tiller was shaped like a short, fairly straight gunstock, and the bowstring was a thick length of hemp or flax strands, usually well waxed to withstand exposure to dampness. The string had to be tremendously strong to withstand the great tension when the bow was drawn.

The earliest wooden crossbows were flexible enough to bend by hand. However, those made of steel or composites such as whalebone, horn, and sinew required some sort of mechanical aid. Some early forms made use of a belt hook-and-pulley arrangement. Fairly weak bows could also utilize simple lever devices known variously as goat's-foot levers, dog's-foot levers, or gaffles. For really powerful bows, there were windlasses with winding arms and a series of pulleys or a gear-and-rack arrangement known as crannequin. To offset pressure against the nut, sears were often added to the trigger assembly; and for precision shooting, complete "set triggers" were sometimes installed, especially during the late 1500s. These worked much the same way as more modern set-trigger arms: pulling one trigger would position the sear of another for hair-trigger let-off.

Since it was necessary to use a mechanical device to bend the powerful crossbows, they were not nearly as fast-shooting as the famed English longbow—and most of them shot only slightly harder. However, they had another advantage that endeared them to most military commanders: A soldier could learn to shoot a crossbow reasonably well in far less time than it would take him to become a skilled archer with the longbow. Aiming, in particular, was vastly simplified. Holding a crossbow to his shoulder—as one would a rifle—a shooter could learn to put bolts into a target the size of a man's chest at 100 yards. In many cases, the bolt itself, positioned in a straight, shallow groove, served as a sight. But on bows of late manufacture (especially those used for target shooting) there was sometimes a bead or aperture sight.

Modern scientific tests have uncovered much information about the performance of military crossbows employed in the early 1500s. One such antique bow was found to have a 470-pound pull. Its 1¼-ounce bolt traveled at the rate of 138.7 feet per second. This compares with 133.7 feet per second for a longbow with a 68-pound pull. The reason for this small difference lies in the fact that the string of the longbow pushes against its arrow for a much greater distance than the cross-

Flemish crossbow of about 1600 with windlass.
Author's collection.

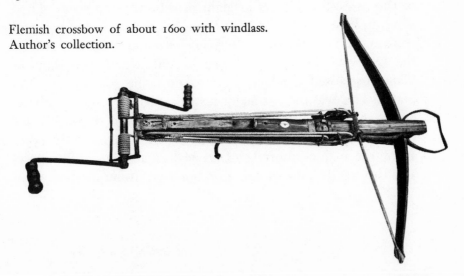

bow string before the arrow leaves the bow. The longbow is therefore more efficient in transmitting velocity to the projectile. While the crossbow bolt travels with only about a tenth the speed of a .22 bullet, it is much larger and can therefore inflict surprisingly great damage despite its comparative slowness.

Although the short arrow of a crossbow does not have a high initial velocity, it retains its speed well. The point-blank range for an average military or hunting crossbow—the distance at which a target can be hit without elevating the point of aim—has been estimated at 60 to 75 yards. And one recent test of a really heavy siege crossbow found it capable of sending its bolt completely through a ¾-inch plank at this distance.

Such power may not seem tremendous by today's firearms standards, but it was sufficient to penetrate armor if the arrow struck squarely. In tests at the H. P. White Ballistics Laboratory in Bel Air, Maryland, crossbow bolts easily pierced metal.

It might seem reasonable to suppose that a 470-pound pull would make a crossbow effective at very long range, and it is true that an aiming elevation of 45 degrees could stretch the maximum range to about 350 yards; accuracy and hitting power, however, were poor at such distances.

Crossbows were used for military purposes throughout almost all of Europe. Even in England, where the longbow was a national weapon and a matter of pride, crossbows were commonly used at least for siege purposes. In America, the earliest of the Spanish explorers brought crossbows with them. They were, in fact, among the arms brought over by Columbus, and were the principal projectile weapons on such heroic treks as the De Soto, De Vaca, Coronado and Narváez expeditions that crisscrossed much of what is now the southern United States. This was the last major historical role for the crossbow, however. As firearms became more reliable and reasonably accurate, they superseded both crossbow and longbow. By 1550, all of the major powers of Europe had abandoned the bow, and the last listings of military bows in America date from the 1570s. Even then they appear to have been obsolete arms stored in the Spanish forts of Florida.

But crossbows have been popular for sport as well as military purposes since their early development. Heavy bows similar to the military type were used for big game, while light bows—some designed for throwing stones or even lead balls instead of arrows—were manufactured for hunting birds, rabbits, and other small game. There were special target bows, too, and these were often very heavy affairs with peep sights and set triggers. Such sporting bows continued in use well after the military bow had disappeared. In fact, target shooting with the crossbow is still an active sport. There is crossbow target competition in Germany, Austria and Belgium.

Meets are held by the Crossbow Guild in Bruges, Belgium, for example, to pursue the ancient sport of "popinjay" shooting. Originally, the popinjay was a wooden bird tied as a target atop a pole. In some contests, the same type of target is still used, but at Bruges the popinjay is a cluster of feathers fastened to the top of a 90-foot tower, and sometimes several such popinjays are hoisted up on a kind of target rack. The object of the game is to knock them off, using a special crossbow with target sights and a blunt bolt.

The tradition of crossbow competition has even survived in the United States, where groups of target shooters use mod-

Shooters with crossbow and early hand cannon, from a manuscript of 1430–40.

ern, streamlined crossbows with nylon strings and rifle-shaped stocks. For a while, it seemed that crossbow hunting would become popular in this country, but it has now been outlawed in almost all states because this arm is silent as well as powerful. The authorities feared that it might be used for poaching and night hunting. And so, with the exception of targetry, there is little use today for the weapon that once horrified the entire civilized world with its dreadful power and accuracy.

Chapter 2

The First Handgun

No one knows who invented the hand cannon. It may have been a solitary genius in Central Europe or a number of men working independently who grasped the fact that a small cannon fired by a single soldier could be an effective weapon against enemy troops. The big guns then in use were fired at forts and castle walls; with the little pieces, human beings became the prime target.

The development of the hand-operated gun came slowly. Gunpowder was first described in Europe by the Franciscan monk Roger Bacon around 1250. Cannon are known to have been in use at least by 1326, possibly as early as 1300. After a time, much smaller versions of these weapons began to appear—actually the forerunners of today's handguns. "Hand cannon," as they were often called, must have appeared before 1350, for mention of their use dates from mid-century.

It is hard to understand why their development took so long, for at the start they were simple affairs. The big guns had merely been scaled down to a size that one or two men could hold and operate. Certainly there is nothing complicated about a tube of cast bronze or wrought iron closed at one end and with a touchhole for lighting the charge drilled in the top of the barrel near the breech. The only difference between the big guns and the small ones lay in the fact that the latter were frequently attached to a pole, or "tiller," the forerunner of the modern stock.

This pole had two purposes: it provided leverage to help control recoil and it afforded a cool handle when the metal became hot from repeated firing. At first the barrel was simply laid atop the end of the tiller, and iron bands were wound around to join them. In later and more sophisticated patterns the end of the tiller was scooped out to receive the barrel before the bands were applied. In still other forms the end of the barrel was forged into a tang that could either be driven into the end of the pole or provided with a socket which held the pole.

The earliest examples of these guns were usually very short and light. In 1364 the town of Perugia, Italy, ordered five hundred of them, each to be no longer than the palm of a man's hand. A specimen from Sweden is eight inches long, and the moat of a robbers' stronghold in Germany recently yielded the largest one of all—a .70-caliber barrel 12¼ inches long. The length of the tiller depended somewhat on the size of the barrel and also on the build and preference of the shooter, but most tillers averaged from three to four feet.

A German manuscript of 1390 tells how these hand cannon were loaded. First came the powder, poured in at the muzzle. Since gunpowder was apt to be weak in those days, an alarming quantity of it was used—enough to fill three-fifths of the barrel! This was rammed down well; then a space was left before a wooden plug, or *sabot*, was inserted with the ball on top. By this time there was very little bore left to guide the ball in flight. The gunner knew it would go generally forward when he fired, but that was about all he could count on.

This lack of accuracy probably did not bother the fourteenth-century soldier as much as we might think, for he couldn't look where he was pointing anyway. In the first

Hand cannon with socket for attaching tiller, fourteenth century. Courtesy Museum of Art and History, Geneva.

place, he was busy trying to hold the gun and steady it against the recoil. He did this by bracing the end of the tiller against the ground or clamping it between his left arm and body while holding it with his left hand just behind the breech of the barrel. With his right hand he held the red-hot firing wire or glowing coal which he was about to thrust into the touchhole to set off the charge. This meant he had to keep his eyes fixed on the hole to make sure he applied the fire to it rather than to his left hand. He could not possibly look at his target.

The only way a gun could be aimed was to have one man hold it and another apply the fire. This was sometimes done, especially after bigger pieces began to appear, but by then barrels had also been lengthened to give more guidance to the ball.

Gradually hand cannon improved. The touchhole was moved from the top of the barrel to the right side. A ledge or pan to hold a little priming powder was added below it, which made ignition more certain. Then a cover was added to this pan to protect the priming powder from the weather and to keep it from spilling out.

Next came a great advance—the invention of the match. This was a twisted rope of hemp or other fiber that had been soaked in a solution of saltpeter so that it would burn slowly and steadily and maintain a glowing coal, much as punk does. Now the gunner was free to move around. With either the glowing coal or the firing iron, he had had to stay near a fire and seize one or the other at the last second before firing. A length of match, however, would burn for some time, and once it was lit the gunner could walk around as he pleased.

All these developments had appeared by 1400 or shortly thereafter. In the years that followed, hand cannon became an important part of most major armories. Johann Ziska, the Bohemian general, demonstrated their value in the Hussite civil wars of 1423–24 when his peasants beat back the fully armored German and Hungarian knights of the Holy Roman Empire. Further improvements came with a movable holder for the match, which ensured that the burning end would strike the pan and so permit the shooter to look where he was aiming. By 1475 the first real gun lock—the matchlock—had appeared; there is a picture of one in a German manuscript of that year.

Still the simple hand cannon continued in use. Large specimens were made for wall guns; small, cheap ones were used to arm peasant levies. When Christopher Columbus set foot in the New World, an old "hand gonne" and a Turkish bow were among the weapons of the landing party. Fragments of others have been found on the sites of the first Spanish settlements in the Caribbean. Thus, a century and a half after its introduction and already obsolete, the hand cannon, earliest of the small arms, took its place in the history of American guns.

Chapter 3

When Matchlocks Were Modern

Many a hunter today considers himself a skilled woodsman, conversant with the habits of the game he seeks and capable of outwitting his quarry. Realizing the importance of good equipment, he wants the best available weapon. It must be accurate at the desired range, quick to load and fire, safe to carry yet ready for instant action. He could not conceive of a firearm that took minutes to prepare for use, required a wick burning in the midst of loose powder, and with luck might hit a man-sized target at 60 yards! Yet this was the gun—the matchlock—carried by most of the early immigrants to these shores. With it the Pilgrim shot his wild turkey and deer, the Virginian defended himself against hostile Indians, and other settlers along the Eastern seaboard employed it for both hunting and soldiering.

The matchlock was developed in Europe around the time Columbus left Spain to seek the Indies. Crude as it was, it represented a great advance in weaponry. The principle was simple. Loose black powder was poured into the barrel and rammed to the bottom—but not hard enough to form lumps that would burn slowly instead of exploding. A ball and wad were rammed in on top and finer powder was poured into a priming pan on the outside of the barrel, from which a touch-hole gave access to the charge within. To fire the gun, the shooter opened the cover of the pan and touched the lighted end of a wick, or match, to the fine priming powder. As this ignited, the flame passed through the hole in the barrel and set off the charge inside.

In some of the earliest types the shooter simply held the match in his hand—a very unsatisfactory method, since when he looked to make sure he was putting the match in the right place he had to take his eye off his target. The next step was the invention of a little vise on the end of a movable arm to which the wick could be clamped. This arm, called the serpentine, was connected to a lever trigger in such a way that pressure on the lever lowered the end of the vise toward the pan. When the pressure was released, a spring raised the arm again and took the lighted wick away from the pan.

While the wick did ignite the powder, it was anything but efficient. Friction matches were unknown in those days, so a fire had to be kindled with flint and steel in order to light the wick—a slow process that made it necessary to have the match burning well in advance of the actual shot. The gunner also had to light both ends at the same time so that if one end went out, the priming powder could be kindled from the other end of the match. Rain, of course, extinguished the match, making the gun useless, so there was no shooting in wet weather or even in a high wind, which was a terrific handicap. For example, Henry Hudson's men aboard the *Half Moon*, exploring in 1609 the river that now bears his name, were badly mauled by Indians when a shower put out the Dutchmen's matches without affecting the Indians' bowstrings.

The Indians quickly saw the colonists' dependence on the lighted match and took advantage of it. In 1607, as Captain Raleigh Gilbert and his men were exploring the coast of Maine, an Indian pretending friendship picked up the firebrand kept to kindle the matches as if he were going to light his pipe, but instead threw the brand into the ocean, rendering the party's guns useless. Down in what is now South Carolina, twenty Spanish soldiers marched on an Indian village to force the natives to give up some corn. They were met by

the Indians outside the village and told they could have all
the corn and other food they needed if they would just put
out the matches of their guns, which terrified the squaws. The
gullible Spaniards complied; all but one were promptly killed.

And there were still other drawbacks to the lighted match.
Its glow at night and its odor in the daytime prevented taking
enemy or game by surprise. Worst of all, the burning match
was always a hazard in the presence of powder. It had to be
removed from the lock each time the gun was loaded so that
there would be less danger of a premature discharge. Even so,
the glowing coal sometimes set off all the charges in the ban-
doliers which soldiers often wore around their necks to hold
ammunition. So redoubtable a warrior as Captain John Smith
of the Jamestown Colony in Virginia was injured and forced
to return to England when loose powder he was carrying in
his pocket accidentally caught fire in this way.

Italian matchlock musket of about 1580–1600 used at the Plymouth
colony. Courtesy the Pilgrim Society.

German matchlock musket, circa 1590–1620. Courtesy Robert Abels.

German matchlock musket, circa 1620–60. Author's collection.

From this it is obvious that the matchlock of the early explorer and colonist was in many ways inferior to the Indian's bow, for only extremely wet weather interfered with the latter's archery and he could shoot both faster and more accurately than the musketeer. The advantages of the gun lay in the psychological effect of its noise, flame, and smoke, the size of the hole it tore and the bones it smashed when it did hit, plus the fact that several balls could be loaded at a time. With all its disadvantages, the matchlock remained the standard military firearm in Europe for more than 150 years. It was an inexpensive gun to make and it was easy to keep in repair—factors that have always influenced officials.

In America, however, the situation was different. Here a man's life and that of his family depended on his ability not only to defend himself against the wily savage and wild beasts but to obtain fresh meat for his table. A gun was more valuable than any other weapon or implement, and he wanted the very best one he could get. Therefore, he was not so apt to be deterred by cost as would be a European war office. He started off with the standard gun—the matchlock—and he managed to survive, defeating Indians and shooting wild animals for food and clothing. One Massachusetts colonist is even reported to have hit a crow, which must have been blind luck unless seventeenth-century crows were a lot dumber than their present-day counterparts.

But the early settler was not satisfied with this clumsy, unreliable, unsafe, and inaccurate firearm. Better guns were available in Europe, though they were not in general use. Conditions in America demanded them, and by the time of the first Thanksgiving there were a few flintlocks and wheel locks in Plymouth. The next fall there were more, and within fifteen years the matchlock had all but vanished—well over a century before European armies finally decided to abandon it.

Chapter 4

The Complicated Wheel

To gun designers, the ideal firing mechanism is one that does its job as efficiently and as simply as possible. Throughout the long history of firearms, every new ignition system has reflected this desire for simplicity—every one, that is, except the wheel lock. This mechanical marvel started out as a complicated device, and succeeding years saw it become even more complicated. For over two hundred years, from the early sixteenth to the eighteenth century, it pursued its own course in the opposite direction from the usual evolutionary path.

Strangely, the principle of the wheel lock was simple: the wheel produced sparks to ignite the priming powder through the friction of stone and steel. This was the manner in which the average European householder had started his fires for centuries. But the wheel lock did it the hard way, much in the manner of the modern flint-and-wheel cigarette lighter. Contrary to popular belief, iron pyrite and not flint was the striking substance generally used. A piece of this mineral was held in a "dog-head" clamp at the end of a pivoted arm and was pushed against the roughened edge of a steel wheel by spring pressure. A key turned this wheel, winding it up against another spring, to which the wheel was connected by a chain. A series of cams, sears and smaller springs then held the wheel in its wound—cocked—position and released it when the trigger was pulled, at the same time automatically opening the cover of the pan to expose the priming powder as the spinning wheel and iron pyrite produced a shower of sparks. A "simple" wheel lock consisted of thirty-five to fifty separate parts. More complicated models occasionally had two or three times that number.

No one knows exactly when this mechanic's delight (or nightmare) was invented. It may have developed slowly, with more than one designer contributing to its creation. The earliest evidence of such a lock, however, comes from the sketchbook of one of history's most prolific inventors, Leonardo da Vinci, who lived from 1452 to 1519. In his famous *Codex Atlanticus*, there are drawings of a primitive form of the lock showing several alternate methods for attaching the connecting chain from the mainspring to the wheel spindle. These are obviously design drawings. Da Vinci may have been trying to improve an existing lock, or he may actually have been sketching a lock that he had invented himself. It is intriguing to think this might have been one of the old master's inventions that actually got into production before his death, unlike so many of his other dreams—submarines, flying machines and so on—that had to wait centuries for technology to catch up with his imagination. The exact date of these first diagrams for the wheel lock is uncertain, but the best guess of his-

German wheel lock pistol, circa 1590. Courtesy the Smithsonian Institution.

Italian wheel lock pistol, early 1600s. Courtesy the Smithsonian Institution.

torians is 1508. It is possible that other designers were working on the same idea at about this period but there is no way to know for sure.

Within a few years, the wheel lock had become well known throughout central Europe. The earliest surviving specimens that can definitely be dated were made between 1521 and 1526, but there are some Italian wheel lock guns combined with crossbows and some primitive Hungarian locks that may very well be a decade older. Charles V of Spain imported wheel lock makers to his country, and before the end of the century the new lock was also being made in workshops as far off as England and Sweden. Throughout the history of the system, however, its true home remained southern Germany and northern Italy. This was the center for wheel lock production, and this ignition system continued in use there after it had been abandoned elsewhere.

The mechanism had several drawbacks as well as advantages in comparison with the earlier matchlock. To a shooter who didn't want to be seen, the lack of a telltale match might be an advantage. But without the glowing wick to indicate that a gun was ready to fire, accidental discharges increased, and the famous excuse that "I didn't know the gun was loaded" made its appearance. Furthermore, the wheel, with its springs and cams, was such a complicated device that it was difficult and expensive to repair. And if the indispensable winding key, or spanner, was lost, the gun was out of commission until a replacement key could be obtained. Despite its involved construction, however, the wheel lock functioned very efficiently. Ignition was exceptionally quick—much faster, in fact, than in many later systems. It was also certain; wheel locks seldom misfired. Wind and even light rain were no hindrance as long as the powder charge in the barrel remained dry. Most important, the wheel lock could be loaded and wound whenever convenient. It would then stay ready for use at any moment, without further preparation.

This was a far cry from the cumbersome matchlock with its need for a burning wick, and the effect on both warfare and everyday life was great. Since there was no need to hold a burning match in the fingers of the left hand, guns could be managed with only one hand. This made the pistol a practical cavalry weapon, and horsemen began to carry firearms on a large scale for the first time in the history of warfare. Since a wheel lock could be kept ready to fire at the touch of a trigger, booby traps and trip guns also came into use. And it was possible to carry a concealed firearm ready to shoot, a fact that caused grave concern to the legal authorities throughout Europe.

Despite its tremendous advantages, the wheel lock never supplanted the matchlock as a standard infantry arm because the cost of manufacture was too great. Thus it remained the weapon of cavalry and elite organizations such as princely bodyguards, or the personal arm of a gentleman who could afford the best. One major exception, however, was the American colonist. Guns were so important in this wild country that the settlers were often willing to pay whatever it might cost to get the most up-to-date type. There was probably a greater proportion of wheel locks to population in colonial America than in any other place in the world.

The cost factor also had an interesting effect on the guns themselves. Since these were expensive arms, customers demanded quality workmanship. There were many plain wheel locks, it is true, but a crudely made specimen was a great rarity. There was a tendency for the buyer to spend a little more and get an extra-special weapon, and this brought the art of decorating firearms to a new state of development. Probably no other type of firearm has ever boasted such a high percentage of decorated specimens. It also led to demands for special features, and so the complicated wheel lock became even more complicated. There were multi-shot arms with several barrels and sometimes two or three locks. There were revolvers and there were even some "machine guns" that

Wheel lock musket, early 1600s. Courtesy the Smithsonian Institution.

worked on the Roman-candle principle, with the first ignition setting off successive shots in a chain reaction. Such a gun might have four barrels and as many as sixteen shots, with one ball and powder charge in front of another in some of the barrels. A powder train connected each load to the next one, so that a single trigger pull resulted in sixteen fast firings. Little chimneys were added to carry the smoke from the priming powder up and away from the shooter's eyes.

Especially popular were self-winding locks that eliminated the need for a key. Several variations of this type were designed, but the most common was wound up by pushing the doghead—the arm and clamp that held the pyrite—forward and pulling it back so that it rested on the pan cover.

There were also enclosed locks, with all parts of the mechanism inside and protected from both dampness and damage. The height of all this striving for something extra was undoubtedly achieved in arms made in the early 1600s for Louis XIII of France by Pierre Bergier. These guns would fire underwater! The locks and pans were hermetically sealed, and as long as the shooter kept the muzzle above water (and surfaced to load and prime) he could bang away while completely submerged. Of course, such guns had about as much practical submarine use as today's pens that write underwater, but the point is that wheel lock ignition made possible more variations and refinements than ever before. The majority of fine wheel locks were nevertheless made according to the traditional design, and the system owed its popularity to its basic advantages rather than to any eccentric features.

The flintlock eventually emerged to supplant the wheel for both everyday and special purposes. By 1650, the changeover was well under way, and by 1700 it was almost complete. There are always a few admirers of "the good old days," however, and one staunch conservative had a pair of wheel lock pistols made by LePage of Paris as late as 1828! They were probably the last ever ordered, for new inventions had long since ended the usefulness of the most complex ignition system ever employed in firearms.

Chapter 5

An Invention of Genius—
The Flintlock

The flintlock was clearly a superior gun action—a great achievement for its time. Compared to the unwieldy matchlock, it must have seemed the ultimate in a fast-handling, rapid-firing arm. Contrasted with the mechanical intricacies of a wheel lock, it was a paragon of simplicity, offering the advantages of greater safety, increased reliability and a smoother action, and for two hundred years it was the finest gun lock made. But the flintlock was more than this. It was truly a "handmaiden of history."

More than any previous firearm, it played a decisive role in events that shaped the world. It was used to fight the great wars of the eighteenth century, wars that determined monarchs to rule Spain and Austria and that established France as the leading power on the Continent. In India and North America, British and French troops armed with flintlocks fought for control of a colonial empire. Americans used these guns to gain their independence in the Revolutionary War and to defend that freedom in the War of 1812. And flintlock muskets brought the French and English rivalry to its climax at Waterloo. These were years of tremendous struggles, and it was the flintlock that determined the method of fighting and the outcome of battles.

Spark-striking actions—forerunners of the true flintlock—

had appeared during the first half of the 1500s. Italy and Spain produced the miquelet. The Scandinavian countries developed the Baltic lock and the so-called Scandinavian snaplock. Germany and the Low Countries favored the snaphaunce, which spread across into England and Scotland, where it was joined by two native systems, the English lock and the Scottish lock. All of these devices produced the necessary spark for igniting the gun powder by striking a chunk of flint against a piece of steel. All were generally effective, faster than the matchlock, less complicated (and therefore less expensive) than the wheel lock.

Still, there was a need for refinement. Some firing mechanisms, like the snaphaunce, utilized a "steel" (the striking plate) that was separate from the cover of the priming pan. Thus, the pan had to be opened by hand, or an extra device had to be included in the lock to open it automatically as the cock holding the piece of flint struck the steel. Other mechanisms, such as the English lock, boasted a combined steel and pan cover that opened automatically when the steel was struck, but these locks usually lacked an efficient safety device to prevent accidental firing when the pan was primed and the steel in position. Still other systems, such as the Scandinavian snaplocks, had outside mainsprings that were subject to damage. And there were other inadequacies as well.

All of these defects were clear to Marin le Bourgeoys. As an artist, sculptor, locksmith, clockmaker, "worker in moving globes and other mechanical inventions," and above all as a gunsmith, le Bourgeoys was familiar with all sorts of weapons and their mechanisms and with the latest scientific and artistic developments. Even though he lived in the provincial town of Lisieux in Normandy, far from the bustling city of Paris, his fame as an artist and craftsman was so great that King Henry IV appointed him a *valet de chambre* in 1598, and added a warrant granting him the privilege of lodgings in the grand gallery of the Louvre itself in 1608. This was a signal honor—and a long step up from his previous position as official painter to the Governor of Normandy—but the talented

Norman artist preferred to go on living in his native town, making only occasional trips to the capital to deliver the fruits of his genius. Shortly after 1600, his interest seems to have turned more and more from painting to gunsmithing. He invented an air gun, designed a new kind of crossbow, an improved hunting horn, and a new kind of arquebus.

This firearm is not described in any detail in contemporary documents, but it may well have been the first flintlock, for it is highly probable that Marin le Bourgeoys invented that world-shaking mechanism. The evidence is circumstantial but impressive.

The oldest known flintlock—probably made during the first decade of the seventeenth century—bears his name. The second oldest was made by his brother, Jean, and the next earliest group of flintlocks was made by the brothers and their apprentices, some thirty years before the use of the new lock became widespread in the mid-1600s. These facts, combined with Marin's reputation as a mechanical genius and a firearms inventor, make an excellent case for naming him the father of the flintlock.

In this new lock, le Bourgeoys combined the best features of the older spark-striking systems. From the miquelet, he took the combined striking steel and pan cover (or frizzen, as it is called today). From the Dutch snaphaunce, he borrowed the idea of a well protected inside mechanism. But at this point his own genius took over. He redesigned the sear so that it operated vertically instead of horizontally, as had all previous sears, and he made it engage notches in a tumbler attached to the cock. This mechanical change permitted both a safety, or half-cocked, position and a full-cock step that could be released smoothly and quickly by the pull of the trigger. Here at last was a strong, simple lock with a smooth, fast action and a good safety device.

Earliest known flintlock gun, made by Marin le Bourgeoys who probably invented the lock. Courtesy the Hermitage Museum, Leningrad.

Even Marin's earliest surviving flintlock boasts all of these advantages, and it is also a work of art that displays his many talents. The stock is embellished with beautifully sculptured metal and the wood itself is carved and inlaid with equal skill.

The lock plate, side plate, barrel and other metal surfaces are beautifully etched with scenes, vines, and arabesques. The main piece of sculpture on the stock is a helmeted female figurine, and the stock itself is gracefully shaped to represent a stag's leg and hoof. A metal reinforcing bar, extending straight from the trigger guard to the butt, helps to retain something of a traditional stock contour in spite of the unusual stag-leg sculpture.

Detail of the butt of the Bourgeoys flintlock showing the lock and some of the exquisite decoration. Stock is shaped like a deer's leg. Courtesy the Hermitage Museum, Leningrad.

Interior of the Bourgeoys lock showing the simplicity of the action. Courtesy the Hermitage Museum, Leningrad.

This flintlock is truly an arm fit for a king, and it actually did belong to one—or possibly even to two. The gun is today in Russia, in the Hermitage Museum in Leningrad, where it found its way long ago from the collection of King Louis XIII of France. According to tradition, however, it had originally belonged to Louis' predecessor, Henry IV, who died in 1610. This is the date usually assigned to the gun, but it might have been made even a few years earlier, for le Bourgeoys is known to have presented an arquebus "completely of his own design" to King Henry in 1606. Two more flintlocks showing Marin's handiwork are in the Musée de l'Armée in Paris, and another, exceptionally beautiful gun made for Louis XIII by Marin's brother, Jean le Bourgeoys, is in a private collection in the United States. Since Jean died in 1615, the date of the flintlock's invention is closely bracketed.

From le Bourgeoys' town of Lisieux, the design of the flintlock was brought first to Paris, where pattern books were published for the new mechanism in the 1630s. It was still essentially a French lock, but within the next thirty years it had migrated to most of Europe and had begun to supplant the native locks. It had even made its appearance in America. By 1700, it was the standard action in the New World and in almost all of western Europe, and it was applied to all sorts of guns from muskets and blunderbusses to dueling pistols, Kentucky rifles, and even revolvers. The genius of the provincial Norman gunsmith had come to dominate the firearms of almost all the civilized world.

Chapter 6

The Discovery of Percussion

Shot-dodging ducks may well have ushered in the era of modern firearms. In about 1800, the Scottish lochs and marshes abounded with wildfowl of all sorts, but the Reverend Alexander John Forsyth, an ardent hunter, kept missing his birds. According to family legend, the good minister decided that his marksmanship was not at fault. The ducks could see the flash from the priming of his flintlock fowling piece, he believed, and the split second between this and the firing of the main charge gave them time to evade his shot. He grew tired of returning to his home at Belhelvie with smaller bags than he thought he merited, and he determined to do something about it. First he tried to hide the telltale flash by building a hood over the lock. It helped, but it was a clumsy arrangement. The ideal solution, he felt, would be to eliminate the free sparks and the flash altogether. He had heard of some chemical substances that exploded when struck sharply, and he wondered if some of them might be adaptable for setting off a firearm. At least it was worth a try.

These new materials about which the Reverend Forsyth had read were made by dissolving metals in acid. The salts that resulted were called fulminates. Chemists had discovered them many, many years before and had found that they were violently explosive. Some experimenters had thought of mixing them with gunpowder as a substitute for saltpeter—or perhaps even using them in place of gunpowder. They had tried fulminates of gold, silver, mercury and various other metals, and even potassium chlorate (an oxidizing agent used in matches and explosives), but none of them worked well. They were too violent, too unpredictable for use as the main charge, and none of the chemists thought of adapting one of the new substances as a primer only. That remained for Forsyth, inspired by the dodging ducks.

The Scottish clergyman was not a brilliant scholar, nor especially learned in the field of science, but he was persistent, observant and ingenious. These were the qualities that were to bring Forsyth success where others had failed. His first idea was simply to use one of the fulminates as a substitute for gunpowder in the priming pan. This was not satisfactory. The sparks from the flint sometimes ignited the new primer, but it did not flash as reliably as common gunpowder. Worse still, this primer frequently failed to set off the charge inside the barrel. Redesigning the cock of the gun so that it became a hammer and struck the fulminate directly brought better results. The primer detonated more readily and dependably from the blow than it had from the sparks. Still, it frequently failed to send sufficient flame through the touchhole to ignite the charge inside the barrel. The open pan of the flintlock seemed unsuitable for percussion ignition.

Patiently trying one shape and then another, Forsyth redesigned the part of the lock that was to hold the primer until he developed a confined area that directed the full force of the flame through the touchhole to produce sure ignition.

By 1805, he had produced a workable percussion lock. It had a tiny trough to hold the primer and a hammer with a flanged nose that closed off all possible routes for the flash except that which led to the bore. All that season Forsyth tested his new gun on the wildfowl of the nearby lochs and marshes. He was delighted with the results, and when he visited London the next year, he showed his fowler to fellow sportsmen and friends of a scientific bent.

That trip brought radical changes to both the Scottish clergyman's life and the whole field of firearms design. One of the cronies to whom Forsyth showed the gun was so intrigued that he persuaded him to exhibit it to Lord Moira, England's Master General of Ordnance. His Lordship was impressed with the gun and with the man who had invented it. He thought he saw military possibilities in the new system, so he asked Forsyth to stay in London and try to strengthen and simplify his lock. In short order, a leave of absence was obtained from Forsyth's parish, a workshop was established at the Tower of London, and gunworkers were hired to assist in the project. For the next year, Forsyth labored over percussion locks, both for small arms and cannon, but success eluded him. The mechanism remained delicate and expensive, and his one official test produced a disappointing performance. To make matters worse, Moira was replaced by a new Master General who lacked his vision and understanding of experimentation. Forsyth was ordered to settle up his accounts and clear his "rubbish" out of the Tower.

Though official sponsorship of percussion ignition had come to an end, the persevering Scotsman was by no means ready to give up. With the help of his friend James Watt, who had invented the steam engine and was familiar with mechanical engineering, Forsyth obtained a patent on the use of fulminates as primers for firearms. This patent was so broadly drawn that it covered all forms of fulminates and every method of using them for the purpose of ignition. It did, however, specifically illustrate the lock which Forsyth then considered his best design. The mechanism boasted a small pivoting magazine that held a reserve supply of the detonating compound and was shaped somewhat like a typical perfume bottle of the period. It was this feature that has caused collectors to give the lock its popular name—the "scent bottle." In addition to the primer, the magazine also held a striker—somewhat on the order of the modern firing pin.

To use the lock, the shooter turned the pivoting magazine upside down, then righted it again. This deposited a small

amount of the fulminate in the tube leading to the bore of the
piece, directly below the end of the striker. When the trigger
was pulled, the hammer struck the external end of the striker
and drove it against the priming compound, detonating the
fulminate and sending a spurt of flame into the bore. Forsyth's
patent was granted in April 1807, and with his invention
protected, he returned to his home in Scotland.

The scent-bottle lock may have been too expensive and
delicate to interest the military, but it delighted sportsmen.
Those who could afford it ordered arms with the new locks
from London gunmakers licensed by Forsyth to manufacture
his system. By 1811, business was prospering sufficiently for
the clergyman to set up his own "Patent Gun Manufactory"
in Piccadilly, London. From this establishment, he supplied
the demands of hunters and other gun fanciers for percussion
shoulder arms and pistols equipped with the scent-bottle lock
—or with a later version that utilized a sliding magazine for
the primer—until better systems were devised.

Forsyth apparently never thought of using the detonating

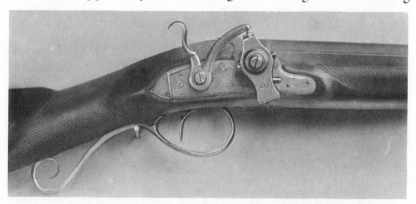

Forsyth scent-bottle lock. Courtesy the Smithsonian Institution.

Forsyth fowling piece with scent-bottle lock and interchangeable barrels.
Courtesy the Smithsonian Institution.

compound in any form but a loose powder that required a carefully machined and delicate magazine. Contemporary inventors apparently had more vision. Within a few years, dozens of other methods had been devised. There were pellet primers, patch primers, tube primers and a host of others, including the percussion cap and eventually the modern metal-cased cartridge. Every one of these innovations was a direct result of one Scottish hunter's exasperation with dodging ducks.

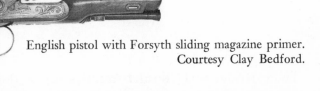

English pistol with Forsyth sliding magazine primer.
Courtesy Clay Bedford.

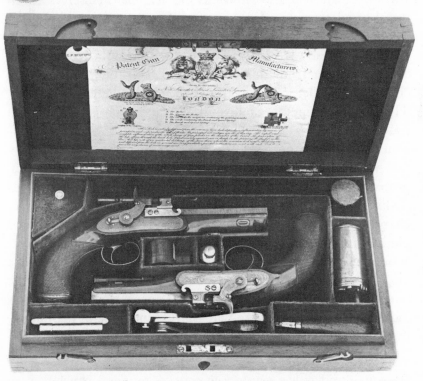

Cased pair of pistols manufactured by Forsyth's company with sliding magazines. Courtesy Clay Bedford.

Chapter 7

Old Yet New

The cartridge breechloader seems as new as today, and in some ways it is. But it is also almost as old as guns themselves. Even metal-cased cartridges have been used for centuries with varying degrees of success. In the beginning, of course, these cartridges were not self-primed. That is, they relied on a spark or flash of fire from some outside source, but they held the charge of powder, and sometimes they held the bullet as well. The modern principle of loading at the breech emerged from four centuries of experiment with methods of inserting self-contained ammunition.

The first cartridge breechloader was really a little cannon, probably used as early as the 1400s, and the cartridge was nothing but a separate chamber that could be loaded with a charge of powder in advance. This separate chamber looked like an iron beer mug complete with a handle, and it was about the same size as a pint mug. The mouth end tapered a bit, however, so that it could be inserted into the rear of the bore to form a reasonably tight joint when the chamber was locked in place. Also, there was a little touchhole in the device, through which the shooter ignited the charge. The cannon

Opposite: Breechloading cannon with separate "cartridge" chambers, from a print of the late 1600s.

that used this separate breech, or "cartridge," was usually a small swivel gun firing a spherical iron ball that weighed half a pound or perhaps a pound. The bore measured 1½ to two inches in diameter. Two men were needed to load and fire it. One man took a ball and inserted it into the base of the bore, followed by a ready-loaded chamber containing the powder charge. He locked this in place with a little wedge. Then he aimed the piece at the target and held it steady while his companion put a burning match to the touchhole of the chamber and fired the gun. While such cannon probably first appeared in the fifteenth century, they continued in use for over three hundred years.

Small arms, too, soon began to employ little metal cartridges or chambers. Matchlocks, wheel locks and flintlocks are all known to have utilized them. Sometimes a little trapdoor on top of the barrel flipped up so that the loaded cartridge could be inserted; sometimes the gun broke open like a modern double-barreled shotgun. Once in a while, these cartridges were designed to hold both the bullet and the powder, but

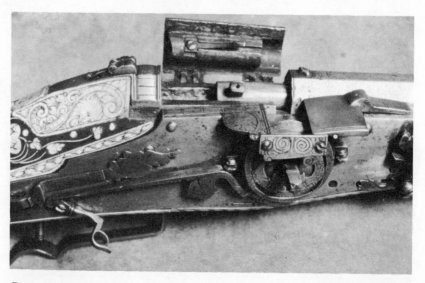

German breechloading wheel lock of about 1550. Note the separate chamber, or "cartridge," which is partially inserted. Courtesy Joe Kindig, Jr., and Ridge Press.

most often the projectile was inserted into the breech separately and followed by the cartridge. Always there was a touchhole in the side of the little cylinder so that the flash from the powder in the priming pan could set off the charge inside. The earliest surviving guns of this type date from the first half of the 1500s. They are wheel locks, and they all have hinged trapdoors on the barrel. King Henry VIII of England owned two of these breechloading wheel locks, and one of them is dated 1537. Henry also owned a large group of combination pistol-shields which were made toward the middle of the fifteenth century, probably for his personal bodyguard. The center of each shield boasts a small breechloading matchlock pistol that was loaded with a metal powder cartridge after a pivoted breechblock was lifted. Flintlock break-open guns appeared in the next century, and most seem to have been made in Austria or eastern Germany. A number of them survive in public and private collections today.

None of these early metal-cartridge systems ever became popular. Since cartridge cases offered a tight breech seal, and these guns were probably better than any other breechloaders of the time, their lack of success is a mystery. Shooters may have had trouble lining up the touchhole of the cartridge with that of the barrel, and there may have been the matter of expense since each metal case had to be made by hand and carefully fitted to the gun. Whatever the reasons, the fact remains that they never caught on, and all models are relatively scarce today. The collector who owns one has a rare prize.

It was after 1800 when really successful metal-cartridge breechloaders appeared. Even then, the new system did not look promising. The first major breakthrough was actually a dismal failure. In Paris, Samuel Jean Pauly (who sometimes called himself Johannes S. Pauly) invented a breechloader that utilized a metal cartridge which held a bullet and even carried its own priming mixture, though outside the case. In 1805, Alexander John Forsyth had developed a percussion compound that went off when struck, and Pauly made use of it in his invention of 1812, which utilized a firing-pin blow for ignition instead of the traditional spark. Pauly took a small dab of the priming mixture and placed it in a little depression on the outside of the cartridge base, where the firing pin could strike it directly. A tiny hole carried the flash from this priming to the charge inside. The firing pin was concealed inside the breech of the gun, and the outside "hammer" was used only for cocking the piece. Both shoulder arms and pistols were manufactured on the Pauly system. The long guns had lift-up breeches that exposed the rear of the chamber for insertion of the cartridge; the pistols had barrels that tipped down for this purpose. Pauly's guns worked very well when they were handled by a skilled man who loaded and operated them carefully. The French Army judged them too fragile for military use, however, and civilian sportsmen apparently agreed. Also, the percussion priming compound had a distressing habit of drying up and falling out of the little depression in the cartridge, so the ammunition sometimes failed to ignite at the critical moment. This bothered a great many shooters, and the Pauly gun joined its predecessors as an interesting but unsuccessful attempt.

The next few years witnessed the turning point. In the 1840s, a Frenchman named Flobert took the standard percussion cap of the period and squeezed a tiny bullet into its mouth. He didn't bother with a charge of powder; the explosion of the primer propelled the bullet. It was a very weak cartridge, but it was a completely self-contained unit, and it worked well enough for use at indoor shooting galleries.

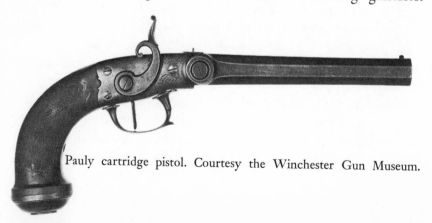

Pauly cartridge pistol. Courtesy the Winchester Gun Museum.

Flobert designed a simple gun to fire his cartridge, and it attained some popularity for its limited purposes. Even more important were pin-fire cartridges, which placed the primer inside the cartridge and under the end of a pin that passed through the case. When the pin was struck by the gun's hammer, it ignited the primer. Such cartridges became quite popular, for they contained a charge of powder and were therefore much more powerful than Flobert's invention. Shotguns, rifles, pistols, and even revolvers were made on the pin-fire system. And there were dozens of other cartridge variations—and guns to fire them as well. When two Americans by the name of Horace Smith and Daniel Baird Wesson developed both a rim-fire cartridge and a revolver for it in the 1850s, the era of the cartridge gun began in earnest. Interestingly, many of the designs for the new metal-cased cartridge guns featured the same moving breechblocks, trapdoor and break-open systems that had been used on the relatively unsuccessful cartridge guns of the sixteenth and seventeenth centuries. Some of these systems are still in use today. The basic breech concepts are old as the hills. Only the efficient and powerful cartridges are new.

Part II

THE
TWO GREAT
AMERICAN
CONFLICTS

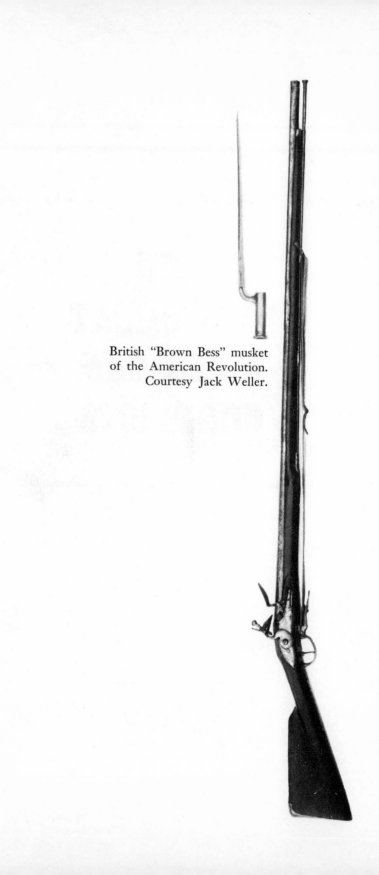

British "Brown Bess" musket
of the American Revolution.
Courtesy Jack Weller.

Chapter 8

The Revolutionary Gun

It was hot. The June sun beat down on the ragged, weary line of Americans stretched across Breed's Hill above the Charles River. All night long they had dug trenches. Morning found them still digging, strengthening fence rows, piling hay, improvising defenses of all sorts. There had been artillery fire, hard for green troops to take, but these men had stood it without stopping their work. Now they crouched behind their fortifications, peering along their musket barrels as 2300 magnificently disciplined British soldiers moved to the attack. On they came, line companies, light infantry, grenadiers and marines in perfect formation. Here was invincibility. No one could doubt it. Now they were 100 feet away. It was time for untrained men to run, but no one fled. Now a distance of only 50 feet was left. Perhaps the Americans were too frightened to move.

Then it happened. The wall, the fence and the ditch exploded in a sheet of flame and lead. A slightly ragged volley by professional standards, perhaps, but it had been shrewdly delayed until the last moment and it had been aimed low. Maybe old Israel Putnam had ordered, "Don't shoot till you see the whites of their eyes!" and maybe he hadn't, but that's what they did. Buckshot and ball tore into the beautiful lines, and they melted away. Caps and muskets flew through the air as the huge balls dropped each soldier they hit. Shocked survivors looked dazedly at the great holes in the line where their comrades had stood a moment before and at the crumpled forms upon the ground. Then they fell back.

Three times the British climbed that terrible hill and faced the deadly volleys. Then, their ammunition exhausted, the Americans were forced to retreat. But before they ran out of bullets they had killed or wounded 1054 of the Redcoats, almost half of the attacking force. The British had won the Battle of Bunker Hill but they had paid so dearly that they wanted no more such victories.

The guns that did so much damage at Bunker Hill and in other battles of the Revolution were no secret weapons. They were the standard muskets of the day, and all of them were remarkably alike, whether they were of American, British, French, or German origin. They were flintlocks, and they were smoothbores. In length they ran from four and a half to a little over five feet, and they weighed from 12 to 14 pounds. Calibers ranged from .69 for the French through .75 for the British to a little more than .80 for some of the German models. At the beginning of the war, Americans followed the British patterns, but after 1777 and the alliance with France, they shifted to the French models.

The chief characteristics of all the muskets involved were their large bores and the fact that they were not rifled. A big ball had tremendous stopping power. Modern pointed bullets of small diameter and high velocity may pass through the fleshy part of the body without dropping the victim, but a ball three-quarters of an inch in diameter will almost always knock a man to the ground, no matter where it hits him. This

French "Charleville" musket, Model 1763. Author's collection.

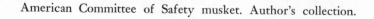

American Committee of Safety musket. Author's collection.

was important in breaking up an attack such as that on Bunker Hill. In addition to the large ball, it was often the practice to use three or four buckshot, a quarter of an inch in diameter, in the charge, thus adding more missiles and increasing the chances of a hit.

The fact that the barrels were not rifled allowed the guns to be loaded quickly. For a rifle to function, the ball had to fit tightly. This was achieved by centering the ball in a patch of greased linen and forcing it down the barrel, which took a good deal of time. Smoothbores, however, permitted the use of a loose-fitting ball which dropped down the barrel. With such a bullet it was possible to prepare paper cartridges containing a ball and a measured charge of powder, all ready for instant use. To load, the soldier pulled a cartridge from his box, bit off the end, poured a little powder into the flash pan, dumped the rest down the barrel and followed it with the ball and the remnant of paper to serve as a wad. The ramrod was necessary to make sure that the ball was seated firmly, but no real force was used in the process.

Using such cartridges, a well-trained soldier could load and fire with remarkable speed. In most European armies a recruit had to fire fifteen shots within 3¾ minutes—a sustained rate of fire of one shot every 15 seconds—before he was excused from the "awkward squad." Astounding as this may seem when one considers all of the motions involved, students today have found that they can match it with relatively little practice.

In accuracy, however, the musket left much to be desired. Since the ball fitted loosely, it bounced down the barrel and might leave it at any one of a number of angles. Major George Hanger, a British soldier during the Revolution and an expert marksman, summed up the accuracy of the standard musket:

A soldier's musket, if not exceedingly ill-bored (as many of them are), will strike the figure of a man at eighty yards; it may even at 100, but a soldier must be very unfortunate indeed who shall be wounded by a common musket at 150 yards, provided his antagonist aims at him; and as to firing at a man at 200 yards with a common musket, you may just as well fire at the moon and have the same hopes of hitting your object. I do maintain and will prove, whenever called on, that no man was ever killed at 200 yards, by a common soldier's musket, by the person who aimed at him.

Such a verdict would frighten the average shooter today, but the eighteenth-century trooper was not worried about accuracy. As at Bunker Hill, attacks were made in close formation against an enemy who also stood shoulder to shoulder. Shooting was done in volleys by command. Individual targets did not matter, for with a tight mass of the enemy attacking it was more important to fire as many bullets in their general direction as possible; a good percentage would be bound to take effect. This is much the same theory on which automatic weapons are employed today, creating fields of fire through which an enemy must pass. For this task the musket was admirably suited, as the results of many Revolutionary War battles proved in deadly fashion. When accuracy was needed, there was the rifle, an excellent arm in the hands of skilled marksmen for scouting, sniping and other special functions. But for the usual stand-up battle of massed bodies of men, the musket, with its four crashing bullets a minute and its vicious bayonet thrust if necessary, was the ultimate weapon.

Chapter 9

The Redcoats' "Hunting" Rifle

Lieutenant Colonel St. George Tucker was an officer in the Virginia Militia, and he had experienced British fire before—but never anything quite like this. It was dusk, the poorest time of the day for visibility. Tucker and his fellow American soldiers were scattered in open order at a considerable distance from the British outposts at Yorktown. Enemy fire was light—yet the Americans were suffering. Five or six of them had been wounded, one of them mortally. The militia officer later noted in his diary that a single shot had felled three of his men. Someone was shooting much more accurately and much harder than the Americans had anticipated.

Normally, Tucker and his comrades would have been reasonably safe. A hit from the standard smoothbore musket under these circumstances would have been a matter of sheer luck. But the guns now shooting at them were different; they were rifles.

It has been fortunate for historians that Tucker kept a diary during the American Revolution, for he noted many interesting and historically valuable details. Among these was the amazement of the militiamen at the withering effectiveness of enemy shoulder arms as the siege at Yorktown went on.

Actually, there was little cause for wonder. The rifle that Tucker and his comrades faced was the German jaeger, and it was fired by trained marksmen from Ansbach, Germany. The first of these specially hired marksmen had come to America to assist the British forces back in 1776. Now it was the fall of 1781, and the Revolution was all but over. Many of the Americans were armed with accurate rifles, developed from the same jaeger design, yet they never could get used to the idea that the enemy had accurate rifles, too.

This, then, is the real surprise—that Americans had forgotten the origin of their own rifles. Evidently, they had no realization of the widespread use of military rifles in central and northern Europe, but they might well have remembered the slow evolution of the American rifle from just such arms as these. It had been less than fifty years since typical German rifles had been made in Pennsylvania by immigrant gunsmiths, and more recently similar guns had been brought over for picked British marksmen in the last of the French wars. Communications were fragmentary, however, and traditions died quickly in a new land. Even a man from a "rifle state" like Virginia could be taken aback when he found such a fine weapon in enemy hands.

The rifle that caused Tucker's consternation had developed in central Europe toward the end of the seventeenth century. Its ancestor had been the wheel lock, which had been popular among Europeans for well over a hundred years. The wheel lock, however, had employed a light, straight buttstock designed to be held against the cheek when firing. The new rifle

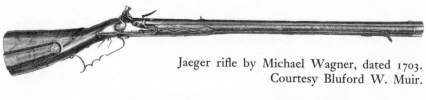

Jaeger rifle by Michael Wagner, dated 1703.
Courtesy Bluford W. Muir.

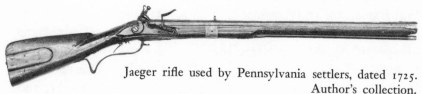

Jaeger rifle used by Pennsylvania settlers, dated 1725.
Author's collection.

had a broad butt made for bracing against the shoulder. This provided greater stability and avoided the damage to the face that often resulted when the cheek stock was not held securely enough. In addition, it utilized the new French flintlock which was then winning almost universal acceptance in Europe and America for all types of firearms. This lock did not provide quite as quick an ignition as the wheel lock once the trigger was pulled, but it could be prepared for firing much more rapidly, and it was simpler and much cheaper to make and to repair.

These were the two characteristics—lock and stock—that set the new rifle apart from its predecessors, but it soon developed other distinct features as well. It was short, with an octagonal barrel averaging between 24 and 30 inches long. Its bore was large, usually between .60- and .75-caliber, for it was a big-game rifle originally designed for deer, wild boar and chamois. Its rifling was deep and multi-grooved, and it had well designed open sights. Normally it had a wide trigger guard, protecting a set or hair trigger; this type of trigger was used because chamois and similar animals were often shot at ranges that required precision marksmanship.

Another of its distinctive features was a box carved into the right side of the stock and fitted with a sliding cover. Here the shooter carried his small tools and perhaps an extra flint. In a few instances, he may also have used it to hold the small greased patches with which he wrapped his bullets to make

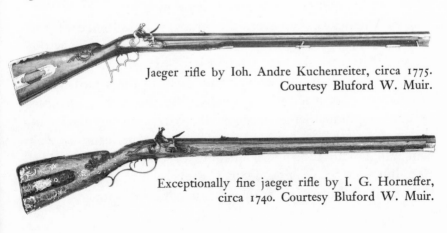

Jaeger rifle by Ioh. Andre Kuchenreiter, circa 1775.
Courtesy Bluford W. Muir.

Exceptionally fine jaeger rifle by I. G. Horneffer,
circa 1740. Courtesy Bluford W. Muir.

them go down the bore easily and still take the spin imparted by the rifling. (Americans normally used the boxes in the stocks of their long rifles for this purpose, but since few European rifles show traces of grease it is thought that the greased patches were normally carried elsewhere.)

The jaeger was the firearm of the professional forester, the gamekeeper and the hunter of central Europe from the 1600s until almost 1850. From these men the rifle took its name, for *Jaeger* is the German word for hunter. Aside from minor stylistic modifications, the gun didn't change until the adoption of the percussion system in the 1820s. It was a fine rifle. There was real stopping power in its large ball, and it could fire tight groups at ranges of 200 yards or more. In the hands of a skilled marksman, it could handle almost any task a rifle with open sights would ever be called upon to perform.

Although it had been designed primarily as a sporting arm, the jaeger entered the military field very quickly. Since King Christian IV of Denmark had begun to arm some of his troops with rifles early in the 1600s, the idea had spread, and the jaeger soon became the preferred type of rifle for most European armies. It was standard for all of the Germanic countries. Norwegian ski troops were equipped with rifles of the jaeger pattern as early as 1711, and other nations of central and northern Europe rapidly followed suit. For more than a hundred years, it set the style for European rifle development. Even the relatively modern British Baker rifle, adopted in 1800, was consciously patterned after it.

For Americans, however, the primary importance of the jaeger lies in its relationship to the Kentucky rifle. It was the jaeger that the settlers from Germany and Switzerland brought with them to Pennsylvania early in the 1700s. Rifles just like it were made in this country by the early gunsmiths before the gradual lengthening of the barrel and lightening of the stock created the famed American gun. Americans are well acquainted with the superb qualities of their own Kentucky rifle, but, like St. George Tucker, they have nearly forgotten the excellent European firearm from which it sprang.

Chapter 10

The Murderous Rifled Musket

The Civil War was the bloodiest conflict in American history. In four years, a nation of 32,000,000 people suffered casualties of 714,245 men killed and wounded, compared with 880,000 dead and injured out of a population of 133,000,000 during World War II. Ranked shoulder to shoulder, heroic soldiers on both sides faced a literal hail of death in gory battles. In one day at First Bull Run, or Manassas, more Americans were killed than in four days at Tarawa; Second Bull Run, only a three-day engagement, resulted in almost as many American casualties as the conquest of Iwo Jima, which took thirty-six days and set a record for World War II.

The tactics used in the Civil War were based upon the old smoothbore musket which had been a standard infantry arm for centuries. But a new weapon had just appeared that was far more accurate and powerful. It piled up the casualties and its singing "minié" ball became synonymous with death. This was the rifled musket.

Ever since the early 1500s, two types of gun barrel had existed. One was smooth on the inside; the other had grooves which gradually twisted in a spiral cut into the sides of the bore. These grooves were called rifling and the guns that had them were known as rifles. Rifling caused the spherical bullet to spin as it left the barrel; this made it carry much more accurately and penetrate deeper when it hit. Since a bullet could take the rifling only if it fitted the bore tightly, a rifle was much slower to load than a smoothbore. With a gun that had no rifling, the bullet could be dropped in loosely and held by a wad rammed in on top of it.

Military men quickly recognized the value of the rifle as an accurate weapon for sharpshooters, but guns that would shoot fast were even more important. During a battle men fired in volleys in order to lay down a blanket of fire. Accuracy was desirable but speed was essential. Therefore, the rifle was used by sharpshooters and other special troops while the smoothbore musket became standard for the infantry.

Still there were those who saw the importance of having both speed *and* accuracy in one gun, and they kept looking for some way of combining the two. The key was a bullet that could be loaded loosely but would nevertheless fit the bore tightly. It was impossible to do this with the old spherical ball; a new shape was needed. A French Army officer, Captain Claude E. Minié, made the breakthrough in about 1851. He invented a cylindro-conoidal bullet with a cavity in its base and a little wedge set into the cavity. This bullet could be easily dropped down the barrel, but when the gun was fired the explosion of powder drove the plug up into the soft lead bullet and expanded it sufficiently to make it fit the bore tightly.

The minié ball as developed by James H. Burton. Author's collection.

Minié's bullet was good, but an American improved it and made it a suitable military projectile. James H. Burton, Master Armorer at the U. S. Harpers Ferry Armory, discovered that if the cavity in the base of Minié's bullet were properly designed it would expand by itself, without the wedge. This simplified the manufacture of the bullet (which of course made it cheaper to produce) and eliminated the danger of losing a plug during the loading operation, making the bullet ineffective. The United States promptly adopted the new bullet, which became known popularly as the "minié" ball even though it was no longer either Minié's invention or a ball. Apparently no one ever thought of calling it "Burton's bullet," though official documents did refer to it occasionally as the Harpers Ferry ball.

The minié ball ended the era of the smoothbore musket. All military firearms could now be rifled, and the U.S. lost no time having new weapons designed to take advantage of this opportunity. In 1855 three arms were adopted, each firing the new bullet: a pistol; a rifle of the short, traditional form; and a longer gun the size of the old musket but with a rifled barrel. This last was the rifled musket. It had a 40-inch barrel rifled with three shallow grooves, and it fired a .58-caliber

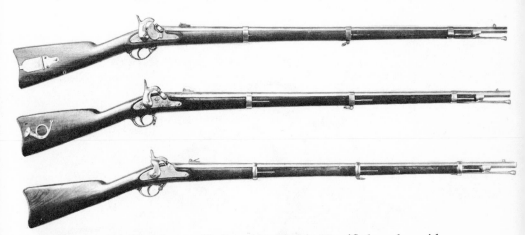

Top to bottom: Model 1855 rifled musket, Model 1861 rifled musket with infantry insignia tacked on by the original owner, the Model 1863–64 rifled musket. Courtesy the Smithsonian Institution.

minié ball. The bullet weighed 500 grains; 60 grains of black musket powder comprised the charge. In spite of its length, the weight of the entire gun was only 9¼ pounds.

An unusual feature of the Model 1855 rifled musket was its priming device. Instead of using loose percussion caps placed individually on the nipple for each shot, the 1855 had an automatic primer invented by Dr. Edward Maynard, a Washington dentist. This consisted of a tape with individual charges of fulminate spaced like the roll of caps in a child's cap pistol. As the hammer was cocked, an arm moved the tape forward and placed a new cap over the nipple ready for firing. Unfortunately, there were drawbacks to this device, and it was abandoned in succeeding models of 1861 and 1863, which readopted the rifled-musket system of putting the individual caps on the nipple by hand.

These were fine arms, the best of the muzzle-loaders. An experienced soldier could load, aim, and fire three times a minute, and under combat conditions he could be expected to keep up a steady fire of two shots a minute. He was also fairly certain of hitting his target, and hitting it hard. A good marks-

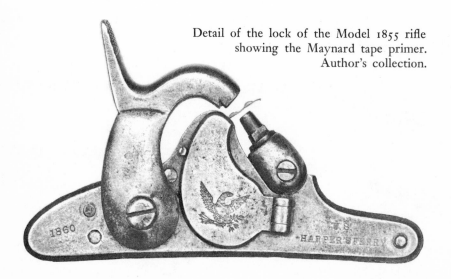

Detail of the lock of the Model 1855 rifle
showing the Maynard tape primer.
Author's collection.

man could put 10 shots into a four-inch bull's-eye at 200 yards. He could hit a six-foot-by-six-foot target at 500 yards, an eight-by-eight target about two out of four times at a thousand yards, and at that considerable distance the bullet had enough power left to penetrate four inches of soft pine.

The rifled musket was used for only a decade, despite its excellence. The new arm arrived on the scene just as it became possible to manufacture effective breechloaders and as the new metallic cartridges were being perfected. The Civil War brought the end of the muzzle-loader as a military weapon; an official breechloader, the Allin Conversion (an altered muzzle-loader), was adopted by the U. S. Army in 1866.

During its ten-year span, however, the rifled musket made its presence felt. Nearly two million were made either at the Springfield Armory or at private armories under government contracts. It was the most common infantry arm on both sides throughout the entire war and accounted for the greatest percentage of casualties. Among all muzzle-loading guns, its record is unequaled.

Chapter 11

Lincoln's Choice for Firepower

The tall, spare man peered at the target, a sheet of U. S. Congressional stationery fastened to a woodpile in Treasury Park. Seven shots had struck the paper or come close to it. "I believe I can make this gun shoot better." As he spoke, President Abraham Lincoln reached into his vest pocket and fished out a tiny wooden sight he had whittled. With the cares of a nation at war upon his shoulders, it had been a relief to turn his mind to a simple mechanical problem and to practice his skill with a pocket knife once more. Now to test the results.

After fitting the sliver of pine over the standard sight of the rifle, he turned and strode back to where his companion, a clerk in the Navy Department, had marked his shooting position. Seven new cartridges slid into the magazine, and the President was ready. Deliberately, he emptied the gun, reloaded and fired seven more times. All but two of the shots struck the paper. He had indeed improved his shooting. Now it was time to go back to the White House and tackle bigger problems. Not that the President's interest in this gun had ended with a plinking session; on the contrary, he was instrumental in putting the same model into the hands of Union soldiers. The gun that had so absorbed Lincoln was a Spencer, the first really successful magazine repeater firing self-contained metallic cartridges. It had been invented by Christopher

M. Spencer, a fabulous little Yankee from Manchester, Connecticut, whose other inventions would eventually include
automatic silk-winding machinery, an automatic screw-cutting
machine, a refinement in drop-forging techniques—and even
a steam-powered automobile which he regularly drove to
work in 1862 (until the town fathers asked him to stop because his machine scared horses). The magazine-loading repeater was just one example of his wide-ranging genius, but it
appeared at a very opportune moment. The patent was granted
on March 6, 1860. War clouds were already gathering, and
the Great Conflict would begin the very next year.

The Spencer was a fine gun. A hole bored through the
butt of the stock received a tubular magazine that accommo-
dated seven cartridges. A coiled follower spring kept the shells
constantly under pressure. When the shooter pulled down-
ward on the lever-action trigger guard, the breechblock
dropped and exposed the rear of the bore. The spent cartridge
case was ejected, and a new one fed in from the magazine as
the trigger guard was returned to its normal position; the cartridge was pushed into the chamber when the breech closed.
It remained only to cock the conventional side hammer to
have the piece ready to fire. An experienced shooter could
empty a seven-shot magazine in nine seconds.

Refilling the magazine took a little time, but trained troops
were expected to be able to keep up a steadily sustained fire
of 14 or 15 aimed shots a minute. About seven times as fast as
the rate of fire expected of a man with the standard muzzle-
loading rifled musket, this was a tremendous increase in firepower.

In order to help soldiers maintain such a steady and rapid
fire over a long period of time, a special cartridge box was
developed. Known as the Blakeslee Quickloader, it contained
a series of tubes (existing specimens hold anywhere from 8 to
13); each tube was filled with seven cartridges, ready to slip
into the hollow stock. With a 13-tube ammunition box slung
at his side and a fully loaded magazine in his rifle, a soldier
could go into battle with 98 rounds quickly available.

The Spencer was a reliable gun, too. Soldiers who used it reported that it almost never got out of order, and a malfunction of any kind was a rarity. It was, they said, the finest repeater of the war, and some maintained it was the finest rifle of any sort, anywhere.

Still, it took many months before the impact of this new gun was felt in combat, and it never armed more than a small proportion of Union soldiers. The principal reason was that the Chief of Ordnance, Brigadier General James Wolfe Ripley, was suspicious of all the new breechloading and repeating weapons which were beginning to appear. In most instances he was right. Many of these new inventions were impractical or downright dangerous. But Ripley could not distinguish the good from the bad. It required a direct order from Lincoln himself before Spencer was given his first contract, and even after that the number of guns called for was reduced time and again on various pretexts. A few privately purchased Spencers probably saw action late in 1862, but it was the spring of 1863 before they arrived in sufficient quantity to make their presence felt.

Then things began to happen. At Hoover's Gap, Wilder's regiment of Mounted Rifles—armed with Spencers they had bought themselves—defeated a whole Confederate brigade. And the Rebels thought they had been outnumbered five to one! At Chickamauga, Hanover, and Gettysburg, the Spencer

Spencer carbine with its action open. Courtesy the Smithsonian Institution.

performed spectacularly. Ripley was removed as Chief of Ordnance. The new chief, Brigadier General George D. Ramsay, reported that the demand for Spencers was tremendous; no soldier who had seen one used, he declared, could be satisfied with any other arm. Ramsay tried to see that the men got them. As a result, the government purchased some 12,471 full-length Spencer rifles and 94,196 carbines. Purchases by states and individual soldiers added more Spencers to the conflict, and some authorities have estimated that as many as 200,000 saw service.

With the end of the war, the market for these arms suddenly collapsed. The Federal government had more Spencers on hand than it knew what to do with, and it sold many as surplus, glutting the civilian market. Spencer added improvements, including a cut-off that would allow the gun to be fired as a single-shot breechloader while holding a full magazine in reserve in case of emergency. But nothing helped. In 1869 all assets of the Spencer Repeating Rifle Company were placed on the auction block. The Turkish government bought 30,000 carbines at the sale, but the biggest buyer was a former shirt manufacturer named Oliver Fisher Winchester, whose light lever-action rifle, with a greater magazine capacity, had won the Western market and helped to ruin Spencer. Having also bought his competitor's patents, he didn't have to worry about Spencer's making a comeback. The day of the Winchester dawned just as the Spencer's day was ending.

Chapter 12

Handguns of the Union Troops

It was spring, 1862, and the Shenandoah Valley of Virginia was alive with troops. Stonewall Jackson's famed Valley Campaign was getting under way, while south of Harrisonburg, Turner Ashby's Confederate cavalry scouted the countryside looking for Yankees. It was an easy search, and soon a group of blue-clad horsemen rose to the bait. A picture-book cavalry charge developed, with the opposing forces dashing at each other across an open field.

One of the leaders of the Rebel attack, Captain Harry Gilmor, singled out a Union officer and galloped toward him, revolver in hand. As they closed, he fired twice, apparently without hitting his adversary. The Union officer in turn missed with three or four shots. Closer they came. Grimly the Confederate saved one shot. Only a few feet separated them. He could not miss at this range. The shot rang out, but still the Yankee kept coming. His saber flashed, and the startled Gilmor needed all his skill to avoid the swinging blade. Returning his empty revolver to its holster, he drew his own sword. Boot top to boot top they fought in the classic cavalry tradition of previous centuries until the horseman in gray, whirling his saber, disarmed his adversary and took him prisoner. It was then he found that a steel vest beneath the blue coat had made his bullets useless. There had been no fault with his revolver or the ammunition.

The sword had won the day in this case, but such instances became fewer and fewer as the war went on. Revolvers were found to be more efficient for mounted combat, and breech-loading, repeating carbines used afoot often prevented an enemy from getting close enough for hand-to-hand fighting. A number of famous Confederate cavalry units, including Mosby's Rangers, dispensed with the saber altogether, while Union horsemen began to fight more and more on foot, using their mounts simply as transportation from one battlefield to another.

The revolver made its biggest impact on the cavalry, where every trooper carried one—sometimes two. But officers of all branches of the service normally carried them, as did some of the enlisted men of the field artillery. Selected seamen were also equipped with them and, especially during the first few months, many an infantry private thrust a personal handgun through his belt.

Yet it is an interesting fact that no revolvers were made in a Federal armory. When the war broke out, the official government-made handgun was the Springfield pistol-carbine that had been adopted in 1855. It was a long weapon with a rifled barrel and a detachable shoulder stock—features that were supposed to make it shoot accurately at longer ranges than the average pistol could. In addition, it was equipped with the patent Maynard primer, invented by a Washington dentist and strongly recommended by Jefferson Davis, who had been Secretary of War when the gun was adopted. This ingenious primer was a tape, encasing small dots of percussion compound and automatically fed over the nipple when the hammer was cocked. In actual use, however, there were too many failures. Also, the point of impact varied according to whether the arm was fired with the shoulder stock attached or detached. Thus the troopers lost confidence in the pistol-carbine. Slightly over 4000 of these guns were made in 1856 and 1857, and then production ceased.

When the war started, the Union needed revolvers for the rapidly expanding cavalry—and needed them fast. Almost anything that would shoot was welcome. Agents purchased handguns in France and England while American manufacturers were besieged by Federal, state, and private buyers. Designs for percussion revolvers, pin-fire revolvers and even a few rim-fire and center-fire cartridge revolvers were accepted. Some were excellent arms; others were so impractical that only a wartime emergency allowed them to get into production at all—and not even that emergency could make them a success.

Authorities differ about the number of pistol models carried by Union troops either as official issue or as personal arms, but fifty is a modest estimate. The most conservative lists cite twenty as "martial," meaning those handguns purchased and issued by the Federal government. Other pistols are classified as "secondary martial" because there were no specific government contracts for them, and the third group is designated "personal."

Ordnance officers charged with supplying ammunition for such a variety of weapons might well have given up in despair, but the situation was not nearly as bad as it sounds because many of these models were bought in such small quantities that they were little more than curiosities. Colt and Remington revolvers made up almost 75 percent of all handguns purchased and issued by the government, and if the Starr single- and double-action models are included, the figure rises to slightly more than 85 percent. Therefore all other pistols comprised less than 15 percent of the total.

Most of these martial pistols were made in two calibers— the .44 (Army) and the .36 (Navy). The designation was purely artificial, for many a soldier tucked a .36 into his holster because he liked the feel of the grip and preferred the lighter weight, while some sailors eagerly sought .44s because of their greater power. Of the two sizes the Army was by far the more popular, outnumbering the smaller .36 by approximately ten to one.

Thus, as might be expected, the Colt and Remington .44-caliber revolvers led all the rest in numbers purchased and issued by U. S. Ordnance. The Colt Army Model 1860 topped the list with a total of 128,697, followed by the Remington with 115,563. In addition, huge quantities of both were bought by states and individuals.

The Colt Army was an excellent handgun and it appeared at the right moment to take advantage of the wartime demand. The first pistols Colt made for the Army were the huge, heavy "dragoons," beginning with the famous Walker Colt of 1847. Through the years this monster had been reduced in size, but it was not until 1860 that a radically lighter and more streamlined version was developed and put on the market. It had an instantaneous success, and with the beginning of the war it began to set sales records.

The Remington, too, was a fine weapon. Many modern collectors claim it was better than the Colt and point to its solid frame as compared to the "open top" of the Colt. Besides adding strength, the top strap of this frame over the cylinder was grooved as a rear sight. On the Colt the rear sight was filed on the lip of the hammer and could be used only when the gun was cocked. Since a moving rear sight is not apt to be as accurate as a fixed one, the Remington would seem to have had the advantage over the Colt in this respect.

But the soldiers who used the two guns disagreed with modern theorists. In the records of the Chief of Ordnance are

Colt Model 1860 Army revolver, .44-caliber, the most popular revolver of the Civil War. Courtesy the National Rifle Association.

Remington New Model Army revolver, .44-caliber, the second most popular revolver of the Civil War. Courtesy the National Rifle Association.

field reports, all of them favorable to the Colt but mixed on the Remington. Surprisingly, the soldiers considered the Colt stronger despite its lack of a top strap, and they criticized the Remington's tendency to get out of order and called it dangerous to carry because of the absence of a safety notch.

Most popular of the smaller Colts was the Navy Model 1851, although only 11,696 of them were purchased—very few in contrast to the huge number of .44s. This was a light weapon, but its angular design made it seem bigger than it actually was when compared with the streamlined Army. In 1861 a new Navy model was developed which copied the smooth design of the .44. It was a fine gun and beautifully balanced, but it failed to win favor, and only 2363 were sold to the government. The Remington Navy also ran well behind the Army version which it copied in design, but its total of 13,101 sales still almost equaled the combined sales of the two Colt Navy revolvers.

Very similar to the Remington Navy was the .38-caliber Whitney, manufactured by Eli Whitney, Jr., son of the inventor of the cotton gin. Its solid frame should have given it strength, but the soldiers damned it as a frail arm that easily got out of order. Some 11,000 were purchased by the government and one was used in an attempt to murder Secretary of State William H. Seward on the night of Lincoln's assassination. Here its weak construction probably saved Seward's life, for the frame bent when the attacker used it as a club, and the gun failed to fire when he finally reached Seward's bedroom.

All the Colts, Remingtons, and Whitneys had been percussion revolvers. They were loaded with prepared combustible cartridges inserted from the front of the cylinders and pushed home with a loading lever pivoted beneath the barrel. These cartridges contained the bullet plus a charge of powder wrapped in paper or collodion, which would burn readily once the priming spark was applied. This spark, actually a jet of flame, was provided by a percussion cap that was placed on a nipple at the rear of each chamber in the cylinder. All were six-shot single-actions with rifled barrels.

The Starr revolvers, however, offered some variations. Invented by E. T. Starr of New York City, these interesting arms were manufactured in three models, and two of these were double-actions—that is, the act of pulling the trigger drew back the hammer and then released it. No longer was it necessary to cock the hammer first. An Army and a Navy model were made with this mechanism, but then it was abandoned in favor of a single-action Army. Perhaps the trigger pull of the self-cocking type had been too long and heavy to suit the ordnance experts' tastes; possibly they were not yet ready for such an advance.

Yet there were other double-action pistols. Adams and Kerr patent five-shot, double-action, percussion revolvers were purchased in England and were also manufactured in the United States by the Massachusetts Arms Company. The Cooper,

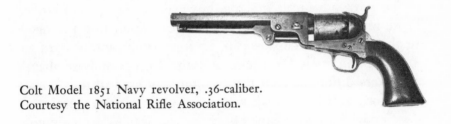

Colt Model 1851 Navy revolver, .36-caliber.
Courtesy the National Rifle Association.

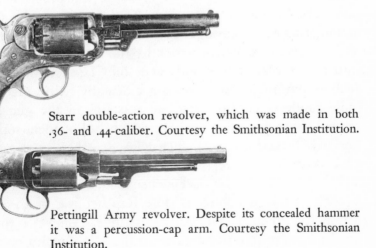

Starr double-action revolver, which was made in both .36- and .44-caliber. Courtesy the Smithsonian Institution.

Pettingill Army revolver. Despite its concealed hammer it was a percussion-cap arm. Courtesy the Smithsonian Institution.

which copied the Colt in almost all other features, was double-action. And then there was the fearful and wonderful Pettin-gill Army revolver devised by C. S. Pettingill of New Haven and improved by Edward A. Raymond and Charles Rob-itaille of Brooklyn. It was not only self-cocking but "hammerless," since its little L-shaped striker was completely enclosed. A single pull on the trigger revolved the cylinder, fired the gun and cocked the striker for the next shot. Unfortunately it was too delicate a mechanism for field conditions, and the invisible hammer that always appeared to be cocked made it dangerous to carry.

Another variant was found in the Savage revolvers. Here two triggers were used, one for revolving the cylinder and cocking the hammer, the other for firing. Savage made three different models, but they all worked on the same principle and were in .36-caliber.

The most advanced designs, however, came from France. These revolvers fired metallic cartridges, eliminating the need for the separate percussion cap. Unfortunately, it was hard to obtain ammunition for them, and the European bore diameters were different from those commonly used in the Army. Therefore, relatively small quantities of them were purchased —not enough to have any effect on the war. Most common were the LeFaucheux pin-fire revolvers, of which some 12,-000 were bought by the government. They were .41 double-action arms with cartridges that had short pins protruding just above their bases. When struck by the hammer, the pin drove into an internal primer and set it off. The trouble was that such a pin might be struck accidentally with exactly the same result when the cartridge was not in the gun, which tended to make a soldier with a pouch full of them somewhat nervous. Nevertheless, the men who used these guns generally gave them a good report.

In addition to the LeFaucheux, there were two other French cartridge revolvers. The Raphael was a .41 double-action that used a center-fire cartridge. Almost a thousand Raphaels were purchased early in the war, but no one seems to know what happened to them after they reached this country, and there are no reports about their good or bad qualities. Another double-action revolver, the Perrin, used a .45 rim-fire cartridge, but only two hundred of these were purchased, not enough for a field test.

Americans could make cartridge revolvers, too. Smith & Wesson had begun production of the .22 Model 1, and the larger .32 Model 2 appeared in 1861. Both were small for military use, but many were purchased individually by soldiers who preferred the ease of their rim-fire cartridges to the more cumbersome cap and ball. No other American firm was able to make cartridge revolvers, however, because Smith & Wesson controlled the patent on a cylinder with the chambers bored all the way through—an essential feature in such a weapon.

Top left, Savage revolver; the lower loop cocked the hammer and rotated the cylinder, then the trigger fired the piece. Top right, Adams double-action revolver, the most popular of the English imports. Center, LeFaucheux pin-fire revolver made in France. Bottom, Model 1855 pistol-carbine with its shoulder stock attached. Courtesy the Smithsonian Institution.

Therefore, the percussion-cap handgun reigned throughout the war as the standard arm. Both Colt and Remington had fine, well-established revolvers that assured them dominance in the field. To catch a buyer's eye it was necessary for new companies and inventors to offer some feature that they could claim as an improvement. Their efforts must have made life miserable for ordnance officers and armorers, but they provide delightful examples of mechanical ingenuity for the collector of today.

Chapter 13

Handguns of the Confederacy

Soldiers went into battle unarmed, officers cursed as they struggled with revolvers that wouldn't fire, but the South fought on stubbornly. Confederate cavalrymen searched the battlefields for dead men's guns and armed themselves with whatever came to hand.

They prized their guns as they prized their lives, and every man tried desperately to acquire extra arms. One pistol might malfunction, a second might be lost in battle, but if a man had four he could face the enemy without even stopping to reload. It was not unusual for a member of Terry's Texas Rangers to carry that many—two in holsters on his belt and another pair in saddle holsters. Some of those men became living arsenals.

The problem was how to provide enough pistols to meet such a demand with the limited facilities available, and the Confederacy showed considerable ingenuity in doing it. Captured parts were incorporated into new pistol-carbines; Colts, Remingtons, and Whitneys were copied—with parts made of brass because of an iron shortage—and men became gun manufacturers overnight. Two of these men even invented new pistols. Thomas Coffer built a gun with a two-piece cylinder that was more or less a cross between the percussion and the cartridge system. Jean Le Mat made one of the deadliest weapons of the war—his famed "grapeshot" revolver with one barrel in .36- or .42-caliber and a second one that spewed a .60-caliber charge of shot.

At the outbreak of war, the North had been flooded with different kinds of guns, and Union ordnance officers had been plagued by the diversity of models. Confederate ordnance officers had problems, too, but of an exactly opposite nature. There were few manufacturers able to make handguns. Machinery was scarce and materials were hard to obtain. Union purchases of revolvers ran to hundreds of thousands, while Confederate production could be counted in tens of thousands.

A few handguns were made in the South before the outbreak of the war, but these were mostly single-shot percussion pistols. It was easy to obtain revolvers directly from Northern makers right up to the start of actual hostilities, and a number of Southern states and many individuals took advantage of this to acquire a basic supply. When war broke out, the first troops in the field carried these guns, along with older models and some imported English revolvers. The Yankees were also obliging enough to leave a good quantity of weapons on the fields of battle during the early years of successful Confederate campaigns.

The capture of Harpers Ferry provided a supply of parts, and these were joyously hauled off to Fayetteville, North Carolina, to be assembled into a Confederate version of the clumsy 1855 pistol-carbine. The Southern product differed from its Union counterpart most noticeably in that it omitted the Maynard tape primer. Jefferson Davis, who had been impressed with this patent primer, was now President of the Confederacy, but his ordnance officers did not approve, and their decision carried. The Fayetteville pistol-carbines were no more popular than the original model had been, but guns were scarce and there was no point in letting them go to waste. After the parts were used up, production stopped, for the military knew that regular revolvers were the type of handgun needed.

To get these arms into production the Confederacy was willing to offer amazing inducements. First of all, there was deferment of active service for men needed to operate an arms factory. Next, the cost of setting up such an establishment would be advanced by the Confederate government, to be repaid from profits, and if Federal troops should capture the plant, the debt would be canceled. Large contracts were offered and soon a number of individuals announced themselves capable of providing these tools of war for the South. Their spirit was willing, but their abilities turned out to be inadequate.

Of all the contractors who hopefully signed agreements to produce as many as 15,000 revolvers apiece within three years, only five succeeded in making any considerable number of weapons at all. These were Griswold & Gunnison, Leech & Rigdon, Rigdon & Ansley, Spiller & Burr, and the Columbus Firearms Company. Harassed by manufacturing problems, material shortages, a lack of skilled labor and the need for frequent movement to avoid advancing Union troops, the total production of all five firms was less than 15,000 revolvers.

Interestingly, while Union soldiers preferred the .44 Colt Army Model of 1860, Southerners favored the .36 Colt Navy of 1851. Most of their arms were copied from it, though variations were made to simplify manufacture and to substitute available materials for those in short supply.

Barrels were almost always round instead of octagonal as in the original Colt, recoil shields were sometimes omitted and, in the case of the Griswold & Gunnison, the frame was made of brass instead of iron. These "Confederate Colts" can readily be recognized by such differences, as well as by a rougher finish than those made at the Colt factory.

One of the top five Confederate gunmakers—Spiller & Burr of Richmond—chose the Whitney Navy revolver rather than the Colt as its model. The company encountered such production difficulties, however, that it was finally bought out by the government of the Confederacy and the machinery was moved to Macon, Georgia, where production was resumed at the Confederate armory. Some of these Whitneys are marked "C.S." or "Spiller & Burr" or both; others bear no markings whatever, but their brass frames identify them as Southern products.

In addition to these "primary" revolvers made directly under contract to the Confederacy, there was a secondary group made for sale to private citizens. Most of these were made in Texas by such firms as Dance Brothers, and Tucker, Sherrod & Company. Dance Brothers copied the Colt but omitted its recoil shield and produced a flat frame immediately recognizable to the student of arms history. Tucker, Sherrod, on the other hand, copied the big Colt .44 Dragoon of the prewar era.

Had these been the only Confederate handguns made, this would be a story of woefully inefficient copies of Yankee revolvers. But there were two innovators who set out to make an improved product and added a new dimension to Southern gun design.

These were Thomas W. Coffer of Portsmouth, Virginia, and Dr. Jean Alexandre François Le Mat of New Orleans. Coffer attempted to build a cartridge revolver that would cir-

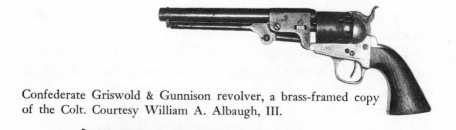

Confederate Griswold & Gunnison revolver, a brass-framed copy of the Colt. Courtesy William A. Albaugh, III.

Confederate Spiller & Burr revolver, a copy of the Union Whitney revolver but with a brass frame. Courtesy William A. Albaugh, III.

cumvent Smith & Wesson's patent, and Le Mat devised the 10-shot percussion "grapeshot" revolver.

It seems odd that a gunsmith in a country at war should be worried about a patent held by the enemy, but Coffer went to great lengths to avoid using a bored-through cylinder—a device that was covered in a patent to which Smith & Wesson held the rights. He invented a two-piece cylinder, one part of which contained the chambers for the charges while the other was pierced by smaller holes that could be lined up with these chambers. Special cartridges with narrow projections were inserted in the chambers, after which the rear part of the cylinder was slipped on so that the cartridge projections stuck through its smaller holes much in the manner of the percussion caps on other revolvers. It was necessary to remove the cylinder to load the gun and this was, of course, an inconvenience. More important, the metal shortage in the Confederacy made a cartridge arm impractical. Probably for these reasons only a few pilot models of this ingenious arm were made before Coffer gave up and began producing percussion revolvers with a standard cylinder. The frames were solid, as on the Whitney and the Remington, but they were made of brass and had spur triggers without a guard. Such specimens

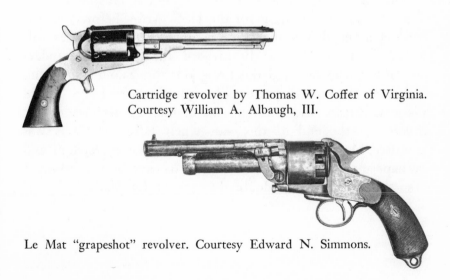

Cartridge revolver by Thomas W. Coffer of Virginia. Courtesy William A. Albaugh, III.

Le Mat "grapeshot" revolver. Courtesy Edward N. Simmons.

are now extremely rare, for invading Federal forces captured Portsmouth in May 1862, and ended production of the Coffer revolver after an estimated total output of only fifty guns.

Dr. Le Mat was much more successful. Actually his patent had been granted by the United States back in 1856, almost five years before war broke out, and he had tried without success to interest the Federal government in it. Once war began, he had no difficulty in obtaining a contract from the Confederacy, however, and he promptly set out for France, where he felt he could have his arms manufactured more easily than in the South—and without the danger of capture by Union troops.

From all accounts, the Le Mat was a very deadly weapon. Made in .42- and .36-caliber, its cylinder was bored for nine loads fired in the normal fashion through a rifled barrel. Immediately beneath this conventional barrel was a second, smoothbore, barrel of .60-caliber which could be loaded with buckshot and put into operation by turning down the nose of the hammer. It was this feature that gave the pistol its nickname of the "grapeshot" revolver. At close range such a charge must indeed have been "formidable," as the good Doctor claimed.

The Le Mat was not only formidable but reliable as well. The officers who tested it for the U. S. Army before the war had recommended it highly, even though no purchases followed. General P. G. T. Beauregard, the colorful Confederate officer who directed the firing on Fort Sumter and who had at one time been a partner of Le Mat's, carried one. So did General Patton Anderson and the dashing cavalry leader Jeb Stuart. At the end of the war, when Jefferson Davis was captured by Union troops in his final dash for freedom and perhaps another try, he was reported to have been carrying a "ten-shot revolver"—undoubtedly one of Le Mat's.

Chapter 14

Berdan's Sharpshooters

The foliage is lush and green along the banks of the James River in Virginia during the early weeks of summer. The green-clad riflemen blended well with the natural cover as they lay in their position on the slopes of Malvern Hill, far below the main Union line. It was July 1, 1862, and the woods were alive with Confederate soldiers anxious to drive McClellan's army back into the river. The men in green were in an advance position, their job to watch for the Rebel drive to start.

Suddenly things began to happen. A battery of the Richmond Howitzers swept out of the woods in front of the Union troops. As it whirled to unlimber, it came within range. This was what the riflemen had been waiting for, and their rifles piped a staccato overture of welcome. Horses dropped on all teams. The cannoneers tried to manhandle the pieces into position, but they too were felled by the rapid and accurate fire from the Union marksmen. Soon the guns and their carriages stood alone, abandoned by all but the motionless bodies of men and beasts that lay all about them. "We went in a battery and came out a wreck," lamented one of the survivors. "We stayed ten minutes by the watch and came out with one gun, ten men, and two horses, and without firing a shot."

In this action, as in all their engagements throughout the Civil War, the men of the United States Sharpshooters showed the world what trained marksmen with good rifles could do to change the character of warfare.

The idea for this unique organization was developed by Hiram Berdan, a young mechanical engineer and noted marksman from New York City. Berdan called on General Winfield Scott almost as soon as war broke out and convinced the old soldier to authorize a special corps of sharpshooters for the United States Army. The special unit had rigid requirements: In addition to being physically fit, each volunteer had to be able to put ten consecutive shots into a 10-inch circle at 200 yards. On this there was no compromise. Eager candidates flocked to the recruiting places, and eventually there were enough competent marksmen to form two full regiments, the first commanded by Berdan, the second by Colonel Henry A. V. Post, also of New York.

The men were of the highest quality, and Berdan determined that their uniforms, arms and equipment should also be special. Green seemed a fitting color for snipers, and eventually each volunteer was equipped with a coat and trousers of that color. For a time they wore gray hats and overcoats, but these led to unpleasant mistakes by fellow Union soldiers, who mistook the sharpshooters for Confederates. After a few such embarrassing errors, these garments were abandoned. Instead of the usual painted canvas knapsack, Berdan's men carried cowhide packs with the hair still on the outside, and each man had a mess kit as well. No other unit in either army remotely resembled the United States Sharpshooters, and this was exactly what Berdan desired. He wanted his men recognized by friend and foe, for he was sure they would perform heroically and win fame—just as soon as they could obtain guns and get to the front.

It was the guns that caused difficulty. To Berdan and his men it seemed only logical that a Sharpshooter needed an accurate rifle. Brigadier General James Wolfe Ripley, the hidebound Chief of Ordnance, didn't see things quite the same way. He felt the Sharpshooters should make do with the regulation muzzle-loading rifled musket, and he refused to budge from that position even when President Lincoln ordered him to give the men the breechloading rifles they wanted. Finally a near-mutiny and more forceful directives from the President broke the stalemate. Rifles were provided, and the Sharpshooters left their camp in Washington to join General George B. McClellan in his Peninsular Campaign against Richmond. It was early in 1862, many long months after the regiments had been organized. But at last the Sharpshooters were in the fight. And there they stayed until February 1865, when there were not enough men left to form even one separate unit. The casualties the Sharpshooters endured during those three years finally took a terrible toll, but the damage inflicted on the forces of the Confederacy was infinitely greater—in psychological punishment and men taken out of the fight—than what those heroic units suffered.

In their spectacular service, Berdan's men used three different kinds of rifles. First there were the heavy target rifles that some of the men brought with them and continued to use throughout the war. Those who did not have their own guns were issued Colt revolving rifles for a short time until the Sharps rifles, which Berdan preferred, could be procured. Toward the end of the war Berdan tried several times to obtain

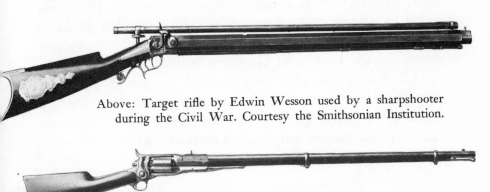

Above: Target rifle by Edwin Wesson used by a sharpshooter during the Civil War. Courtesy the Smithsonian Institution.

Colt revolving rifle such as many of Berdan's men carried early in the Civil War. Courtesy the Smithsonian Institution.

Spencer repeaters, but failed. The civilian target rifles and the Sharps remained the standard weapons.

Heavy target rifles were hardly the arms one would expect to find on a battlefield. Some of them weighed more than 30 pounds; usually they had telescopic sights. None were equipped with bayonets, and trying to perform the manual of arms with such a weapon would have been ridiculous. Regardless of these unmilitary aspects, they shot magnificently. Even if they had to be carried in wagons while the Sharpshooter himself walked, they soon proved their worth.

At the siege of Yorktown in the spring of 1862, a recruit from New Hampshire, George H. Chase, kept a Confederate cannon silent for two days all by himself with just such a gun. Lying under cover, he shot at least one cannoneer each time a crew tried to fire the piece.

Chaplain Lorenzo Barber of the 2nd Regiment also proved the value of his heavy rifle time and time again. At Mine Run in November 1864, for instance, he used his telescopic sight to establish the range for a group of the Sharpshooters armed with open-sighted Sharps breechloaders.

Most of the men, however, carried the rapid-firing Sharps. This was a simple gun with a breechblock that was lowered by using the trigger guard as a lever. When it was down, a cartridge was inserted in the chamber, and then the block was raised by returning the guard to its normal position. It was a strong action and almost foolproof. With it the Sharpshooters decimated the Richmond Howitzer battery at Malvern Hill. At Chancellorsville they gave part of the famed Stonewall Brigade its first taste of disordered retreat. At Gettysburg a hundred Sharpshooters faced the advance of Longstreet's entire corps for twenty minutes and fired an average of 95 shots

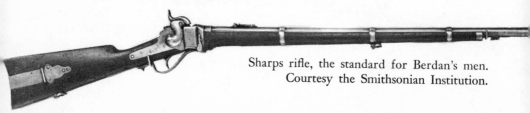

Sharps rifle, the standard for Berdan's men.
Courtesy the Smithsonian Institution.

per man. It was such an astounding performance that the Confederates thought they faced two whole regiments. At Kelly's Ford in 1863, two Sharpshooters from different companies both aimed at and hit the same running Rebel at a range of 700 yards. A captured Alabama soldier told the Sharpshooters ruefully that a man in the lines opposite them could get a furlough just by holding up his hand, but that he was lucky if he could get to the rear without an extension of his furlough to allow a more serious wound to heal. At Petersburg the Confederates learned to recognize the sound of the Sharpshooter's rifles, and one veteran remarked, "you can bet your boots we were mighty careful how we got in their way."

The Sharps was sighted only for a thousand yards, but the Sharpshooters managed to get even more range. During Grant's Wilderness Campaign, for instance, a party of Sharpshooters were ordered to disperse a group of Confederate observers on a signal tower 1500 yards away. Precise aim was impossible at that range, but they carved wooden extensions for their sights and posted an officer with field glasses to watch the results. At the first shot he reported the Rebels all looked down. The men cut longer extensions and tried again, firing higher and higher. This time the Rebels looked up (as the bullets passed overhead) so they continued whittling and shooting until the officer reported the Confederates dodging all over the tower. With that they went to work in earnest and soon cleared the platform. It was a trick that became standard for the unit.

With both their heavy civilian rifles and their Sharpses, Berdan's men added a new dimension to warfare. The Kentucky rifle of the American Revolution had been a fine, accurate weapon, but it could not match the long-range shooting power of the target rifles with their telescopic sights. At lesser distances the open-sighted Sharps shot just as well and much more rapidly. Artillerymen, signalmen, and observers could no longer relax in the open, out of range. If they could be seen, they could be hit. With the coming of Berdan, no man could be safe unless he was completely hidden.

Chapter 15

Mankind Was Horrified

The civilized world was shocked. Cannon shells and hand grenades had exploded for centuries, hurling jagged fragments of iron in all directions. But an explosive musket ball was a different kind of killer. Somehow it seemed more horrible for a small lead projectile to contain a bursting charge, especially since it might well go off inside the victim's body. There was something more personal about firing one at an enemy. The North and South each accused the other side of using these barbarous bullets, and various spokesmen denied the charges. After the war, European nations gathered at St. Petersburg, Russia, and solemnly outlawed the use of such small explosive missiles. The United States did not sign the agreement, but never again were these projectiles used in any major conflict.

There were two principal types of explosive bullets. One was detonated upon contact. The other had a burning fuse and exploded when the flame reached its charge, whether the missile was still in the air or had already entered its target. Externally, both resembled the standard hollow-based minié ball of the period.

The bullets that detonated upon contact were perhaps the earlier type. General Delvigne Jacobs of England had described their use against big game and large military targets several years before the Civil War. In making one of these bullets, the usual practice was to scoop out a cylindrical cavity in the nose and insert a small copper container. This container was filled with a detonating compound such as that used for the standard percussion cap which fired the gun. In some instances, the bullet was cast around a small iron tube, which was then filled with gunpowder and sealed with a percussion cap. Sometimes one of the recently invented .22 rim-fire cartridges was inserted into the bullet. This was a very handy device, for it was a ready-made copper container with both primer and explosive charge. All that had to be done was to drill a hole in the bullet and insert the cartridge (with the .22 slug removed).

Any of these devices would explode if struck a sharp blow, but there was some question as to how hard this blow had to be. The descriptions in manuals mentioned that contact with a hard substance such as wood or bone would detonate them, but there is evidence that human flesh was hard enough to do it if the range was not too great.

A great disadvantage of these bullets, however, was that any number of shocks could set them off. The act of ramming one down a rifle barrel was especially dangerous, and this factor considerably dampened the soldiers' enthusiasm.

Because of the dangers involved in carrying and using shock-sensitive bullets, the type with time fuses soon became more popular. In these, a small bottle-shaped chamber was cast inside the body of the projectile, with its neck opening into the hollow base of the bullet. The chamber was filled with powder and the neck was packed with a slow-burning fuse composition. When the gun was fired, the flash of the explosion ignited the fuse. This burned approximately 1¼ seconds and then set off the explosive charge in the chamber.

There were difficulties. Sometimes the force of the gun's discharge blew the fuse composition right back into the chamber and exploded it while it was still in the rifle barrel. In 1863, Samuel Gardiner, Jr. of New York City, patented improvements in such explosive bullets or musket shells which he believed would provide a solution to these problems. He lined the inside of the chamber with copper and lengthened the neck into a narrow tube that projected out into the hollow base of the bullet. This tube, particularly, was effective in preventing premature explosions, and a few of the later Confederate specimens also utilized it, although without the copper lining in the chamber.

To be fair to the advocates of this barbarous missile, it should be emphasized that the enemy soldier was not their principal target. They believed that these bullets would be particularly useful in blowing up caissons and ammunition wagons at a considerable distance. Indeed, General Jacobs, who had described the explosive bullets before the war, actually succeeded in using them to blow up caissons at 2000 yards. These, of course, were valid military targets and it was unfortunate that soldiers frequently got in the way.

The Gardiner musket shell and other fuse types of bullets had an additional, though neglected, military advantage. The burning of the fuse made it possible to follow the flight of the bullet, thus providing the first tracer ammunition. Oddly enough, no one seems to have understood the value of this, and the idea was not developed until nearly half a century later.

Despite the pros and cons of firing explosive bullets at inanimate targets, they soon were employed for anti-personnel work. Here they did great damage. Even if the bullet exploded before contact, it transformed a smooth projectile into

Left to right: Explosive bullet designed to detonate on contact. Gardiner's musket shell, set off by a fuse. Explosive musket ball extracted from the thigh of a New York soldier.

a twisted and jagged fragment of lead with considerable lacerating power. If it went off after contact, it shattered bones far more extensively than ordinary bullets and inflicted more damage in soft tissue. Bleeding was greater from such wounds, and they healed much more slowly—which meant that a victim would not soon be back in action.

General Ulysses S. Grant mentioned their use by the Confederates at Vicksburg, and made the following comment on such weapons: "Where they hit and the ball exploded, the wound was terrible. In these cases a solid ball would have hit as well. Their use is barbarous because they produce increased suffering without any increased advantage to those using them."

There eventually came to be general agreement on both sides, and the use of the fiendish missiles was gradually ended. These bullets were kept so secret that after the war a congressional investigation committee dismissed as wartime propaganda the charge that the Confederates had employed them; the idea that the North might also have been guilty of their use was completely incredible.

Chapter 16

Arms for Assassination

On April 9, 1865, the Army of Northern Virginia under General Robert E. Lee had surrendered at Appomattox Courthouse. Five days later the jubilation in Washington was still at its height as crowds thronged the city celebrating the return of peace. It was Good Friday, April 14; the air was filled with thanksgiving.

That night a single pistol shot turned the festive North from unbounded joy to bottomless grief. With the aid of a small band of conspirators, a deluded actor named John Wilkes Booth shot and fatally wounded the President of the United States.

For some weeks previously, Booth and his accomplices had been developing their plans and collecting arms. The original idea was not to kill Lincoln but to take him captive and perhaps exchange him for a whole army of Confederate prisoners of war. Appomattox ended that possibility, and Booth then decided on assassination. At the same time, the plot was enlarged to include Vice-President Andrew Johnson, Secretary of State William H. Seward, and possibly General Ulysses S. Grant.

The arms acquired by the conspirators were a miscellaneous lot, but all were good weapons. The guns included a .45-caliber Deringer percussion pistol mounted in German silver and containing a cap box in the butt. This was a small but deadly gun of excellent quality; Henry Deringer had made it at his Philadelphia factory. There were two Colt revolvers: a .36-caliber Navy Model 1851 and a .44-caliber Army Model 1860, both six-shot percussion handguns. A third percussion revolver was a Whitney .36-caliber Navy. There were also two cartridge arms—both seven-shot Spencer repeating carbines firing .52-caliber bullets loaded through a magazine in the butt. Deringer pistols had long been prized for their fine workmanship and their deadliness at close range; Colt revolvers were the most popular handguns of the war; the Spencer carbines had won universal praise from soldiers as the best repeating arms to see service. This was an impressive arsenal.

In addition to the guns, the conspirators had gathered a number of knives. Three of them were of the type normally called "Bowies," heavy fighting or general-utility knives. All three were English-made with antler grips and spear-pointed blades. The one to figure most prominently was manufactured by W. F. Jackson of Sheffield and bore the stamped inscription: RIO GRANDE CAMP KNIFE. An English folding pocket dagger completed the deadly collection.

On the night that the arms were used, President Lincoln and his wife Mary had gone to Ford's Theater to see *Our American Cousin*, starring Laura Keene. General and Mrs. Grant were to have accompanied them, but at the last minute they decided to go to New Jersey to visit their children. Their places were taken by Clara Harris, daughter of U. S. Senator Ira Harris of New York, and her fiancé, Major Henry R. Rathbone.

The party was seated in the state box. President Lincoln occupied a rocking chair at the left. Mrs. Lincoln sat on his right, then Major Rathbone and Miss Harris. The box was decorated with flags and an engraving of George Washington. Directly in back of the President was a small door leading to the corridor from which the box was entered. None of the group noticed that a small hole had been bored through this door so that a person in the corridor could observe both the

Deringer pistol used by John Wilkes Booth to assassinate Abraham Lincoln. Courtesy the National Park Service.

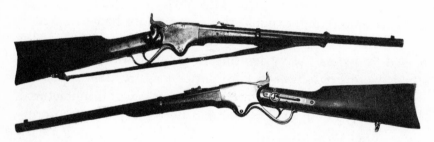

Two Spencer carbines belonging to Booth and his fellow conspirators. One was carried by Booth on his flight. Courtesy the National Park Service.

Top: Whitney revolver used by Payne in his attempt to assassinate Secretary of State Seward. Bottom: Model 1860 Army Colt revolver carried by Booth in his flight from Washington after killing Lincoln. Courtesy the National Park Service.

occupants of the box and the action on the stage. Still another door gave access to the box, and it was through this that Lincoln and his party entered.

At about 10:15 Booth struck. Entering the box silently, he fired the Deringer point-blank at the President's head. The bullet entered the skull midway between the left ear and the mid-line of the back of the head and lodged directly behind the right eye. Lincoln, who was leaning toward the stage with his hand on the rail, slumped forward, then fell back unconscious. Major Rathbone sprang at the assassin, but Booth dropped the pistol, drew the camp knife and wounded the major in the left arm. Eluding the officer's grasp, the assassin gained the railing, aimed another knife blow at the major as he made a second attempt to seize him, and vaulted over the railing to the stage below. Rathbone's efforts, however, prevented Booth from clearing the rail cleanly. His right boot struck the engraving of Washington and the spur caught and tore one of the flags. He lost his balance and fell heavily to the stage, breaking his left leg. Despite the injury, he managed to struggle to his feet, brandish the knife and shout *"Sic semper tyrannis!"* before escaping from the theater. On the way out he slashed at the orchestra leader, cutting his clothes, then with the butt of the knife he felled the boy holding his horse.

In the confusion, Booth got out of the city, even breaking his flight to pick up one of the Spencer carbines he had hidden at Lloyd's Tavern in Surrattsville, Maryland. He also had with him both of the Colt revolvers and the folding dagger. They were found in his possession when he was cornered and shot in Garrett's barn, near Bowling Green, Virginia, on the morning of April 26.

Only one of the other scheduled assassinations was attempted. The man assigned to attack the Vice-President lost his nerve, but Lewis Powell almost succeeded in murdering the Secretary of State, who was confined to bed recovering from a broken jaw and fractured vertebrae which he had suffered in a carriage accident. Powell—or Payne as he called himself at that time—presented himself at the door as a messenger bringing medicine from Seward's doctor. He carried a knife and the Whitney revolver. The ruse worked on the servant, but then things went awry. Near the top of the stairs, Frederick Seward, the Secretary's oldest son, met the would-be assassin and refused to let him enter his father's room. After a brief argument, Powell struck young Seward with the butt of his revolver, fracturing his skull and knocking him senseless. Fortunately for Frederick, the gun's loading lever broke and the cylinder pin bent so that it could not be fired. A soldier-nurse stepped out of the sick room only to be felled by a knife blow. A second attendant was also knocked down. Then Powell leaped on the Secretary.

The steel framework which the doctor had put on Seward's neck to hold the broken bones in place saved his life. The room was dark, and in his excitement Powell succeeded only in gashing Seward's face and shoulders. Then help arrived, and the opportunity was gone. Powell fought his way out of the house with his knife, leaving the useless revolver on the floor. He was captured later in the evening and hanged with the other conspirators.

All of the plotters' weapons were put in evidence at the trial that promptly followed. Most have been in government ownership ever since; and the National Park Service keeps them on permanent exhibition in Washington, D.C., in the restored Ford's Theater.

Part III

FAMOUS EDGED WEAPONS

Chapter 17

The Bayonet

What good is a spear in this day of automatic firearms and nuclear weapons? That was the question the Office of our Chief of Ordnance pondered at the close of World War II. Firepower had increased more than a hundred times since the first crude firearms had appeared on fields of battle; atomic artillery shells and guided missiles now threatened to alter the techniques of war completely, perhaps even eliminating all personal combat. Yet the United States Army was still issuing bayonets to its soldiers. Even some submachine guns were being fitted for them. But when a bayonet is fixed on the muzzle of a firearm, it does nothing more than convert the weapon into a spear, and the ordnance experts seriously wondered if this made sense in the present age.

It had originally made excellent sense . . . three hundred years ago. The muzzle-loading arms of that era required considerable time to reload, and after a musketeer had discharged his weapon, it was useless until he could perform all the complicated motions necessary to ready it for firing once more. In the meantime, he could not defend himself against an attack by enemy cavalry or pikemen. All he could do was to scurry behind the pikemen his own army provided for his protection until he could reload. When attacking, he usually dropped his gun and advanced with sword in hand. It was truly a stroke of genius to think of attaching a dagger to the muzzle of such a musket so that it would serve as both gun and pike. With such a weapon, it was no longer necessary to maintain pikemen as well as musketeers, and to perform the complicated maneuvers necessary to make use of them in battle.

No one knows who first thought of this revolutionary idea, but it is almost certain that it happened in southern France,

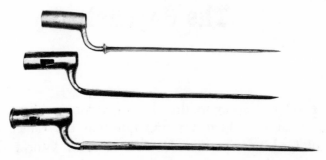

Socket bayonets of the American Revolution, top to bottom: German type with flat blade, American copy of a French pattern, and British bayonet for the Brown Bess. Author's collection.

Dutch socket sword-bayonet, dated 1778. Courtesy the National Park Service.

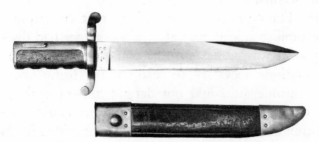

Dahlgren Bowie bayonet made for the U. S. Navy during the Civil War. Author's collection.

early in the seventeenth century. The city of Bayonne in that area was noted for its cutlery, and a type of local dagger came to be called a 'bayonette" in the late 1500s. By the 1640s there are ample references to indicate that such daggers were being attached to firearms. Marshal de Puységur, a famous French soldier and a native of Bayonne, is credited with having first used bayonets in action in 1647. Thereafter, the practice spread rapidly, and by the end of the century almost every country in western Europe had adopted it.

The earliest bayonets were nothing but daggers with tapering handles. Students today call them "plug bayonets" because the soldier simply shoved the handle of the dagger into the muzzle of his musket until it fit tightly. Obviously there were drawbacks to this design. For one thing, the piece could not be fired with the bayonet in place. Also, if the bayonet were pushed in too tightly, it was difficult to get out again. And if it were not pushed in tightly enough, it might drop out or be left in an enemy's body. A better method of attachment was needed, and once the utility of the new weapon was recognized, other designs rapidly began to appear. There were rings, clamps, bolts and other devices, but the method that attained almost universal approval was the sleeve or socket which fit around the muzzle of the firearm and locked in place with a mortise and stud. Marshal Vauban, a renowned military engineer, devised such a bayonet in 1687 and, at his urging, it was adopted for French infantry in 1688. Other nations quickly followed France's example, with socket bayonets of one form or another becoming standard for almost all European armies shortly after 1700. In their most common form, these bayonets consisted of a short sleeve with a locking slot, an elbow bent at right angles and a straight, tapering blade that was triangular in cross section. For some 150 years, this remained the most popular type of bayonet in both Europe and America.

Yet there were other types of bayonets as well; for example, retractable blades either slid in and out along barrels or stocks, or they were hinged and could be folded back along the barrel. Frequently, the hinged kind was activated by a spring so that it would snap forward into position when a catch was released. Blunderbusses and even pistols often carried hinged bayonets of this sort during the second half of the eighteenth century. Some, designed for small pocket pistols, were a ridiculous two inches in length—good only for annoyance, since a lethal stab with such a short blade would depend on luckily penetrating a vital spot. Others, mostly on blunderbusses or carbines, were a full 16 inches long. Almost all were triangular in cross section, useful for stabbing but not for cutting or ripping.

In this respect, they were inferior to the old plug bayonet, which could be used as a knife for general utility and self-defense when not fixed to the gun. Bayonet designers of the eighteenth and nineteenth centuries did not overlook such an obvious advantage, and over the years they experimented with a variety of blade shapes in an attempt to create a weapon with more versatility. Among the types they tried were flat single- and double-edged blades that could be used as swords.

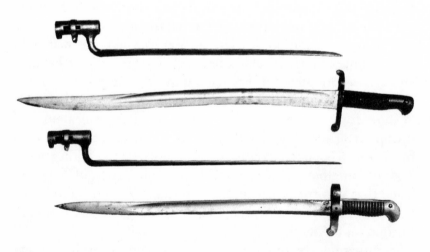

Bayonets of the Civil War, top to bottom: British Enfield angular bayonet, British Enfield sword bayonet, socket bayonet for U.S. rifled muskets, sword bayonet for U.S. rifle. Courtesy Howard Hayden.

Early examples of these sword bayonets had sockets for attachment like the angular models, but these made them awkward to hold, so other fastening techniques were contrived. Most often, the attachment device consisted of a loop at the base of the blade to go over the muzzle of the gun, plus a slot and latch at the pommel, or butt of the handle, to lock onto a barrel lug a few inches from the muzzle. Since these sword bayonets were usually longer and heavier than the angular models, they tended to make a gun muzzle-heavy. For this reason, they were most often used on short firearms such as rifles and musketoons (short muskets).

Other experiments combined the bayonet with a variety of tools. Sometimes saw teeth were added to the back of a sword bayonet for use by engineer or pioneer troops (not to make nastier wounds, as the horror stories would indicate). "Trowel" bayonets were adopted for American troops in the West after the Civil War as an aid in throwing up breastworks in a generally treeless country. Jungle fighting during the Spanish-American War and the Philippine Insurrection brought forth bolo bayonets that could be used for clearing brush when not fastened to the Krag rifle. And there were various other forms as well.

Bowie bayonet for U.S. Krag rifle, 1896. Courtesy the West Point Museum.

Bolo bayonet for Krag rifle, 1899. Courtesy the West Point Museum.

Gradually, however, a trend evolved toward the short knife-bayonet. Long blades might be impressive psychologically, but it takes only five or six inches to kill. Any greater length is superfluous. Short blades are lighter to carry, do not make rifles muzzle-heavy, and are generally more useful for non-lethal purposes such as opening rations, cutting kindling, fashioning field shelters, etc.

It was, in large part, this versatility that swayed the ordnance officers who questioned the wisdom of retaining the bayonet at the end of World War II. Their study revealed that the bayonet had indeed been employed in the classical manner on several occasions during the war, but more often it had functioned as a hand-held knife, sometimes in combat, sometimes as a utility or survival tool. Such a multi-purpose implement, they felt, should be retained despite the advent of atomic artillery and the general use of automatic arms. A well designed, short knife-bayonet, the Mark 4, had been is-

Modern U.S. knife-bayonets, left to right: M4, M5 and M6. Courtesy the West Point Museum.

sued for the .30 carbine in July of 1944. Ordnance decided to continue its use and to adapt it to the Garand rifle. Experiences in the Korean conflict proved the wisdom of their decision. The period of doubt was over, and when the new M-14 NATO rifle was introduced, there was no hesitancy in adapting the Mark 4 to this weapon. This latest version, called the Mark 6, has a checkered plastic handle and its guard has a large hole in one end to fit over the M-14's flash hider, but its blade retains the standard dagger shape.

Even in this day of astounding firepower, such a bayonet still has many uses. For nighttime infiltration, fighting at very close quarters and warding off attacks in the event of firearms malfunctions, the blade is as valuable as ever, and it is eminently suited for utility and survival purposes. Bayonet training continues to be emphasized by our armed forces, for the ancient spear has not yet been entirely replaced by the automatic rifle.

Chapter 18

The Tomahawk

It was a weapon, it was a tool, and at times it was a scepter, a ceremonial symbol, and a peace pipe as well. Indian and frontiersman alike prized it, and around it has gathered the lore of handicraft, battle, ceremony and campfire comfort. No other American arms have combined so many functions. Few other words have conveyed so much meaning as *tomahawk*.

The Algonkian Indians of the Eastern Seaboard, who coined the term, apparently used it to mean a cutting instrument. Captain John Smith said it meant ax—but to thousands of settlers along the frontier it meant terror and sudden death. It became a synonym for war itself. To "take up the tomahawk" was to start a war; to "bury it" meant to make peace, and these phrases are still used today.

What was this fearful and desirable weapon like? Actually it took many forms, although it was originally a wooden club or a stone celt. With the coming of the white man, it became an iron hatchet, and for the next three centuries it constantly changed form, to meet the demands of its users. The first of the iron tomahawks were simple hatchets or "belt axes," small copies of the European felling ax of the period. Even so, they were large by modern standards, each with a head weighing two or three pounds. As the years passed, smaller ones began to appear which were just as useful for cutting kindling on the trail and much easier to wield in combat. By 1700 it was the custom to leave the bigger tomahawks in camp for heavy work, and they soon came to be known as squaw axes. The simple little hatchets remained the commonest of all forms of the tomahawk. Thousands upon thousands of them were traded to the Indians, and they were the most popular type among the white settlers and frontiersmen as well. Morgan's Riflemen carried them during the Revolution, as did other rifle regiments then and during the War of 1812. And they are used to this day in Mexico and Canada.

The early, simple hatchets had a rounded poll, the part opposite the blade. Soon there were improvements and variations. One of the first was the addition of a spike on the poll, which made the tomahawk look something like a geologist's pick or a small fireman's ax. Such spikes began to appear shortly after 1700 and quickly became popular for fighting tomahawks. They permitted a vicious backstroke with a point that would penetrate flesh or pierce a skull with relative ease. The spikes had more peaceful uses too, such as loosening ground or digging small holes. Those with a sharpened underedge could also cut like a pruning knife.

Sometimes these spiked tomahawks were "improved" still further by the addition of a spear point, at the end of the shaft, so that the whole awesome weapon looked like a miniature halberd or medieval battle ax. Actually this extra point was impractical. It got in the way and was apt to stab its owner in the back as he carried it in his belt. Therefore, it lasted only a few years during the mid-1700s. Still another variation was the substitution of a hammer head instead of the spike on the poll, so that the tomahawk resembled a shingler's or lather's hatchet. This version was never very popular—perhaps because few Indians drove nails—but it was made in small numbers for many years.

The most favored of all the specialized tomahawks, however, was the pipe tomahawk. Next to the simple belt ax it was more widely used than any other form, and it was far more highly prized by those Indians fortunate enough to obtain one. Nobody knows what genius devised this wonderful combination of tool and weapon with the comforts and ceremonial importance of the pipe. Probably it was some forgotten Englishman, for the pipe tomahawks first appeared in the English trade areas early in the 1700s. Wherever it appeared, it quickly eclipsed all others except for the simple belt ax, which was vastly cheaper. Even white frontiersmen and soldiers found the combination of pipe and hatchet useful. When the men of the Lewis and Clark Expedition ran out of tobacco on their long trek, they split the handles of their tomahawks and chewed the wood for the last remnants of the tobacco taste. For more than two centuries the pipe tomahawk reigned supreme. When the Crow chief, Holds-His-Enemy, visited the Great White Father, William Howard Taft, in Washington in 1910 he proudly carried his pipe tomahawk just as the "Four Kings of Canada" had held theirs when they went to England and visited Queen Anne in 1709.

But the pipe tomahawk of 1910 was not the same as that of 1709. There had been many changes over the years. The first versions had been true tools and weapons as well as pipes. The blades had been big and strong, the handles heavy enough to deal a stout blow even though pierced through as a pipestem. These were the tomahawks that Lieutenant Henry Timberlake saw among the Cherokees in the 1750s and described as their most "useful piece of field furniture" after watching in wonder while they smoked a pipe ceremonially one moment and the next hurled it at a tree or a fleeing enemy.

Later in the century some tomahawk heads were made out of brass, with only the edge of steel. As the frontier pushed

Halberd-type tomahawk, circa 1750.
Author's collection.

farther west, the tomahawk became more and more ceremonial and less important as a tool or weapon. Trees were few on the plains, and the double-pointed stone club on its long, supple handle was more useful than the hatchet for fighting on horseback. Strictly ceremonial all-brass heads appeared, and sometimes pewter ones as well. Even the iron and steel heads gradually developed thin blades without any edge.

Now and then, however, hostile acts were still committed with this weapon. A trapper, Osborne Russel, was charged by an Indian with an upraised tomahawk in the 1830s. Marcus Whitman was killed by a Cayuse Indian in the Oregon country with one in 1847, and the Army Medical Museum exhibits

Pipe tomahawk with brass head and inset steel edge, circa 1800.
Author's collection.

Plains Indian pipe tomahawk, circa 1850–70.
Courtesy William O. Sweet.

Pipe tomahawk with spontoon blade, circa 1830–50.
Courtesy William O. Sweet.

Plains Indian pipe tomahawk,
circa 1860–80.
Courtesy William O. Sweet.

skulls with tomahawk wounds that were collected even as late as the year 1869.

But by the time of Custer's famous battle at the Little Big Horn in 1876, the hatchet was no longer a factor in warfare for either side. It was at least one weapon the unhappy 7th Cavalry did not have to contend with, though the peace commissioners still gasped from its raw tobacco for the rest of the century.

Chapter 19

Jim Bowie's Blade

Lumberman, slave trader, land speculator, colonel in the Texas Army and defender of the Alamo—Jim Bowie was all of these. But today he is perhaps best known for the introduction of a knife. His name immediately calls to mind a huge and terrifying blade with supernatural powers. Novels, movies, and television have contributed to the legend, but what has history to say of the original Bowie knife and the whole class of cutlery to which it gave its name?

According to Rezin P. Bowie, Jim's brother, the direct ancestor of the famed blade was a knife that he himself developed. He wanted a special hunting knife, so he designed one with a straight, single-edged blade 9¼ inches long and 1½ inches wide. In 1827, Rezin gave the knife to Jim, who had recently been shot while unarmed, thinking his brother might need it for self-protection. As it turned out, he did.

A short time later, members of two warring factions met on a sandbar in the Mississippi near Vidalia, Louisiana. In the ensuing fight, Bowie's friends claimed that he killed one of his opponents with the knife after the man had shot him in the hip and stabbed him in the chest with a sword-cane. Then, after taking a pistol ball in his left arm, he wounded another of the group and chased him off the sandbar. In 1829, Bowie is reputed to have used this same knife in a fight with a notorious Natchez gambler, John Sturdivant. In this encounter the men faced each other with their left wrists tied together; the story goes that Bowie succeeded in disabling his opponent by cutting the tendons of his right arm.

Then, in 1830, came the real Bowie knife. Shortly after the fight with Sturdivant, Jim Bowie went to Texas. On his return, he is said to have visited the blacksmith shop of James Black in Washington, Arkansas; he gave Black the pattern for a knife he had designed and asked Black to make him one. Apparently the pattern was based on the knife designed by his brother Rezin, which had served Jim so well in his previous encounters. In later life, Black always maintained that he had improved on Bowie's model and thus had really invented the formidable weapon himself. As far as can be determined, however, Jim had altered Rezin's knife only by increasing its size, and if Black made any change it was simply to add the short "false edge" along the back at the point—if, indeed, he actually made the knife at all, a matter of considerable dispute.

Evidence is scanty on the appearance of this first Bowie knife, and much of it is unreliable. Certain facts, however, are pretty well substantiated. It was a large knife, suitable for self-defense or general-utility work in the woods. It could be used for lopping off saplings, cleaving the skull of a bear— or an enemy—jointing game or even digging into rough ground. It was single-edged, but a false edge ran along the back for a few inches, permitting a backstroke in combat. The point was probably clipped: that is, the back swooped to meet the edge in a concave arc. And, since this was a fighting knife, there was a guard.

So much is known and nothing more. Romantic stories about magical tempering, secret formulas and techniques of forging, the use of ore from a meteorite and dozens of other myths have grown up, but they all stem from highly suspect sources far removed both in time and place from the actual genesis of the Bowie. Be that as it may, the story of the new knife and tales of the designer's prowess spread far and wide.

Within days after it was delivered, Jim is supposed to have bested three desperadoes who sprang at him from ambush as he rode back to Texas. With his lethal new blade, Bowie struck off the hand of the assassin who seized his bridle. Then, despite a deep stab wound in his leg, he sprang from his horse and disemboweled the second, overtook the fleeing third attacker and split his head in two!

With testimonials as sensational as this on every tongue, knives in the supposed image of Bowie's appeared along the frontier all the way back to the East Coast. Most of the early specimens, made by local blacksmiths, were huge affairs, often between 13 and 16 inches long; they usually had clipped points and handles of wood, bone or antler.

Gradually, however, the knives became more sophisticated in design. American firms along the Eastern seaboard began to manufacture them, and English cutlers from Sheffield produced replicas by the thousands. One such man, George Wostenholm of the famed Washington Works, made several trips to the U.S. to study the needs and wishes of American knife buyers. His knives, bearing the trademark I*XL, were probably the finest produced by the British.

American Bowie knife in its classic form. Courtesy William O. Sweet.

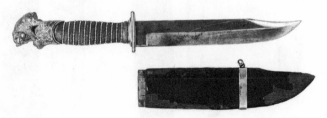

American Bowie knife of about 1850 with California bear pommel. Courtesy William Shemerluk.

Variations in design and materials multiplied. Blades were made with symmetrical "spear" points as well as clipped points. They were beautifully finished, and many were etched with decorations and slogans. Mounts were made of brass, silver, German silver, and white brass; grips were fashioned from ivory, horn, tortoise shell, and mother-of-pearl. Even when the hilts were solid German silver in standard table-cutlery patterns, the knives were known as Bowies—in fact, so far as buyers and sellers were concerned, a knife need only be large, suitable for fighting and general utility work to be

English-made Bowie knife with table-cutlery handle and etched blade, about 1850–60. Courtesy Robert Abels. Below: Group of English-made Bowie knives with spear points. Courtesy Herb Glass.

called a Bowie. The variations were endless, and aside from one or two mass-produced designs, it is rare indeed for a collector to find two exact duplicates.

Jim Bowie died at the Alamo in 1836, but the popularity of "his" knife was just beginning. Throughout the 1840s and 50s, the demand increased as the Forty-niners crossed the plains to California, gamblers worked the river boats, politicians defended unpopular stands, and the average citizen in a good many parts of the South and West simply felt undressed without one.

When the Civil War came, soldiers on both sides carried Bowies. Most of the volunteers had one from the very start; the town of Ashby, Massachusetts, for example, presented a Bowie knife to each man when he enlisted. Company C of the 1st Georgia Infantry was known as the "Bowie Knife Boys."

After the war, the popularity of the knives declined. Buffalo hunters and cowboys still carried them, but the frontier was already vanishing; civilization was crowding out the big knife. It diminished in size and quality until it became the hunting knife of today, shorn of its awesome proportions and a great deal of its grandeur.

Chapter 20

The Clash of Sabers

Epaphras Hoyt was emphatic in his views about weapons. An old cavalry officer who had served during the American Revolution, he scorned all critics of the sword's use in battle and damned those who would rely solely on firearms. The saber, he declared in print, is "indisputably the most formidable and essentially useful weapon of cavalry: Nothing decides an engagement sooner than charging briskly with this weapon in hand. By this mode of attack, a body of cavalry will generally rout one that receives it with pistols ready to fire."

He published these comments in his famous *Treatise on the Military Art* of 1798 for all future officers to read and learn, and many other cavalry leaders of the period agreed with him. Colonel William Washington had commanded the 3rd Continental Dragoons, and he was just as emphatic. So was Light-Horse Harry Lee, and the philosophy of these Revolutionary soldiers guided American cavalry for almost a century—until the time of the Civil War.

The saber on which these great cavalrymen relied was a relatively new weapon when they first came to know it. Before the nineteenth century, horsemen in Europe and America had generally carried broadswords with heavy basket hilts. British dragoon swords, in fact, can hardly be distinguished from the contemporary Scottish *broadswords*, and the two are often confused. Then, under the influence of Eastern Europe where the Polish and Hungarian light horsemen and hussars had been causing a great stir, Western nations began to adopt light cavalry tactics and organization. With the new fighting methods came the light, curved swords that had been popular in the East. The British light cavalry regiments were organized primarily in the 1750s. When the American Army raised horse regiments for the Revolution, they copied the new British styles in both dress and armament, including the cavalry saber, for all of the men. British and American swords never became sharply curved in the Eastern scimitar fashion, but they were often somewhat curved. Also, they were single-edged, designed for cutting rather than thrusting, and they had simple guards consisting only of a strap of metal to protect the knuckles. This type of guard was called, logically enough, a knuckle-bow.

The American cavalry saber of the Revolution was a large weapon. A 35- or 36-inch blade was standard, and the overall length might reach 42 inches, with a weight of three pounds. The blade was either flat-sided or ground with three narrow grooves called fullers. These grooves were not "blood gutters" as they are often mistakenly called; they were intended primarily to lighten the blade and give it better balance.

Hilts were simple, but they came in a bewildering variety of patterns. The commonest boasted a plain stirrup guard. That is, the knuckle-bow looked like half of the typical, simple, cavalry stirrup of the period—which is still used today, for that matter. The pommel (the butt of the hilt) was a plain flat cap. This sword was a loose copy of the usual British pattern. Other sabers had wider guards, sometimes pierced with designs. These guards might be either iron or brass, pommels might look like chocolate drops or even lion heads, and the grips could be plain wood, sometimes handsome curly maple, or wood covered with leather and bound with twisted wire. There were other variations, too, but these were the most common.

After the Revolution was won, the Army was reduced to
an absolute minimum. Horsemen disappeared from its ranks,
and so did the saber. Then, in 1798, trouble arose with
France, resulting in naval actions that have sometimes been
called the Quasi-War. Once again authorizing mounted troops,
the new United States government contracted for its first official cavalry saber. The maker was Nathan Starr of Connecticut, and the sword is now called the Starr Model of 1798.
It was a copy of the British pattern of the Revolution, with
a stirrup guard and a flat-cap pommel. The plain curved blade
was marked on one side with the letters *US* and the date
1799, and on the other with the words *N Starr & Co.* This
saber is a great rarity among American martial arms, for only
two thousand were made; as the very first U.S. pattern, it
commands a high price in the collectors' market. The connoisseur who owns one is fortunate indeed.

For the next twenty-four years, Nathan Starr and a Philadelphia contractor named William Rose made most of the
cavalry sabers purchased by the U.S. government. Throughout this time, the saber retained its primary importance among
cavalry weapons. But there was, nevertheless, some debate

American cavalry saber of the commonest
form used during the Revolution.
Courtesy Dwight Franklin.

Hilt of the Starr Model 1798 saber.
Courtesy Harry D. Berry, Jr.

about the merits of its design. During the Revolution and the early years of the new nation, cavalry leaders had all emphasized the cutting stroke, for which a curved blade was most efficient. New officers were now claiming that the sword was best used for thrusting and not for cutting at all. The edge, they maintained, was ineffective; the only real way to kill was with the point. Even a non-fatal wound from a thrust would be deeper and slower to heal than a cut, they pointed out. Thus, a straight blade would be much better. Most of these new theorists spoke up during and after the War of 1812, but their pleas fell on deaf ears. With the end of this conflict, the government once more abolished regular cavalry regiments. The only sabers that were bought were for militia units, and few procurement officials were ready to make a major design change under these circumstances.

Finally, in 1833, the Army decided to raise a cavalry regiment once again—the Regiment of Dragoons, as it was to be called. The new theorists on saber usage now gained a hearing, but only a partial victory. It was decided to copy a British pattern once again, and this time the blade was to have a reinforced "quill" back (a rounded, thickened spine along most of the back) and only a very, very slight curve. Theoretically, the Model 1833 could be used for either slashing or thrusting, but the truth was that it performed neither function well. It did, however, introduce a brass hilt with a half-basket guard of three bars that was to become standard on American cavalry sabers for almost eighty years.

Model 1833 Dragoon saber, with its almost straight blade contrasted with a curved Model 1812–13 by Nathan Starr that emphasized the cut over the thrust. Courtesy the Rock Island Arsenal.

In 1840, as cavalry troops became more and more important, the United States adopted still another new saber. This time the design imitated a French pattern. The guard remained brass with a half-basket of three bars, but the blade was heavier and curved a bit more than the Model 1833. Once again it was definitely a cutting weapon, though the point could be used. This saber was modified in 1859, when a new, light pattern lessened the curve and narrowed the blade. It was only a slight change, however, for the sword still weighed two pounds. "Old wrist breaker," as the soldiers called it, was the saber worn by American cavalrymen during the Mexican War, the Civil War, the Plains Indian Wars, and the Spanish-American War. It was the last of the important saber weapons, for in the Civil War the revolver suddenly changed all ideas about cavalry tactics. With six shots readily available from a pistol, it became more and more common for a mounted trooper to fire at his opponent and draw his saber only when he had emptied his gun. Classic cavalry charges with drawn sabers opened the Civil War, but they were rare when it ended.

Still the conservative theorists held sway in the matter of arms design. The saber was not relegated to parade duty in

Hilt of Model 1840 heavy cavalry saber
patterned after a French example.
Author's collection.

Model 1913 cavalry sword designed by George S. Patton, Jr. Courtesy the West Point Museum.

their minds even though it was in actual practice, and ordnance officers continued to try to improve the weapon. They learned from studies of battles that the men who had emphasized the use of the point had been right. For example, in the heroic Charge of the Light Brigade back in the Crimean War of the mid-1850s, almost all of the sword wounds inflicted by the British cavalry had been made with the point, not with the edge. European countries were all changing to straight swords that emphasized the thrust. Some even had pistol-type grips that made slashing very difficult.

The United States followed suit, even though the sword had already outlived its combat usefulness. In 1906, Ordnance brought out an experimental model that went part way toward the pure concept of a thrusting sword, and then in 1913 the Army went all the way: One of the service's most proficient swordsmen, George S. Patton, Jr., designed a straight double-edged sword with a huge iron guard and a checkered grip. It was a beautifully balanced weapon and wonderfully efficient. Unfortunately for the designer, who later became the famed tank commander and one of World War II's most colorful generals, the days of mounted combat were over. Patton had no chance to prove the deadly perfection of his contribution. The Army was destined never to use its new edged weapon in battle, but it could at least take pride in the fact that it finally had the best cavalry sword ever designed.

Part IV

AMERICANA

Pre-Revolutionary War Kentucky rifle
with straight, thick stock and simple patch box.
Courtesy Joe Kindig, Jr.

Chapter 21

The All-American

"The most lethal widow and orphan maker in the world" . . . "a superb arm" . . . "deadly at unheard of distances"— these and similar comments brought to the attention of the world the first truly American gun, the American rifle.

Europe was the source of the basic principles of this "superb arm." Rifles had been made there since 1500 and the theory involved was well understood. For good performance the ball needed to fit the barrel tightly, so it either had to be the exact size of the bore and be forced down the barrel with heavy blows of the ramrod aided by hammerlike strokes from the powder flask, or it had to be wrapped in a greased patch of linen or leather. Both methods were used from a very early date and are fully described in books written before 1650. Rifle shooting had at one time been a popular sport in continental Europe, but by the time the German, Swiss, and Dutch settlers reached Pennsylvania it had largely died out except for professional gamekeepers and foresters.

Yet it was these colonists from eastern Europe who brought the rifle here. The settlers began to arrive in considerable numbers after 1710, and with them came the short, big-caliber rifles of their native lands. Some of the newcomers were gunsmiths, and they undoubtedly began to make more of these rifles in their new home. While these were good weapons to begin with, highly accurate at short and medium ranges, the requirements of life on the frontier soon brought modifications that not only perfected the arms but made them things of beauty.

The needs that shaped the new type of rifle were threefold: accuracy at extreme ranges, economy of operation and ease of handling in wooded country. To provide greater accuracy at long range, the barrel was lengthened; this also insured that the powder charge would be completely consumed. Then, to conserve lead and powder—usually in short supply along the frontier—the bore size was gradually decreased. European rifles frequently had bores of .65- or .70-caliber. By the time of the Revolution the average American rifles were .45 to .60, and by the end of the century they were .40 to .45. Decreasing the caliber lessened the diameter of the barrel; this reduced the weight of the gun and made it easier to handle. Stocks also grew lighter as the straight, thick butts gave way to a slender design with a graceful droop and a crescent-shaped buttplate that fitted the shooter's shoulder.

Other changes that were not related to performance helped make the American rifle distinctive. New woods, especially curly maple, became popular. The sliding wood, bone or horn cover on the little compartment in the stock that held the patches was replaced by a hinged metal cover, usually brass. Typical American decorations were carved into the wood of the better specimens or inlaid in brass, pewter or silver along the stock. In the years before and during the Revolution, ornamentation was scanty, confined as a rule to simple relief carving. From 1785 to 1820, however, the arts of carving, inlaying and engraving flowered.

The rifle's evolution was slow, and it was not until around 1750 that enough changes had been made to justify designating it as a new type. Some called it the Pennsylvania rifle because it originated on the borders of that state, and it was also known as the Kentucky rifle because of its popularity with the explorers and settlers of the territory that later became Kentucky and Tennessee. But it was the *American* rifle—as it

was named in the first references to it around the middle 1700s
—no matter which state has the better claim to its name.

From about 1750 to 1820 it continued to develop in the
grace of its design and decoration. Thereafter, although it remained an accurate and efficient weapon, it deteriorated in appearance.

Much has been written about the American rifle's accuracy, and its performance was indeed amazing. When the
first 10 companies of Virginia and Maryland riflemen heeded
the plea of Congress for soldiers and marched to Boston as
the nucleus of the new American Army, they delighted in
demonstrating their skill to city dwellers who were not familiar with these new guns. One Virginian is said to have left
the urbanites goggle-eyed by putting eight consecutive shots
through a five-by-seven-inch target 60 yards away. Indeed, it
was considered no more than average shooting for a marksman
to hit an enemy in the head at 200 yards or place a shot some-
where in his body at 300 to 400 yards (if the wind wasn't too
strong). No wonder the accuracy of the American rifle attracted worldwide attention.

The necessity of centering each ball in a patch before ramming it down the barrel made the rifle slow to load as compared with the smoothbore musket of the day, with its loose
ball and prepared paper cartridge. Because of this fact and
because it did not have a bayonet, the American rifle's use
in the Revolution was restricted to special troops. Its accuracy made it an excellent gun for light infantry as well as
trained marksmen who served as snipers or scouts. In fighting
the Indians along the frontier or dealing with the Indian allies of the British in the northern campaigns, it had no equal
—but in the more formal warfare that characterized most of
the conflict along the Atlantic seaboard, riflemen had to be

Kentucky rifle at the height of its development, with brass
and silver inlays, circa 1815–20. Courtesy Joseph E. Aiken.

backed up by regular infantry with their rapid-firing muskets and bayonets to keep the enemy from overrunning their positions.

One engagement during the Revolution, however, proved an out-and-out rifle victory. At the Battle of Kings Mountain in the Carolinas, a group of frontier riflemen cornered and defeated a larger British force. Here the rifle alone was the instrument of victory; no other firearms were employed by the Americans.

Again, in the War of 1812, the deadly aim of American riflemen combined with superb American artillery to turn back a veteran British army at the Battle of New Orleans. Sheltered by breastworks and supported by regular infantry, these riflemen could use their arms to the best advantage, and the results were staggering: British casualties, 2600; American, 13.

This was the American rifle, a gun that was more than a superior weapon. For it transcended its place in history and became part of the American legend.

Chapter 22

The Hall Rifle

Every time a man squeezed the trigger, flame and hot gas leaped from an opening just inches in front of his face. A maddening, hook-like lever protruded from the underside of the stock, digging into each infantryman's shoulder, tangling with his belt and other equipment, snagging his clothing, catching on brush. And the gun had a reputation for blowing off thumbs. Yet the Hall rifle made firearms history and established a new pattern for industrial technology.

Few guns have combined so many paradoxes. For example, although some of its design elements were primitive, the Hall was the first arm successfully produced on a modern assembly line. It was originally conceived as a flintlock shoulder arm, but it soon developed into a percussion rifle-handgun with a breech that was removable for use as a pistol; it was carried as pocket protection on many a dangerous frontier street. It had drawbacks that would have frightened a modern shooter, yet it was the first breechloader ever adopted as a standard military weapon by any nation. And although it was invented by a man with little gunsmithing experience, it was the first arm with completely interchangeable parts.

With various improvements, the Hall was produced for a quarter of a century, during which time it not only became the world's first major military breechloader but possibly the first regulation percussion arm--certainly the first used by American forces.

This amazing rifle was the invention of a down-East Yankee from Portland, Maine. John H. Hall was his name, and since wild coincidence produced three men of that same name all living in the same general area at the same time, historians have had a terrible time trying to straighten them out and decide which one invented the gun, which one was a jeweler and which one a shipbuilder. There was a John Harris Hall and two John Hancock Halls. For more than seventy years, arms students have believed that John Harris was both the shipbuilder and the inventor, but within the last few years documents have been discovered proving that the younger John Hancock, born January 21, 1778, was entitled to honors as the inventor and mechanical genius.

Little is known about Hall's early life or his background in gunsmithing. Probably he had little training, for he admitted that when he invented his firearm he was "but little acquainted with rifles and . . . perfectly ignorant of any method whatever of loading guns at the breech." The previous three hundred years of experimentation with breechloaders in Europe were wasted on young Hall. He tackled the problem without any background whatever—and, at the age of twenty-three, came up with a successful solution.

His new gun was a flintlock, like all the other arms of the time. It was also a rifle. What set it apart was a pivoted breech-block that contained both the lock mechanism and the chamber of the barrel. This block could be raised by pressing in and up on a little hook-shaped catch on the underside of the stock. Using one of the paper cartridges of the period, a standard load could then be inserted (after first priming the pan with a little of the powder) and the block was pressed back into position, where a spring catch would hold it in place. This was a good deal faster than loading from the muzzle, and it could be done easily while kneeling or prone.

Hall patented his new gun in 1811. In the process he encountered a young Washington architect named William

Thornton who was employed by the Patent Office. Thornton claimed that he was working on a very similar breechloading system, and to avoid trouble Hall agreed to a joint patent although the main ideas were all his own.

The eve of the War of 1812 would seem like a fine time to develop a new weapon, but it was not until peace was restored that young Hall was able to interest ordnance officers in his invention. Then extensive tests were held, and the new rifle performed admirably. In 1819 it was adopted as an official arm and production began at the Harpers Ferry Armory, with John Hall himself employed to supervise its manufacture. In this position he was able to set up the gunmaking machinery he had designed and to create an assembly-line system utilizing completely interchangeable parts. A similar system had been tried in France late in the eighteenth century. Eli Whitney, inventor of the cotton gin, had attempted it in the United States some twenty years before Hall, but mechanization was limited and tolerances were too great. Hall was the first to succeed completely.

As for the drawbacks of the arm, it probably never blew off a man's thumb—despite the rumors—but the little hook on the bottom was really a nuisance. A fishtail key replaced it in the 1840s, and this was something of an improvement; finally a side lever almost completely removed the trouble.

Hall flintlock rifle and bayonet, Model 1819.
Courtesy the Smithsonian Institution.

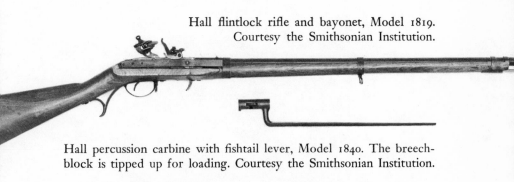

Hall percussion carbine with fishtail lever, Model 1840. The breechblock is tipped up for loading. Courtesy the Smithsonian Institution.

These last two modifications were made only for carbines, however; the infantry rifle was always equipped with the hook catch. Its biggest drawback was perhaps the joint between the breechlock and the barrel. This was a simple butt-joint which became loose enough with wear so that gas and flame could escape, annoying, frightening and distracting the shooter. This difficulty never was corrected.

Despite all these handicaps, the Hall rifles and carbines were made, with both flint and percussion locks, for a quarter of a century. They were used in minor wars with the Indians all along the frontier and in Florida. They served effectively in the Mexican War, and some of the old arms were still in service for the beginning of the Civil War in 1861.

The percussion version of the Hall had one unique advantage. The breechblock could easily be removed and carried as a pistol for personal protection when a soldier was off duty. This was a feature that no other U.S. military arm before or since has ever provided, and many a Dragoon on leave in a captured Mexican city was happy to feel the angular lines of a Hall breech in his pocket. These soldiers, at least, thoroughly approved of John Hall's invention and of their country's leadership in adopting a breechloader for military service.

Chapter 23

Double Death

The third decade of the last century was a wild and turbulent era in American history. Down in Texas, Jim Bowie had just died at the Alamo. His body had scarcely been consumed on the great funeral pyre with the other heroic defenders of the mission, and the Bowie knife was already an American institution. Up in Philadelphia, Henry Deringer, Jr., was busily fashioning the lethal little pistols that made his name famous throughout the land as a symbol of violent death. Together, the big knife and the little pistol became the indispensable companions of almost every adult male in the South and West. In many communities no man—whether he was a hunter, gambler, tradesman or political leader—felt fully clothed without a pistol in his pocket and a knife in his belt or hidden in his coattail. One weapon could strike at a comparative distance; if it fired only one shot, that often turned out to be plenty—and the gun was small enough for easy concealment. The other weapon provided a final defense at close quarters if the pistol failed to stop an attacker.

To George Elgin of Macon, Georgia, it seemed logical that these two arms should be joined together. Such a combination would, he thought, have numerous advantages over the usual custom of wearing two separate weapons: it would be more compact for carrying, and it would be faster and more efficient in use. There would be no more need to drop the pistol and fumble for a knife after shooting. As he explained in his patent application, ". . . in an engagement, when the pistol is discharged the knife (or cutlass) can be brought into immediate use without changing or drawing."

Filled with enthusiasm, Elgin applied for a patent in Washington on March 9, 1837, and received the coveted document on July 5 after successfully defending his right to it against another inventor who had been working on a similar idea. Actually, men had been trying this sort of combination almost since the first handgun had been invented. Even Samuel Colt had experimented with a knife blade on his new revolver a short time before.

If George Elgin was aware of these previous (and largely unsuccessful) attempts, the knowledge failed to deter him. Even before his patent had been granted, he placed an order for a thousand of his new arms, in three different sizes, with the firm of Morrill, Mosman & Blair of Amherst, Massachusetts. By the summer of 1837 he was able to exhibit two pattern pistols to the commandant of a planned U. S. Navy ex-

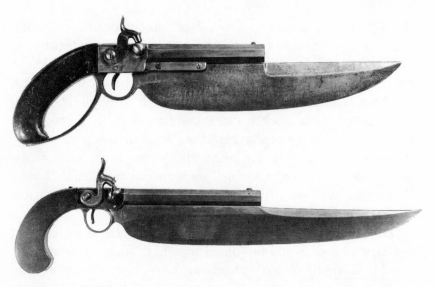

Elgin cutlass pistols, Navy Model above, a civilian model below. Courtesy the Smithsonian Institution.

ploring expedition to the South Seas; he used these samples
to support his argument that he had designed the ideal side
arms for such a venture. On September 8 he received a Navy
order for 150 of his "pistol knives"—on condition that they
could be modified to meet official requirements and delivered
within forty-seven days. Success seemed just around the
corner, for with this contract Elgin's cutlass pistol had become
at one stroke the first percussion pistol and the only combination arm ever officially accepted for the United States Armed
services. It was obvious that such official endorsement would
increase the huge civilian market Elgin anticipated.

Therefore the inventor felt he needed a second manufacturer to handle his Navy contract. Apparently Morrill, Mosman & Blair was so deeply involved with its contract for the
first thousand pistols that the firm could not make the slightly
altered version requested by the Navy. Elgin called upon
Cyrus Bullard Allen of Springfield, Massachusetts, to supply
the pistols and Nathan Peabody Ames, the noted sword maker,
to produce the blades and scabbards.

When finished, the Navy cutlass pistols were truly impressive weapons. The five-inch pistol barrel was .54-caliber. The
special, high-heat-tempered steel blade was 11½ inches long
and fastened to the bottom of the barrel with a tongue-and-
groove joint secured by two screws. The trigger guard was a
one-piece extension of the blade and included an additional
guard to protect the fingers holding the grip, in true sword-
guard fashion. A leather scabbard, tipped with German silver,
held both the pistol and a ramrod. For each of these plus
three extra nipples per pistol, the Navy paid $17.50; Captain
Thomas Catesby Jones, who had signed the contract on be-
half of the United States, delighted in their "unquestionable
superiority . . . over any other [weapon] for arming boat
crews and exploring parties [landing on] islands inhabited
by savages."

Captain Jones may well have been right in his appraisal of
the cutlass pistol. So much gear had been purchased for the
South Seas Exploring Expedition that a lot of it had to be

left behind, but at least some of the Elgin pistols went along when the ships sailed in August 1838. There were landings on hostile islands just as Jones had expected, and in one recorded instance of actual combat the new weapon performed as well as its inventor could have hoped—though the fight ended tragically.

It was July 1840, and a small party under Lieutenant Joseph Underwood and Midshipman Wilkes Henry had landed on Malolo Island to bargain for provisions with the Fiji natives. In the midst of the bartering the natives suddenly attacked. Underwood and Henry sought to cover the retreat of the party to their boat. With a pair of ordinary belt pistols, the lieutenant dropped two of the cannibals and was striving to defend himself with their butts when he was killed. The midshipman shot one of the attackers with his Elgin and cut down another with the blade. Then, seeing that the crew had reached the boat and that Lieutenant Underwood was dead, Midshipman Henry turned to flee but was struck on the back of the head by a missile and killed.

This is the only account of the actual use of the Elgin cutlass pistol in combat. The Expedition made no official report on its performance. Even if such a report had been filed, it probably wouldn't have helped the inventor. The civilian market that Elgin had so happily anticipated never materialized. A great depression began in 1837, and all new inventions, including Samuel Colt's, fared badly during the hard times. When the Expedition returned, George Elgin was already out of business. The firm of Morrill, Mosman & Blair was bankrupt. Cyrus Allen had died. As suddenly as that, one of the nation's most unique and colorful arms had faded from the American scene.

Chapter 24

Magic Gun of the Plainsmen

No one could call it a beautiful gun. Its ancestors had been long, graceful rifles, light of bore, with fine carving and delicate inlays. But this offspring had none of their grace. Its barrel was heavy and its bore large; its stock was thick and chunky, and there was little decoration. In fact, there was nothing to recommend it but performance. It was designed for a special job, which it did superbly. The men of the Western mountains and plains had told the gunsmiths exactly what they wanted in a gun. The plains rifle—or mountain rifle, as it was often called—was the result.

The famed Kentucky rifle developed by the gunmakers of Pennsylvania had served the frontiersmen of the Eastern states well. In the wooded country east of the Mississippi, game was relatively small, with deer and black bear about the biggest animals one could expect to meet. Distances were comparatively short and most men traveled on foot. The small caliber, long barrel and light stock of the Kentucky suited their needs perfectly.

As the trappers and frontiersmen spread out past the Mississippi into the new Louisiana Territory, their needs changed. Here was a vast country with huge distances to be covered in search of furs and supplies. The horse became the standard means of transportation; no one set out on foot if he could possibly avoid it. Game was bigger, too. There were bison and elk instead of deer, and the grizzly was a vastly different proposition from the black bear. These animals took a lot of killing. Small balls and light charges were worse than useless.

Thus the rifle changed. The gunsmiths who moved west from Pennsylvania into Ohio, Illinois—and especially to St. Louis—altered old guns and made new ones to meet the changing demands of their customers. Long guns were a nuisance on horseback, so barrels were shortened; most ranged between 28 and 38 inches. Calibers were made larger to stop big game, generally .45 to .55, and the barrels were heavy enough for a minimum service charge of 100 grains of powder. Stocks were sometimes full-length to the muzzle, sometimes short half-stocks. Either way they were sturdy, thick in the wrist and wide in the butt. This destroyed all grace of design, but it created a stock that would not snap at the first fall from a horse's back. It was still possible to decorate these arms, and a few of them were carved and inlaid. Usually, however, the plainsman avoided any ornamentation that might catch the sunlight and either spoil his aim or attract an enemy's attention. Also he preferred to put his money into features that would insure performance rather than please the eye.

There were other distinctive features about these guns. They were heavy. Since the huge powder charges would have kicked unmercifully in a light arm, many a plains rifle weighed 15 pounds or even a little more. The barrel was soft iron and the rifling grooves were cut in a slow spiral. Balls pushed by 100 grains or more of powder would not always take rifling with a rapid twist; they might skip and fly wild unless charged exactly right. The slow twist with soft iron permitted a wide variety of loads, even up to 215 grains, with no sacrifice of accuracy. Almost always the new guns were percussion arms. Some of the first ones were flintlocks, but by the time the plains rifle had reached its full development the older lock had become obsolete.

This was the rifle of Jim Bridger, Kit Carson, Joe Meek, and their brethren of the high plains and the Rockies. With it

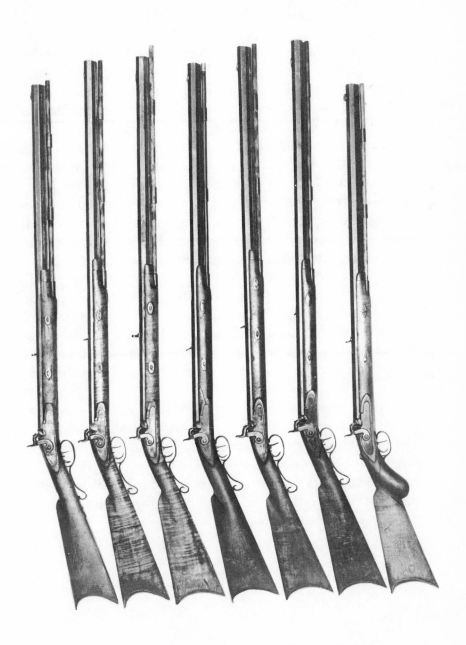

Group of Hawken plains rifles. Courtesy James E. Serven.

they slaughtered the buffalo for food and fur, brought down the mighty grizzly and fought the Sioux and Blackfoot. With its almost foolproof reliability no matter how rapidly and carelessly charged, its superb accuracy and long range, it was a constant delight. Using such a rifle, Henry Chatillion showed the astonished historian Francis Parkman that he could regularly drop buffalo with a clean shot through the lungs at distances beyond 300 yards. And Lieutenant George Brewerton watched in amazement as an old hunter named Lewis winged a Digger Indian on the dead run at over 200 yards.

Perhaps the best summary of the plains rifle's capabilities, however, comes from a much later source. Many years after it had passed from common use, an experienced marksman found a new specimen in St. Louis. Remembering stories of its prowess with considerable skepticism, he determined to give it a thorough test. He, too, was astounded.

". . . I found that it would shoot straight with any powder charge up to a one-to-one load, equal weights of powder and ball. With a round ball of pure lead weighing 217 grains, patched with fine linen so that it fitted tight, and 205 grains of powder it gave a very low trajectory and great smashing power, and yet the recoil was no more severe than that of a .45-caliber breechloader. . . ."

It was a fine arm for its day and purpose, but conditions changed and gradually the plains rifle disappeared as had its Kentucky forerunner. The heyday of the fully developed percussion plains rifle was from 1820 until almost 1870. Then the breechloaders began to move in. The big Sharps, especially, became vastly popular and the slower muzzle-loading rifles were pushed to one side.

Chapter 25

The Most Imitated Pistol

Imitation, it has been said, is the sincerest form of flattery. If this is so, Henry Deringer, Jr. of Philadelphia must have been one of the most sincerely flattered gunmakers of history. Other gunsmiths throughout America copied his designs, imitated his workmanship and even pirated his name and trademark. Within his lifetime, his name became a common noun, applied to a whole class of firearms. No other gunmaker in all history ever achieved such a distinction.

Deringer's famous product was a pistol. More specifically, it was a pocket pistol with a short barrel in a large and powerful caliber. He did not hit upon this concept suddenly, in a moment of inspiration; rather, it developed over a number of years as part of his regular line of gunmaking.

Henry Deringer, Jr. was born in 1786 in Easton, Pennsylvania. The son of a gunsmith, he was apprenticed to his father's trade in Richmond, Virginia, when he was still a boy, and after completing his apprenticeship, he moved to Philadelphia in 1806 and set up in business for himself. Mostly, he made muskets and rifles on order for private citizens and on contract for the United States government. He also made a few handguns—flintlocks at first, then percussion guns when that new ignition system became known in Philadelphia. His dueling pistols were of such high quality that they achieved a measure of fame (as did many of his other guns), but he was still known primarily as a maker of shoulder arms.

According to Deringer's own recollections, in 1825 he began concentrating more extensively on handguns—though not yet on very small models. In that year, he made a pair of percussion pistols for a Major Armstrong, a man he recalled as being "Governor of some of the Indian tribes west of Arkansas" at the time. Actually, Armstrong was not made agent to the Choctaws until 1831, but the date of the pistols that Deringer gave, 1825, may be the correct one, nevertheless. These were undoubtedly large guns of the type collectors now call "greatcoat" or "coaching" pistols, and these new percussion arms quickly attracted attention. Deringer's name became recognized as a symbol of pistol quality, and in succeeding years he gave more and more of his attention to such arms.

The exact birth date of the pocket pistol that brought Deringer his greatest fame is unknown. Probably it was in 1848 or 1849, when the veteran gunmaker was already well into his sixties. The distinctive style of this model had been developing slowly ever since the pair of percussion pistols for Major Armstrong had first brought the name Deringer to attention in the civilian pistol field: The back-action locks—

Deringer pistol, as seen from the left and right side.
Courtesy the Winchester Gun Museum.

with the firing mechanism inletted into the wood behind the hammer rather than in front of it—had appeared probably in the mid-1830s. The checkered grips and big hammer spur had also become characteristic of his work. Even the foliate engraving and the trademark "DERINGER/PHILADELA" were in use at least by the early 1840s. All that remained was the matter of size, the "bird's-head" contour of the butt and the characteristic barrel shape—flat-topped for its entire length and octagonal at the rear with the sides and bottom rounded near the muzzle. And perhaps even these unique elements evolved gradually as the other basic features had.

When the classic Deringer did appear, it was a deadly little weapon. Its barrel might vary in length anywhere between 27/32-inch and four inches, and calibers ran all the way from .33 to .51. The over-all length of the pistol varied from tiny vest-pocket sizes of 3¾ inches to greatcoat-pocket dimensions at nine inches. The barrel was always rifled, with seven grooves twisting in a clockwise direction. The stock was black walnut, and the mountings were German silver, except for a few extra-fancy guns with gold or gold-plated mountings. Deringer considered the construction and decoration of his barrels as a significant characteristic by which legitimate specimens, made in his own shop, could be separated from spurious copies. His barrels were wrought iron, and they were etched and browned in swirls to simulate a Damascus twist. There was a very low blade sight at the muzzle and sometimes a raised notch sight at the rear.

The little pistol packed a man-sized punch. The shortest specimens might not be accurate for more than six or seven feet, but they were deadly at close quarters. Their size was such that they could be concealed with ease, fitting into a pocket with scarcely a wrinkle showing. Some men fastened them inside their waistcoats, tied them in their coat sleeves, stuck them in their boots or even hid them down the backs of their collars. A Deringer would fit almost anywhere, ready for any short-range emergency. Here was a wonderful weapon for the man who wished to appear unarmed but knew better than actually to go without a gun. Here also was just the sort of arm to use as a second, hideout, weapon in the event that an unconcealed arm had to be surrendered to an adversary.

Despite these many advantages, it took a number of years for the Deringer to achieve wide acceptance. Sales grew through the early 1850s, reaching their peak in the years from 1855 to 1861, with a total of about 8000 pistols finding purchasers during this period. By now, imitators were brazenly copying Henry Deringer's style and even his name. To avoid lawsuits, some of his competitors called their guns "derringers"—spelling the name differently so that they could not be convicted of trademark infringement.

The Civil War and the advent of breechloaders brought a decline, but in its brief heyday the Deringer pistol made its presence felt on a wide scale. The greatest markets were in the South and West, especially in California where the *Army and Navy Journal* reported that "the sharp crack of the Deringer . . . [was] heard in the land much more frequently than the voice of the turtle." Almost everyone in the Territory seemed to carry one, or sometimes two—gamblers, lawmen, newspaper editors, politicians, and just plain citizens. Deringers figured in homicide after homicide, ranging from slayings of anonymous miners in the gold fields to the murder on February 27, 1859, of Philip Barton Key, the son of Francis Scott Key, by Congressman Daniel Sickles within a stone's throw of the White House—and finally, six years later, the assassination of Abraham Lincoln by John Wilkes Booth. Everyone in the country came to know Deringer's name from reading of these crimes in the newspapers.

When Henry Deringer died in 1868 at the age of eighty-one, he was a wealthy man, highly respected in his community. By then, cartridge guns had nearly driven his percussion pistol off the market, but his idea of a small pocket gun with a large bore had been accepted all over the country. And these new arms were—and still are—called derringers, even though the later ones utilize self-contained ammunition.

Chapter 26

Lindsay's Double-Loaders

There is no denying that John P. Lindsay hit upon an excellent idea, but it came to him just a little too late. In the mid-1800s, when he first began toying with the notion of loading a single-barreled gun with two charges, other inventors were already working on more sophisticated repeaters. Lindsay's contribution was clever—in fact, unique—yet it was doomed from the start.

For centuries men had been experimenting with the idea of loading a series of charges one on top of another in a single barrel and then firing them off either singly or in series. Pistols and shoulder arms adapted for that sort of shooting had been made ever since the 1500s, but always there had been some drawback, some danger of malfunction, that made them unsatisfactory for general use. Sometimes these guns refused to fire at all; sometimes only part of the load ignited and left one or more charges in the barrel which could not be fired until the gun was loaded all over again. Worst of all, some devices had a tendency to fire the rearmost load first, putting a tremendous strain on the gun and on the shooter and often injuring one or both.

Lindsay knew all about these troubles, but he devised a way to eliminate them and make a gun that would fire two consecutive charges out of the same barrel with complete safety.

The trouble was that by the time he accomplished it, almost no one was interested any more.

As a young man, Lindsay got his start as a gunsmith at the Springfield Armory in the 1850s, making guns for the United States government. It was there that he devised the general plan for his new arm. Legend has it that he was inspired by the death of his soldier brother in a campaign against the Indians. Armed with a single-shot muzzle-loader, this soldier had been at a considerable disadvantage when the Indians drew his fire and then charged before he could reload. Supposedly, Lindsay was driven by this sad event to devise a gun that would fire twice and so disconcert the wily savages. There may be a germ of truth in this story, but it is unlikely that the course of developments was quite so simple. After all, other people had worked on such guns, and some of these experimenters were undoubtedly known to Lindsay. It is possible, however, that his brother's death prompted him to join their ranks. Even so, his first model, produced in 1860, was a very unmilitary pocket pistol.

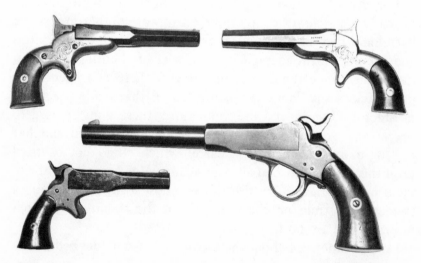

Lindsay's big .44-caliber pistol and three Lindsay "Double Deringer" pocket pistols with spur triggers. Courtesy Samuel E. Smith.

Lindsay's arms were muzzle-loading percussion-cap weapons with the loads set off by the detonations of caps placed on nipples that led directly to the charges. To make his invention a two-shot pistol, Lindsay used two nipples and two hammers. One nipple led straight down in the normal fashion to ignite the rear (second) charge, while the other was connected to a tube that ran a short distance up the barrel before it entered the bore in a position to ignite the front charge. In his earliest models, Lindsay also used two triggers, one for each hammer. The right trigger fired the first load and the left one fired the rear load; to avoid accident, it was important for the shooter to pull them in the proper order.

Lindsay also designed a special bullet that was a real wonder to behold. It consisted of two spheres joined by a short bar so that they looked like a miniature exercise dumbbell. The loading sequence was a powder charge, then one of these double-ended bullets, then another charge and a second bullet. The space between the two spherical ends of each projectile was designed to be filled with a lubricant. If this was packed in well and the rearmost bullet was rammed down properly, it effectively prevented the fire of the front charge from leaking back and setting off the second load. Lindsay supplied brass molds to cast these unusual bullets, and today the molds are a real collector's rarity.

With his pistol designed, Lindsay began production almost at the same time he applied for a patent, late in 1859 or early in 1860. Before the patent was granted, however, he had perfected his gun still further, and the original application appears to have been withdrawn in favor of a new one covering his improvement—a lock with a single trigger that would fire first one hammer and then the other with no chance for confusion about pulling the right trigger before the left. It was an ingenious device that not only assured the proper firing order but also prevented the accidental fall of both hammers in quick succession on a single pull of the trigger. Safety was built in because it was necessary to release the trigger after the first pull before the second shot could be fired. The patent was granted October 9, 1860. Lindsay saw no reason to wait for this formality, however, and he seems to have put his new single-trigger arms into production well before that date. Double-trigger specimens, in fact, are quite rare.

Lindsay had picked a good time to start manufacturing arms. War clouds loomed very plainly on the horizon. There was unrest in the newly settled frontier regions, and even many a citizen in the civilized East thought seriously about being properly armed. If there was ever a seller's market in firearms, this was the time, and Lindsay's new guns got off to a good start. The inventor arranged for manufacturing facilities in Naugatuck and New Haven, Connecticut, to produce the arms, but for snob appeal he used a New York City address in his barrel stampings. He manufactured two kinds of pistols; one was a pocket model with a spur trigger which he called a "Double Deringer" in his advertisements and marked "Lindsay's Young America" on the barrel. This was a powerful .40-caliber handgun, often with a rifled barrel. It would command respect in any emergency. But there was an even bigger model in .44-caliber with a conventional trigger and trigger guard. For some reason, Lindsay called this hefty handgun his Navy Model, but collectors today generally refer to it as the Lindsay Army pistol since .44 was the standard caliber for Army weapons—while the Navy traditionally preferred the .36.

Probably Lindsay hoped to sell this big pistol to the government, especially since the Civil War had broken out and there was a great clamor for almost anything that would shoot. Although he was disappointed in this hope, he did manage to sell the Army a two-shot rifled musket based on his principle. In fact, he sold a thousand of them for $25 apiece.

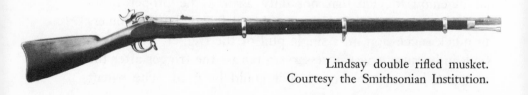

Lindsay double rifled musket.
Courtesy the Smithsonian Institution.

They performed very well in the intensive tests the Army gave them. In all of these tests, however, they were carefully loaded, and the manufacturer's directions were followed precisely. Apparently the Ordnance officers feared that soldiers in the field might not be so careful, for the Army bought no more of the double rifles.

The Lindsay double pistols and rifles were good arms. In spite of the Army's doubts, they were safe and reasonably foolproof. Even if the rear charge went off first, the shooter needed to fear no worse consequence than a ferocious "kick." The trouble with Lindsay's idea, as noted above, was that it came too late. He was trying to sell a muzzle-loading arm at a time when metallic cartridges had begun to render them obsolete. He might have made a terrific success fifty years earlier. As it was, he failed.

Chapter 27

B. Tyler Henry's Rifle

Oliver Winchester was worried. Ever since he had ventured outside the world of shirt making and invested in the arms industry, he had been in trouble. In 1855, he bought eighty shares of stock in the Volcanic Repeating Arms Company; the name had a fine ring to it, but the performance of Volcanic rifles and pistols left a great deal to be desired. Mechanically the guns were good, but the ammunition they used was poor. The cartridges were weak, and misfires were frequent. There had been managerial difficulties as well, and finally the firm went into bankruptcy. In 1857, Mr. Winchester organized a new corporation—called the New Haven Arms Company—with which to buy Volcanic's assets; and in the process, he personally retained eight hundred shares of the stock. This was a controlling interest, and so Oliver F. Winchester, shirt maker, found himself president of a firearms company manufacturing guns that few people wanted to buy.

Something had to be done. From previous experience, Winchester understood management and merchandising. Even though he knew nothing about guns, he could—and did—apply his skills to this new field. He sought fresh sales outlets, he insisted that his products be sold at list price, and he advertised heavily. But all this was not enough. The new firm soon found itself in the same dire straits as the old one. The only thing that could save it was a new product, a gun that worked well enough for people to want it.

This was beyond Winchester's capabilities. Fortunately, he found help in the person of B. Tyler Henry, the new plant manager he had appointed to bring efficiency to the operation of the factory. Henry was a good designer and administrator, who knew guns and the gunmaking business thoroughly. But more than that, he had the spark of true mechanical genius. In 1858, Winchester called upon this gunsmith to put his genius to work in an effort to save the New Haven Arms Company. He asked Henry to develop a new cartridge that would be powerful, safe and self-contained, and he asked for an improved gun to shoot the new loads.

This was a tall order, but Henry was equal to it. In a matter of months, he developed a .44-caliber, rim-fire, metal-cased cartridge. Then he made a few simple alterations in the Volcanic rifle that was already in production, both to overcome its weaknesses and to adapt it to the new ammunition. On October 16, 1860, he patented his improvements (which included a new locking bolt and a firing pin that struck both sides of the cartridge rim at once to lessen chances of a misfire). With minor retooling, the New Haven Arms Company was soon ready to go into production, and the re-designed rifle, now called the Henry, made its debut early in 1862.

It was a light, sleek, brass-framed arm, just like its predecessor. A tubular magazine under the barrel held fifteen cartridges, and a lever action fed them into the chamber and cocked the gun just as it had in the Volcanic. But the subtle improvements were reflected in better performance. The Henry weighed only about 9¼ pounds—less than most rifles of its time—and it was very fast-handling. In government tests, it was quickly proved that a reasonably skilled man could fire 120 rounds from the Henry in five minutes and 40 seconds—including loading time. This meant an average of one shot every 2.9 seconds. A highly proficient shooter could do even better. Winchester claimed that two shots per second were possible, but this figure was based on shooting a single magazineful from an already-loaded rifle. At any rate, the Henry was a very rapid-firing arm, offering a large number of shots. It was possible, in fact, to carry a cartridge in the chamber in addition to the full magazine load, thus making 16 shots instantly available. This was awesome firepower in an era that was dominated by single-shot rifles.

Speed and lack of weight were not the only advantages offered by the Henry. Its cartridge also performed well. The 216-grain bullet was lighter than many hunting and military projectiles of the period, and the 26-grain black-powder charge was almost diminutive by contemporary standards. Nevertheless, the slug had a muzzle velocity of 1200 feet per second, and it actually retained enough force to kill at a thousand yards. This was more than sufficient for the shorter ranges at which it was generally used, and the small cartridges meant less weight for the shooter to carry.

Once his new rifle was ready, Oliver Winchester lost no time in starting to sell it. He had special presentation models elaborately engraved and plated in gold and silver as gifts for men whose influence might be helpful. Abraham Lincoln got one. So did Secretary of War Simon Cameron and Secretary of the Navy Gideon Welles. The Civil War was building to its climax, and large government purchases seemed a logical and profitable goal for the company. Unfortunately, there was no

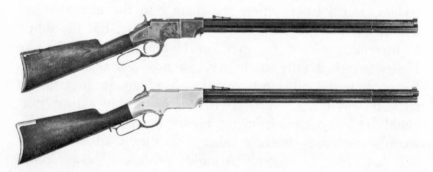

Henry iron-frame rifle (above) and the more common brass-frame rifle. Courtesy the Winchester Gun Museum.

chance of success. The Chief of Ordnance, Brigadier General James W. Ripley, was a staunch supporter of muzzle-loading rifled muskets, and he despised all newfangled breechloaders and repeaters. As a result of his attitude, the Federal government bought only 1731 Henrys. Sales had to be sought elsewhere, and Winchester quickly found them.

At the time of the Civil War, it was common practice for individual states to equip their own regiments before sending them off to fight for the Union, and several Northern states bought the new guns for their troops. In addition, individual officers and enlisted men (even some of those in the Regular Army) purchased these repeaters in quantity. Outside of the military, the market also grew rapidly. Cowboys, mountain men, prospectors and miners bought the new rifles. So did lawmen—and bandits. Wells Fargo issued Henrys to some of its stagecoach guards and presented specially engraved models to heroic employees. In just three years, more than ten thousand of the new rifles were made and sold.

The New Haven Arms Company prospered mightily. After teetering on the brink of bankruptcy, the firm suddenly found itself quite solvent, with a net value of about $354,000.

Detail of Henry rifle presented to President Abraham Lincoln. Courtesy the Smithsonian Institution.

Moreover, it had a network of dealers established throughout the Northern and Western United States, and it was ready to move into the area recently governed by the Confederacy. Because the Henry's reputation resulted in a growing demand for the gun, inquiries were now beginning to come from Europe, raising the possibility of large sales abroad. It was time for another reorganization in New Haven, and once again Oliver Winchester was ready. In 1866, he formed the Winchester Repeating Arms Company—absorbing New Haven Arms—with himself as president, and sold all his remaining interests in the shirt business. He then brought forth a slight modification of the Henry, the Winchester Model 1866. A firearms dynasty had been established, and although B. Tyler Henry retired that same year, the factory continued to stamp the head of each rim-fire cartridge it manufactured with a large letter H—as it does to this day—in tribute to the man whose genius had rescued the company from disaster.

Chapter 28

The Trapdoor Springfield

The single-shot trapdoor Springfield was an expedient, and expedients are never ideal. They are seldom even good. This one was an exception. Designed for fast, easy production, it was a strong and simple rifle that handled easily, shot well and hit hard.

The decision to adopt a breechloader as the official shoulder arm of all United States troops came toward the close of the Civil War. Experience gained in that conflict had proved conclusively that breechloaders were practical, and they had outperformed the old muzzle-loaders in every way. At the end of hostilities, however, the Union arsenals were full of perfectly good muzzle-loading arms. It seemed a shame to waste these guns, especially in view of the post-war military economizing that began in 1865. Funds were scarce, and the obvious expedient was to try to convert these old firearms to breechloaders rather than to develop some "ideal" new rifle. Erskine S. Allin, Master Armorer at the Springfield Arsenal in Massachusetts, invented a practical method of altering muzzleloaders for breechloading, and the conversions began in 1865. With further minor improvements, the Allin-altered rifle became the trapdoor .45/70 Springfield a few years later.

As designed by Allin, the new arm had a strong, simple action. A breechblock—which included the firing pin—was hinged at its forward end. A simple latch released the block so that it could be flipped upward, exposing the chamber and ejecting the spent case after a cartridge had been fired. A fresh load could then be slipped into place, the block snapped shut and the side-mounted hammer cocked, all in just a few seconds. The unusual upward opening of the rifle's action explains why this Springfield was called the trapdoor design.

The first 5000 rifles altered to Allin's system retained the .58-caliber bore that had been used during the Civil War. Then, in 1866, an improved extractor was designed and a liner was brazed into the bore to reduce the caliber to .50. The next 25,000 trapdoors, known as the Model 1866, were manufactured with these refinements, and the new .50-caliber barrels were used for the Models 1868 and 1870. Then, in 1873, the bore size was reduced to .45 and, except for minor variations, the famous .45/70 trapdoor Springfield rifle of the Indian wars had reached its final form. The .45/70 designation of course described the cartridge, which boasted a .45-caliber bullet propelled by 70 grains of black powder. This was an excellent load that provided a hard-hitting slug and a flat trajectory, making the Model 1873 Springfield especially useful for firing at the long ranges that were often encountered in the American West.

Raw recruits particularly welcomed the rifle's simplicity of operation and the bullet's flat trajectory. Using live ammunition for marksmanship training was considered wasteful at that time. It was better to save the cartridges for actual fighting, the officials believed, and field commanders apparently agreed. (Or at least they complied.) One report stated that the men had been allowed a total of twelve cartridges apiece for testing and target practice during a full year. Thus, city

Springfield .45/70 infantry rifle. Courtesy the
Winchester Gun Museum.

boys and immigrants who had never handled a gun before they enlisted might suddenly find themselves pinned down in a Western gully, fighting for their lives with a weapon they had used only once or twice in practice. In such a situation, they delighted in the .45/70, which worked easily, shot where it was pointed and did not have to be aimed high to compensate for a sharply curved trajectory.

For almost thirty years, the trapdoor Springfield served in the field with few complaints from any source. The one major criticism concerned an occasional difficulty in extracting spent cartridge cases after prolonged periods of firing. This fault received considerable attention in the press following the disastrous Battle of the Little Big Horn, in which General George Armstrong Custer and five troops of the 7th Cavalry were wiped out by Sitting Bull and a force of Sioux and Cheyennes on June 25, 1876. A shocked nation read that the .45/70 carbines carried by the troopers had jammed in the desperate struggle. Cartridge cases had been found on the field with their heads torn off by the extractors. This fact was magnified as the nation sought a scapegoat for the catastrophe. So was the fact that the soldiers were armed with single-shot rifles while at least a few of the Indians apparently carried lever-action repeaters. The ammunition difficulty proved to be rare in actual occurrence (and the number of repeaters used by the Indians proved to be greatly exaggerated). The trapdoor system therefore weathered the storm of criticism as professional soldiers rallied to its defense. It continued in use throughout the entire period of the Indian wars; many volunteer units carried it during the Spanish-American War in 1898, and some state militiamen were still armed with it at the outbreak of World War I.

The most common form of the trapdoor Springfield was the infantry rifle (Models 1866, 1868, 1870, 1873, 1879, 1880, 1882, and 1889), but it appeared in a number of other designs as well. "Cadet rifles," slightly smaller than the standard versions, were made for West Pointers, beginning in 1868. Carbines for cavalry were adopted in 1870, and successive varia-

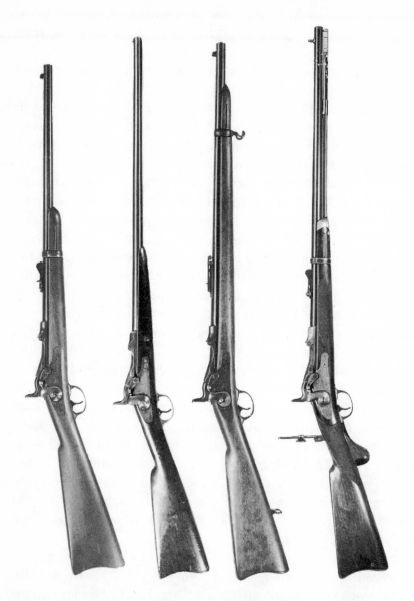

Left to right: Springfield .45/70 carbine, Model 1879; Springfield 20-gauge shotgun; experimental 1882 rifle-carbine, an attempt to make one arm suitable for both infantry and cavalry; Officer's Model .45/70 Springfield. Courtesy Archer L. Jackson.

tions appeared in 1873, 1879, 1884, and 1890. These carbines, along with Colt or Schofield Model Smith & Wesson revolvers, constituted the primary armament of the United States Cavalry throughout the West. There were also rare patterns of the .45/70, including an Officer's Model with a sporting half-stock, adjustable peep sight and handsome engraving, and there was even a 20-gauge shotgun variation. A few trapdoor shotguns were manufactured in 1881 for issue to frontier scouts and guides who could use them to supplement regular rations with fresh meat. Both the Officer's Model and the shotgun are rare, but possibly the rarest of all the trapdoor Springfields is the short rifle, Model 1882, which is readily recognizable by its 28-inch barrel. This was an experimental weapon made in an attempt to produce a single shoulder arm that would be suitable for both infantry and cavalry. The trapdoor short rifle was never manufactured in any quantity.

The models described thus far were the government arms, but private enterprise also produced trapdoor guns, sometimes even complete with the Springfield Arsenal marks. Manufacturers did this by purchasing surplus locks and sometimes receivers from the government and fitting them with new stocks and barrels. Frequently, these are handsome arms with engraved mounts and nicely checkered stocks. They look, in fact, very much like the Officer's Model Springfield, except that they usually have octagonal barrels—a feature by which they can quickly be recognized. All the government models had round barrels.

In 1892, the United States government adopted the Krag-Jorgensen magazine rifle, and two years later the Krags began to reach troops in the field. Erskine Allin's single-shot action had become obsolete, though it was not to disappear entirely for more than twenty-five years. In the whole history of U.S. martial arms, few long guns have performed their function more efficiently or in more colorful surroundings. And few indeed can offer the collector such a variety of models and types—ranging from the simple to the ornate and from the common to the very rare.

Chapter 29

Saga of the Six-Gun

Tucked into a low-slung holster, its plow-handle grip close to the marshal's hand, the single-action Colt revolver has become a symbol of the Old West to millions of television viewers across the United States and to many people in foreign lands. Its efficiency has been exaggerated beyond all possibility as actors fire away at impossible ranges, seldom bothering to reload after firing the six shots that a cylinder holds. So widespread is the Colt's reputation that American airmen during World War II who carried the Colt Single Action found it commanded enormous respect even in remote parts of China. The Chinese, who were not at all impressed by the issue .45 automatic, recognized the super-weapon they had seen perform remarkable feats in Hollywood Westerns.

But what was the gun really like and what role did it play in American history? When production began in 1873, the Colt factory designated it the Model P. It was a sturdy revolver with a solid frame, a cylinder bored for six cartridges and, usually, an ejector on the right side. It was single-action —that is, the hammer had to be pulled back and cocked before the gun could be fired. Calibers varied. The first revolvers were .45. In 1878 a second line was chambered for the .44/40 Winchester cartridge so that the Westerner who wanted to carry both a rifle and a revolver needed to carry only one type of ammunition. The manufacturer added other calibers until there was a spread from .22 to .476.

Barrels ranged from three to seven inches in standard models, and longer ones could be had on special order. Other variations soon appeared on the market. Some short-barreled versions, known as "house" or "storekeeper" models, didn't have ejectors; some models were fitted for shoulder stocks. When smokeless powder replaced black powder, the Colt was strengthened to withstand the greater pressures. Standard and flat-topped frames, custom sights and finishes, plating, engraving, custom grips of many materials—all of these became available.

The first trade name adopted by the Colt company was the Peacemaker, which applied to the pistols it made in .45-caliber. By the middle 1880s, however, the revolver had become the standard Army side arm and was known officially as the Single Action Army Revolver. The variant chambered for the .44/40 Winchester cartridge was called the Frontier Six Shooter or just the Frontier Model. In 1896, a target version— the Bisley—came out. One of the most famous, though short-lived, modifications was the Buntline Special with its extra-long barrel and detachable shoulder stock. There were also a number of nicknames that applied to any and all of the models—"thumb-buster," "plowhandle," "hog leg," "equalizer," "six-gun," and many more.

Colt single-action Peacemaker revolver, serial No. 1.
Courtesy John S. du Mont.

Even if it couldn't perform all the feats attributed to it in the movies, the single-action Colt was and is a magnificent arm. It provided accuracy at normal pistol ranges; it had the stopping power necessary to drop an adversary or a wild animal with one shot; it was ruggedly built. Westerners depended on its strong construction, for handguns might be dropped, stepped on by a horse or be subjected to other harsh treatment. Furthermore, the Colt "S.A." was designed with tolerances that permitted it to operate even if dirt or sand got into the action—a distinct asset, since this eliminated the necessity of taking the gun apart and cleaning it before it could be used again. In a tight situation, there might not be time for disassembly.

The Colt had another advantage immediately recognized by the modern industrial designers and packagers. It looked like a gun and felt like a gun. Just to hold it imparted a sense of power—a factor that has much to do with its popularity today, long after more powerful, more accurate and faster-shooting pistols have become generally available.

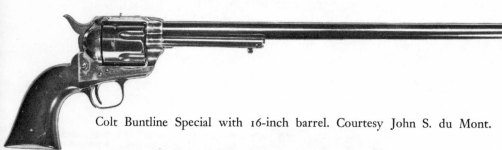

Colt Buntline Special with 16-inch barrel. Courtesy John S. du Mont.

Colt single-action "Storekeeper" Model
with short barrel and no ejector.
Courtesy John S. du Mont.

The Colt Single Action has played an important role in military as well as civilian history. It was the standard pistol for the Army throughout the major Indian campaigns after 1873. No other revolver even came close to rivaling it in the West, for sheriff and outlaw, cowboy and miner, homesteader and storekeeper preferred it to all others. Even after the Army discontinued issuing single-action revolvers in favor of double-actions and then automatic pistols, many officers continued to buy and carry the old Model P. General Patton, with his fully engraved silver-plated Peacemaker fitted with ivory grips, was a notable example. He purchased his in 1916, wore it on the Mexican border and during both world wars.

Colt discontinued production of the famous revolver in 1941, but the gun was too good to die; the demand for it continued and prices for antique or just plain "used" specimens soared. After the war, imitations and variations by other firms reached the market. And, finally, Colt's executives heeded the demand and decided to revive the company's most popular arm in .45 as well as other calibers. Thus, almost a century after the first production model was completed, it is still possible to buy a brand-new Colt Single Action revolver.

Chapter 30

The Knuckleduster

To an Irishman, the finest weapon in the world has always been a stout oak shillelagh—or so the popular myth would have it. But James Reid of Belfast thought otherwise. A club was fine for a more or less friendly brawl, but if the situation got really serious, a man needed a gun. The ideal weapon for hand-to-hand fighting, according to Reid, had to be small, yet combine two purposes—shooting as well as head or jaw cracking. In the end he designed and manufactured just such an arm; but it was for Americans, not Irishmen, and he perfected it years after he had left his native land for a home in the New World.

James Reid was born April 9, 1827, the son of a prosperous textile manufacturer of County Antrim. He grew up among the machines of his father's Belfast factory, and the life of an industrialist seemed to appeal to him. He married and he sired a daughter before suddenly deciding to emigrate to America at the age of thirty. The reason for this decision is unknown, but James, his wife and daughter Annie arrived in New York City in February 1857. Aside from the birth of a son, James, Jr., a month after he arrived, there is no record of Reid's life during the first five years in America. Probably he worked in various mechanical occupations to support his family. Then, in 1862, he blossomed forth as a firearms maker, specializing in cartridge revolvers.

It was a long jump from textiles to guns, but in December of '62 he applied for his first patent on a revolver. The gun utilized removable percussion nipples so that it could be fired either with percussion caps or with self-contained metallic cartridges.

The Civil War was now in progress. Hundreds of thousands of men were locked in the national struggle. And there was violence as well in Reid's bailiwick. Draft riots plagued New York City, and a family legend has it that the Reids watched these brawls from the second floor of their building, at 171 East 26th Street. It was an opportune period to be making guns, and business prospered.

Then the time came to move again. Annie, Reid's daughter, was in bad health, and the doctor recommended that the family move out of the city. They chose a site in Catskill, New York, beside a creek that could provide power for a grist mill and a series of gun shops. During the spring and summer of 1865, Reid worked to establish his new factory and mill. There was a mansion for his family as well as fifteen houses for his employees, for by this time he was a man of substance, a successful businessman, but at heart he remained a mechanic and inventor. In the evenings he worked over designs for a new kind of revolver. This would be his ideal all-purpose weapon, and on December 26, 1865, he obtained his patent.

It was indeed a new and different kind of gun. Reid called it "My Friend" but it became generally known as a knuckle-duster or knuckler. It had no barrel, merely a cylinder supported in a frame that had a peculiar ring grip. The rear edge of this ring was not circular but protruded backward, in an out-of-round curve, to form a grip for firing or a knuckler for fist fighting. When the hammer was cocked, a little spur trigger popped forward out of the front edge of the ring grip so that the gun could be held in the normal manner and fired. As the cylinder revolved, each chamber in turn lined up with the firing pin, and a hole in the frame acted as a barrel— if it could be called that.

But the user could easily take advantage of his other option

—holding the gun by its cylinder, with his little finger through the ring, and clubbing away with the brass knuckles. It wasn't a particularly efficient design for this use since it required a back-handed swing to bring the metal ring up for a direct blow. Except at close range, it wasn't a very effective gun either, since there was no barrel to guide the bullet. It could be deadly at close quarters, but a man across the room would have a good chance of escaping all of its seven shots unscathed.

Despite its shortcomings, however, the knuckleduster found a market, and Reid coined the trade name "My Friend" in keeping with the fashion of the times which saw other pistols dubbed "Bull Dog," "Tramp's Terror," "Red Jacket," and the like. Three calibers were made—.22, .32, and .41. The smaller ones boasted seven shots while the .41 was limited to five. The large-caliber specimens are the rarities among the early models; only about 300 of the .41s were made, in contrast to perhaps 3400 .32s and a much larger quantity of .22s. Most of them had brass frames, but toward the end of production iron frames were introduced, and these iron-framed knucklers are also scarce.

The real rarities among knuckledusters, however, are those with barrels. According to well accepted legend, a guard at Sing Sing Prison suggested to Reid that he add a barrel to provide a better grip when using the weapon as a club. Actually, the barrel only gets in the way for this purpose, and it is far more likely that Reid tried it in an effort to obtain at least a little accuracy. Barreled models, manufacturecd on a trial basis, ranged from a five-shot .32 with a three-inch barrel to a .41 without a fully enclosed ring guard, but they never caught on. Probably no more than a total of 575 of them were ever finished, and today they are choice items for any collector of American revolvers.

The low production which ultimately made these guns a joy to collectors, however, brought sorrow to James Reid. During the 1870s the knuckledusters enjoyed considerable success, and other manufacturers began producing them. Per-

haps a total of 14,000 of all makes were manufactured. The
knuckler was even imitated abroad; the Belgians produced a
copy that they called "The Fisticuff." Then the market suddenly dried up. Production ceased in 1882 or 1883, and the
depression of 1884 brought ruin to the inventor. Debts could
not be collected and arms could not be marketed. He was

Selection of "My Friend" knuckledusters. The barrelless types range from
a .44-caliber model (top) to .22-caliber models (lower left). The knuckledusters with barrels are .32-caliber (top and bottom) and .28-caliber
(center). Courtesy Herschel C. Logan.

forced to sell the gun shops, the grist mill, the workers' homes and even the mansion house. Packing his remaining goods, he made his final move to West Troy, New York, where he took a job in the Watervliet Arsenal, working for the Federal government. There he died on May 28, 1898. His little gun was to become a welcome friend to collectors in the next century, but it had hardly been a friend to James Reid.

Chapter 31

Injuns!

European writers romantically idolized the North American aborigine as a noble savage. His physique was comparable to the classical ideal of the ancient Greeks, his other traits worthy of the citizens of Tartary. But to those who lived closest to him he was often an implacable foe, bitterly hated though fascinating. Admired or loathed, viewed with scientific detachment or through the rosy haze of romanticism, the American Indian has aroused the interest of the civilized world ever since the first explorers brought back word of his existence.

Of all the aspects of Indian culture, the native weapons and methods of warfare have attracted the most attention throughout the centuries. It was essential for those who fought the red man to understand these things. From the very beginning, the colonists and explorers who wrote books devoted a great deal of space to arms. Collections were formed. One of the oldest surviving Indian artifacts collected by a European is a wooden tomahawk club sent home by an Englishman in Virginia more than three hundred years ago. Famous Indian fighters such as General George Armstrong Custer and General George Crook collected Indian weapons. Old soldiers reminisced aloud and in print, and usually they discussed battles and arms. With an avid audience, imagination was encouraged. Tall tales grew and were repeated until they became accepted as fact. Myths were born. This was especially true of Indian firearms.

One of the first tales that every gun enthusiast hears concerns the arms traded to Indians by early fur buyers. According to this hoary legend, the Indian obtained his gun by piling one valuable beaver pelt on top of another until he had a stack equal to the height of the gun he sought. The wily entrepreneurs, seeking greater profits, therefore kept increasing the length of the guns they offered while the poor Indian kept paying out more and more skins in a sort of hairy inflation. This story has been spread for years by word of mouth, in catalogues, magazines, and even in books. It is sheer nonsense.

The Indian knew exactly what he wanted in a gun and he insisted on getting it—otherwise no fur. The records of the fur-trading companies are specific on the point that the guns had to meet the Indians' requirements. These specifications are listed and the contracts the companies wrote with gunsmiths contain them.

The last thing an Indian wanted was a long, heavy gun. If he were an eastern aborigine, it would get in his way in the woods; if he were a Plains Indian, it would be unmanageable on horseback. He wanted a light gun that he could handle easily and carry all day without tiring. He preferred a smoothbore to a rifle because it was easier to use and could be adapted to a variety of purposes. Rifles had to be loaded carefully with a patched ball, and powder fouling could quickly become a problem; Indians were not noted for the care they gave their guns, and they seldom cleaned the barrels. Also, the rifle's bore was comparatively small and would not hold enough shot if an Indian wanted to hunt small game. A smoothbore, on the other hand, could be fired with ball or with either buck- or birdshot.

To meet these requirements, a special and easily recognizable type of gun was developed. Collectors have given it many names—Northwest gun, Hudson's Bay fuke, Mackinaw

gun, Indian musket, Indian gun or just plain trade gun. A flintlock of about .58 caliber with a barrel ranging from 30 to 42
inches, it appeared early in the 1700s and was made almost
without change until well after 1850. Both stock and barrel
were light in weight. The trigger guard was unusually deep,
and on the side opposite the lock was a serpent-shaped side
plate. Often the figure of a sitting fox (the mark of the Hudson's Bay Company) was stamped on the barrel or lock.

This was the Indians' favorite gun for more than a hundred
years. They preferred it to the newer percussion-cap and cartridge arms because caps and cartridges had to be obtained
from traders and were expensive, while an Indian could make
his own flints. And on a running horse a flintlock could be
loaded more easily than a percussion arm. Placing a tiny cap
on a nipple was a delicate operation, but with its large touchhole a flintlock could be primed by slapping the butt and jarring some of the charge out of the barrel and into the pan.

Once the Indian obtained his gun, he usually set about altering it and making it really his own. Sometimes he shortened
the barrel to carbine length and fashioned the cut-off portion
into a tent peg or hide scraper. Frequently he removed the
buttplate—another scraper. For decoration he applied brass-
headed tacks or wrappings of rawhide. These wrappings were
also used to mend broken stocks.

Although this was the most popular arm, all sorts of guns
found their way into Indian hands through trade, gift, capture,
or theft. Army muskets and carbines, rifles, repeaters like the
Spencer, Henry and Winchester, pistols and revolvers. Each
underwent a change just as the trade guns had. (The Indians
even learned to reload cartridges without the benefit of the
usual tools, using phosphorus soaked from match heads to
prime rim-fire cartridges and percussion caps for center-fires.)
Such weapons, however, were in the minority, for the trade
gun was by far the most common firearm. And even in the
late 1800s bows and arrows were still widely used.

This leads us to another myth—that in the 1870s and '80s
the Indians were frequently better armed than the U.S. troops.

While this may have been true in one or two small encounters, the soldiers were far better armed in all the major battles, including the humiliating defeat of Custer on the Little Big Horn. Stories to the contrary were usually attempts to explain reverses. As a rule, the cavalryman carried both a carbine and a revolver. The Springfield .45/70 carbine issued to the troops was an accurate and dependable gun with good ballistic qualities; both the Colt single-action and the Schofield Smith & Wesson were excellent revolvers.

In most instances, fewer than half of the opposing Indians had firearms of any kind, and most of those they did have were muzzle-loading smoothbores in poor condition; breech-loaders and repeaters were rare. In the Fetterman Massacre in Wyoming on December 21, 1866, for example, only six of the eighty-one white men killed suffered gunshot wounds. In

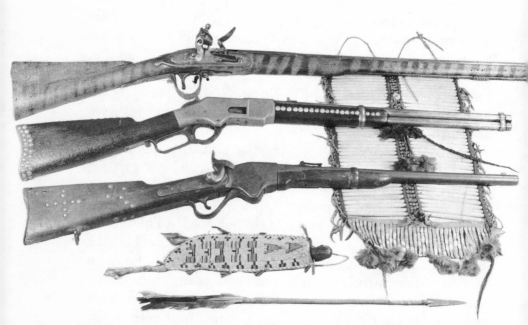

Three Indian guns. Top: Northwest gun cut to carbine length; at one time it was studded with tacks, but these have been removed. Center and bottom: Winchester and Spencer repeaters with tack decoration. Courtesy Mary du Mont.

the rout of Custer, the best-informed estimates put the number of Indians carrying breechloaders and repeaters at only 25 to 30 percent; another 25 percent had flintlocks and the remainder nothing but bows and arrows. All the soldiers had good firearms.

There is no real basis for the traditional picture of Indians either as dupes of grasping traders who inveigled them into struggling through the woods with seven-foot muskets or as splendid light cavalry armed to the teeth with the latest repeating rifles. If an Indian had a gun at all, it was probably a light flintlock smoothbore studded with brass-headed tacks, its stock wrapped with rawhide, its barrel rusty and its general condition such that the average gunsmith would declare it unserviceable. And this was true from colonial times to the winning of the West.

Chapter 32

Guns of the War Chiefs

Geronimo! Sitting Bull! These names were among the few that chilled the spines of even the bravest frontiersmen. Great Indian warriors became symbols of bloodthirsty battle, of death and destruction to all who stood in their way. They were the leaders of some of the fiercest fighters the world has ever known. Few warring groups have ever aroused so much interest and curiosity as the fighting Indians of the West.

From dime novels to Wild West shows to motion pictures, legend has lumped all tribesmen together—Apache, Sioux, Pawnee, Ute, and dozens more—into one anonymous mounted warrior in feathered war bonnet. And the legend almost always depicts this redskin as carrying a better gun (supplied by a whiskey-peddling white trader) than the arms of the soldiers and settlers he fought.

Facts have only just begun to win the battle against such legend and to present Indians as they actually were, with all their variety of customs, dress and attitudes. Their weapons, too, have come in for attention, and the true picture is gradually emerging. Guns were scarce and highly prized. Old muzzle-loading flintlocks were most popular until late in the nineteenth century, when quantities of metallic cartridges began to show up on the frontier. The repeating carbine of every movie redskin was in reality a treasure worthy of a fighting

F. REMINGTON.

chief. A short-barreled lever-action was, after all, light, fast-handling and capable of firing shot after shot without being reloaded.

Here are the firearms, both single-shots and repeaters, that were actually taken from the West's most savage fighters after the last uprisings. They range from a rifle that was used by an unknown warrior of the Hunkpapa Sioux through the weapons of some of the greatest Indian leaders in American history. The Winchester .44 carbine that belonged to Sitting Bull is now in the Smithsonian Institution, in Washington, D.C. The other guns shown are from the collection of the Museum of the American Indian (Heye Foundation), in New York City.

Some braves owned more than one gun, but the rifles pictured were the ones in their possession when their fighting days were ended. They kindle the memory of a bloody past.

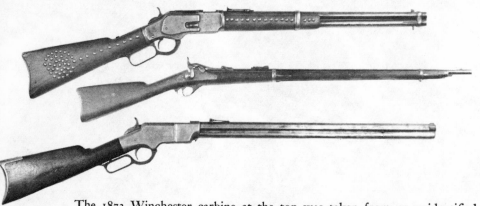

The 1873 Winchester carbine at the top was taken from an unidentified Hunkpapa Sioux at the Dakota Territory's Standing Rock Reservation; it's a tack-decorated .44/40 16-shot repeater. In the center is a .45/70 Springfield used by Lame Deer, chief of the Minneconjou Sioux. He was killed in an attack on Colonel (later General) Nelson A. Miles at Fat Horse Creek, Montana Territory, in 1877, and this rifle was taken from his body. The rifle at bottom is a .44 rim-fire Henry, presented to Sitting Bull the Minor by President Ulysses S. Grant in 1875. Often confused with the famous Hunkpapa Sioux Sitting Bull—whose gun is also shown in this chapter—the Oglala Sioux Sitting Bull the Minor, or the Good as he was sometimes called, was a friend of the white men. He was killed by enemy Crow tribesmen in 1876 on the Tongue River, and the rifle was recovered by Miles.

Sitting Bull's .44 Winchester Carbine

Probably the most powerful chief of all the Plains Indians was Sitting Bull of the Hunkpapa Sioux. A warrior who "counted his first coup" on the body of an enemy at the age of fourteen, he also became a highly respected medicine man and tribal councilor. He was the principal organizer and commander of the combined tribes that went on the warpath in 1876, terrorizing the entire Montana region, defeating General George Crook at the Rosebud River and wiping out Custer's command at the Little Big Horn only a week later. Sitting Bull himself did not, however, fight in either battle, but stayed in the rear, "making medicine" instead. The Hunkpapa medicine man is often pictured as a fighter, but once he became

Sitting Bull. Courtesy the Smithsonian Institution.

Sitting Bull's .44 Winchester, Model 1866. Courtesy the Smithsonian Institution.

prominent he rarely appeared on a battlefield and seldom fired a gun; rather, he acted from behind the lines as councilor and strategist. Faced with increasing pressure from the Army, Sitting Bull and his followers retreated to Canada. Gradually, however, bands of his hostiles deserted and returned to the United States to surrender. At last, Sitting Bull himself came back with what was left of his group, surrendering to Major David Brotherton at Fort Buford, Dakota Territory, on July 21, 1881. He remained at peace, but was suspected of trying to stir up trouble among some tribal factions; in 1890, he was shot and killed by Indian police, who claimed he had resisted arrest. The gun that Brotherton took from Sitting Bull at Fort Buford is shown here; it is a .44 Winchester repeating carbine, Model 1866, and it bears the traditional Indian decoration of brass-headed tacks.

Chief Joseph's .45/60 Kennedy Rifle

One of the greatest Indian military leaders of all time, Chief Joseph led his band of Nez Percés on a thousand-mile flight toward Canada during the widespread uprisings of 1877. On the way, he outwitted and defeated three forces commanded by famous Civil War officers; fighting against Colonel Nelson A. Miles, he seriously bloodied an Army that had four times the strength of his own group. Joseph's feat has been compared with some of the greatest organized retreats in history. At last, when he reached Bear Paw Mountain, Montana Territory—only thirty miles from the safety of the Canadian border—he was surrounded and besieged. Indian messengers managed to get through the Army lines and reach Sitting Bull, who was already in Canada; they appealed to him for help, but their pleas went unheeded, and on October 5, 1877, the Nez Percés surrendered. Miles, who was afterward made a general, said Chief Joseph "was the highest type of the Indian I have ever known, very handsome, kind and brave." Joseph led his people in peace, as he had in war, until he died at the Colville

Chief Joseph. Courtesy the Smithsonian Institution.

Chief Joseph's .45/60 Kennedy repeater.

Nahche, son of Cochise and his second wife. Courtesy the Smithsonian Institution.

Reservation in Washington in 1904. The rifle shown was surrendered to Miles at the time of the chief's capture. It is a .45/60 Kennedy repeater, an octagonal-barreled lever-action gun manufactured by the Whitney Arms Company.

Nahche's .45/60 Winchester Carbine

Son of the famed Cochise, Nahche (sometimes spelled Naiche or Nai-chi-ti) was hereditary chief of the Chiricahua Apaches of whom Geronimo was medicine man. The name Nahche, appropriately, means "mischief." To the white settlers of Arizona and New Mexico, he was that and more. Nahche was one of the most resourceful leaders during the Indian depredations of the late nineteenth century, when the Chiricahuas raided the southwestern United States and northern Mexico until they were finally subdued by General Nelson A. Miles in 1886. The war chief was imprisoned and, even after his release, was kept under constant, close surveillance. He became a peaceful leader of his people until he died, on the Mescalero Reservation in New Mexico, in 1921. This picture of him was taken in 1884, just a few months before the last great outbreak. He is shown with his wife, E-clah-heh. The gun he is holding in the photograph is a Frank Wesson carbine; it may have been his own, or it may have been a studio prop that was kept on hand by the photographer, along with the dried cactus and painted trees, for pictures such as this. The gun that Nahche actually surrendered at Fort Bowie, Arizona Territory, in 1886 was the other rifle pictured here. A lever-action carbine, it is a .45/60 Winchester repeater, Model 1876.

Nahche's .45/60 Winchester repeater, Model 1876.

Rain-in-the-Face. Courtesy the Smithsonian Institution.

Rain-in-the-Face's .52 Sharps Carbine

The West still vividly remembers the blood bath that took place when Sioux war parties gathered under Rain-in-the-Face, a chief of the Hunkpapas. An almost implacable enemy of the white man, he participated in two of the most devastating battles ever fought against the troops sent to guard the frontier—the 1866 Fetterman Massacre in Wyoming and the Custer slaughter in Montana a decade later. Both were total defeats for the whites. It has often been claimed that Rain-in-the-Face personally killed Custer, but there is no evidence to support such an assertion, and the warrior himself always denied it. Like many of the other Indian leaders, Rain-in-the-Face eventually realized that he was fighting for a hopeless cause; he had never been one to give up, but he saw that victory for his people was impossible and he finally surrendered in 1880. He remained at peace until he died in 1905. In this portrait by the famous Western photographer D. F. Barry, the Indian is holding what appears to be an 1873 Winchester. The rifle may have belonged to Rain-in-the-Face, or it may have been Barry's. The gun that the noted chief surrendered to General Nelson A. Miles at Fort Keogh, Montana Territory, in 1880, at the end of his hostile career, was the single-shot .52-caliber Sharps breechloading carbine pictured here. Its hammer, you will note, is missing. There is no record of whether the rifle was in this condition when it was surrendered—but if it was, the Indian may have deliberately chosen it as his surrender gun, merely turning in a worthless weapon.

Rain-in-the-Face's .52 Sharps.

Geronimo's .45/60 Winchester Carbine

Geronimo was medicine man and prophet of the Chiricahua Apaches. His name became so famous a symbol of warlike ferocity that it has been adopted by the U.S. paratroops as their battle cry. Contrary to popular belief, however, Geronimo was not a chief; he was a leader and councilor of the Chiricahuas, while Nahche was actually their chief. Throughout the 1870s and 1880s, the Army made strenuous attempts to subdue and pacify the Apaches in Arizona. For short periods, the soldiers would succeed; then the Indians would suddenly leave their reservations to terrorize Arizona and New Mexico, often crossing the border to plague Mexico, too. A warrior as well as a medicine man, Geronimo often led the raiding parties. In 1882, he surrendered to General George Crook, and for a while became a peaceful (and successful) farmer. But in 1885, he was back on the warpath for his last campaign. It lasted eighteen months, as he consistently eluded more than 5500 troops. It ended on September 5, 1886; on that date, he surrendered to General Nelson A. Miles—and was promptly shipped from prison to prison, on various Army posts. The rest of his life was spent under close watch, although he was finally freed. He died at Fort Sill, Oklahoma, in 1909. Geronimo had many guns. In the photograph opposite, he stands at the far right, holding a single-shot .45/70 Trapdoor Springfield, Model 1873. The warriors pictured with him are all his relatives: From the left, they are a brother-in-law, Yanozha, carrying a Winchester 1873 carbine; a son, Chappo, also with an 1873 Winchester (there is no way to

Geronimo's .45/60 Winchester repeating carbine, Model 1876.

tell the caliber of these guns from the picture); and a second cousin named Fun, who has a .45/70 Springfield carbine. This group portrait was taken in March of 1886, during a series of conferences with General Crook. These negotiations almost brought peace but the talks broke down, fighting began again and Crook was replaced by Miles. Other pictures have shown Geronimo holding a Springfield carbine and a Dance Brothers percussion revolver. The gun shown by itself is the .45/60 Winchester repeating carbine, Model 1876, that Geronimo presented to Crook during the abortive 1886 peace conferences in northern Mexico.

Geronimo, on the right, with three Apache warriors in the Sierra Madres. Courtesy the Smithsonian Institution.

Part V

SHOOTING AT MARKS

Chapter 33

Matchlock Marksmen

Skilled civilian shooters are vital to the national security of any country. In the event of war, today's civilian may become tomorrow's soldier. This is why the U.S. government supports such competitions as the National Rifle and Pistol Matches at Camp Perry, Ohio. The importance of marksmanship may be obvious, yet few modern shooters know that as long ago as the sixteenth century, European governments promoted target contests to assure themselves of skilled shooters.

Even more startling is the fact that the firearms enthusiasts of that era became so accurate that they could often center a ball in a five-foot target at more than 200 yards. This may not seem like extraordinary shooting by modern standards, but the contestants were using smoothbore arms and primitive black powder. Rear sights were almost unheard of, and a shooter could not even brace the gun stock against his shoulder.

In the late 1400s and early 1500s the guns used were matchlocks, some of them triggerless at first. Such an arm was fired by pivoting a clamp called a serpentine, which held the wick, or match, to ignite the powder. Soon, however, the trigger came into general use; it permitted better gun support and a less awkward hold because it enabled the shooter to keep his hand under the stock. Gradually, these early arms

Target shoot in Zurich—September, 1504. From a contemporary drawing.

were superseded by the wheel lock, which replaced the match
with a wheel that struck sparks from a piece of iron pyrite
for ignition. This made for faster ignition and fewer misfires,
but was still relatively crude. The average gun, whether it
utilized the match or wheel system, was about four feet long
and weighed 10 or 12 pounds. Calibers ranged from about
.60 to as large as .80. The stock was straight, designed to be
held at hip or chest level or sometimes pressed against the
cheek.

Let's look at a typical shooting contest in which early
matchlocks were used. It was held at Zurich, Switzerland, in
September 1504. Three men at a time came forward and stood
tensely inside small cubicles at the firing line, guns at the
ready. The roofs and walls of their shooting boxes were designed to provide shade and eliminate distractions; they also
isolated each man, making him realize he was completely on
his own once he stepped inside.

The boxes were open at the rear, but if a shooter glanced
back over his shoulder, he would see nothing to reassure him.
There stood a group of gimlet-eyed officials watching his
every move, checking to make sure he violated none of the
strict rules of the contest. Behind the officials, he could see
more competitors, guns in hand, awaiting their turns and obviously not wishing him well. Scorekeepers, clerks and regis-
trars sat imperturbably at their tables ready to record either
success or failure. To the rear were spectators, serious and
intent.

It was better to look ahead. There, some 202 yards away,
stood three targets—three circles, each 58 inches in diameter
with a nail in the exact center and a black bull's-eye around
it. Next to each target was a little tower protecting the spot-
ters. If the shooter scored a hit, a wand from the tower would
indicate the location. If he should miss completely, there
would be a humiliating gesture from the spotter and a deri-
sive hoot from the spectators. Other signals indicated good
shots that still might not be counted for one reason or another: A bullet that failed to penetrate the target completely,

for instance, was void; so was one that struck the nail dead center, though points were awarded on the basis of how close to center each shot landed. Disqualified shots were deducted from a contestant's total of twenty-eight chances. Some of the regulations (the number of shots allowed, for example) might vary from city to city, but they were always strict.

There were dozens of rules that the shooter had to bear in mind. Disobeying one could cause his disqualification. His gun had to be a smoothbore with only a simple globular front sight and no special gadgets for holding or steadying it. Officials inspected each gun before the shooter took his place, and they also checked his ammunition and watched him load. They permitted only one ball for each load, and that ball had to be a simple sphere. Elongated and twisted projectiles were forbidden.

It was the technique of shooting that the officials watched most closely, however. The shooter had to hold his gun free-hand; he could use no straps or shooting rest. Although he could not brace the butt against his shoulder when firing, he was allowed to lay his cheek against the side of the butt when aiming, or he could hold the piece in front of his body at

Three marksmen, from a painting of 1533, showing methods of loading and holding firearms in competition.

chest or hip level. But the weight of the gun and the force of the recoil had to be absorbed solely by the arms and hands. As if these rules did not impose sufficient difficulties, the shooter had only a limited time for firing. There was constant pressure on him from the moment he stepped into his shooting stall. That's how it was at Zurich, and tensions were as great at matches all over Europe.

The attitude of the public greatly increased these pressures. Shooting contests were serious matters. Competition among cities throughout Switzerland, Germany, and Austria was intense. Prizes for the best shots were often lavish: gold, silver, rich cloth, livestock, and other coveted awards.

What spurred the shooters even more than the prizes, however, was a dread of the ridicule heaped upon the competitor with the lowest score. That unfortunate man was seized by jesters, who acted as prizemasters, and was hauled before the crowd to hear his shame proclaimed loudly and listen to sneering comments about his talents, his probable depravity and his home life. Into his arms the jesters thrust a sow with piglets—the traditional booby prize for shooting events—and the final indignity came as they threw him upon a bench, beat him with bladders, slapsticks and other clowning gadgets and berated him for having had the nerve to enter the contest. This was humiliating treatment, but it was meted out to anyone—prince as well as peasant—who was so unfortunate as to come in last. Shooting contests were surprisingly democratic in this respect.

With all of these handicaps, both mental and physical, it is remarkable that the shooters could perform at all. But they shot remarkably well. In 1558, at Rottweil, Germany, 218 shooters fired eighteen shots each. One contestant placed all of his bullets in the target. Five others scored seventeen hits apiece and seven made sixteen each. In all, thirty-seven marksmen placed thirteen or more shots where they counted. Similar scores were recorded at other contests, truly remarkable records when you consider the arms used, the method of holding the guns, the time factor and the almost complete lack of any aid for the naked eye.

Such skill did not develop overnight. Marksmanship contests had offered popular sport since the fourteenth century. The first of these were for archers and crossbowmen. Shortly after 1400, guns began to appear, usually at the end of the other contests, and with inferior prizes. By 1472, the Swiss were holding all-gun meets, and soon these began to predominate throughout central Europe, although the crossbow continued as a popular target arm. When rifles first appeared, they were expressly forbidden for competition because they were so accurate. As they became more common, however, they were gradually accepted for special all-rifle events—with the targets sometimes a remarkable 805 feet away!

Most often, these targets were circles, similar to those of today, but there were other kinds as well. In one type of contest, the shooters fired at wooden birds called popinjays, fastened to the tops of tall poles. Scores were determined by the sizes of the pieces knocked off. Most elaborate of all, however, were the cut-out wooden figures of Turks or mounted warriors which were hauled along a track to give the shooter a moving mark.

Marksmanship contest in Prague, 1585, from a contemporary print. The target was a figure of a mounted knight drawn along a track to give the contestants a moving mark.

The large meets were usually invitational, and hundreds of people—contestants as well as spectators—attended. The visitors often traveled long distances; occasionally, the host city offered a special prize for the shooter who came from the greatest distance. The contests were regarded as instruments for keeping peace, because citizens of one principality became acquainted with those of another through healthy competition. Therefore, it was a matter of good politics and civic pride to attract as many visitors from as wide an area as possible.

This promotion of peace and mutual understanding was one of the greatest reasons for the shooting contests, but there were other factors as well. The sheer joy of sport was one. Another was the previously mentioned realization that a ready cadre of skilled shooters was a tremendous asset to a government in case of war. Principalities encouraged the practice of marksmanship during the entire clear-weather season. Sunday afternoons from Palm Sunday until the end of October were customarily devoted to shooting practice, and in many places sufficient powder and bullets for three shots were provided free each week to every shooter.

Many changes have taken place in target shooting since these first beginnings. By the middle 1500s, the rifle had joined the smoothbores in competition. By 1600, peep sights had been allowed, and shooters were permitted to brace their guns against their shoulders for a steadier aim. From this background, the early settlers of Pennsylvania brought with them their knowledge of the rifle and their love of shooting, to produce here the traditional American rifleman of frontier days. Later, immigrants from the same central European area brought with them the more refined shooting techniques that produced the *Schuetzen* contests—using extremely accurate target rifles—so popular throughout America in the 1800s. Other types of competition, permitting different positions and even rests, developed into the wide variety of shooting contests recognized today.

More important, however, are the things that have *not* changed: the recognition of target shooting as an enjoyable sport; the belief that the friendly competition of marksmen can promote international understanding and good will; and the knowledge that a trained body of civilian marksmen is a vastly important asset to national defense. More than five hundred years have tested these theories and proved them to be as valid now as they were in 1400.

Chapter 34

The Grand Old Schuetzen

Spectators drank beer by the gallon. They sang *Schatz mein Schatz* and other old German favorites, and they helped themselves generously to such delicacies as *Sauerbraten* and *Kartoffel Kloese* from heavily laden tables in a dining hall that could seat 1500 people. Festivities were noisy and convivial in and around the tree-shaded pavilions and refreshment stands. In the two houses just outside the fringe of trees, however, the atmosphere was tense and serious. There, fifty-seven men at a time took their places, raised heavy rifles to their shoulders and fired offhand at the row of targets 200 yards away. This was a *Schuetzenfest*, a shooting festival that was fired according to rules that had originated in the 1400s, when firearms matches were added to the traditional crossbow contests of central Europe. But these marksmen were in America, competing in the ninth National *Bundesfest* (convention or meet) at Glendale, Long Island, July 3–11, 1898.

Rifle contests had been popular in America ever since the first German and Swiss settlers had brought their short but accurate flintlocks to these shores in the early 1700s. These events began as informal meets at local crossroads—often with shingles for targets and beef for a prize. Then the frontier turkey shoot developed as a variation. Old formalities and rules were forgotten in the sparsely settled new land until a wave of immigrants from central Europe came to America toward the middle of the nineteenth century. These marksmen had been accustomed to shooting in the traditional manner, with all its regulations, and they brought their version of the sport with them. This time highly formal shooting matches flourished, because the frontier had moved west; there were now cities and parks where groups could gather and where the necessary facilities could be obtained.

Local target-shooting groups were organized, at first in the centers of German population—Milwaukee, Chicago, New York. In these cities, the immigrant riflemen had a chance to meet with others of the same background, to speak their native language—and to do a little shooting. But the interest in marksmanship was strong among the native-born population, too, and soon these people began to join the German groups in increasing numbers. So did newcomers from other nations. *Bunds* or *Vereins*, as they were called, spread in ever widening circles, until the first national *Schuetzenfest* was held in New York in 1866. It was such a success that others followed at Baltimore, Philadelphia, Union Hill (New Jersey), Newark, and St. Louis, all building up to a great national meet in 1898 at Glendale, which boasted luxurious facilities and an astounding $25,000 in prizes. In an era when many men worked for less than 50¢ a day, this was big money indeed, and it attracted the best marksmen in the land.

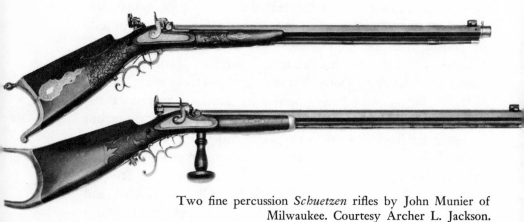

Two fine percussion *Schuetzen* rifles by John Munier of Milwaukee. Courtesy Archer L. Jackson.

Like their fifteenth-century counterparts, these *Schuetzen* contests were fired strictly offhand and at long range. Palm rests could be used, but no separate supports or holding equipment of any kind were permitted, and no contestant was even allowed to place the butt of his rifle under his coat, vest, or suspender when aiming. Targets varied: Silhouettes, American Standard patterns and the Honor Target Columbia (sometimes called the German ring target) were often employed. Some of these targets consisted of a series of small concentric rings, while others utilized rectangles as the aiming areas. One of the most popular types was the Stitch Target Germania, a 12-inch circle with a six-inch bull's-eye. At 200 yards, only hits in the bull's-eye counted! For this kind of shooting, a man needed excellent vision, a steady hand—and a strong arm to support the heavy rifle that was preferred by the best shooters.

Under the rules, many types of rifles might be used, but a specialized form appeared that lent itself especially well to long-range offhand work. This was the celebrated *Schuetzen* rifle, a colorful arm but also a precision machine. It had a caliber of less than .50, since this was a requirement at most matches. (In general, the most popular bores ranged between .32 and .45.) Regardless of bore size, it was a heavy gun; the thick octagonal barrel frequently measured an inch in diameter, and a complete arm often weighed 12 to 16 pounds. The

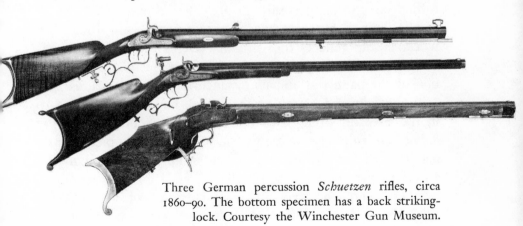

Three German percussion *Schuetzen* rifles, circa 1860–90. The bottom specimen has a back striking-lock. Courtesy the Winchester Gun Museum.

most striking feature of a *Schuetzen* rifle, however, was its stock, especially at the rear end. It is by this structure that most collectors immediately classify a *Schuetzen;* once seen, it is never forgotten. To begin with, such a stock was always quite broad, and the buttplate was deeply curved, with long protuberances, or "horns," at both the heel and toe. These projections were designed to pass over the shoulder and under the arm of the shooter and help him to steady the heavy rifle. Another special—though optional—feature was a hinged palm rest for the left hand, attached to the underside of the barrel. This rest might terminate in a ball, a bar, or whatever shape the target shooter considered most convenient for supporting his particular gun.

As a rule, the front sight was a bead, sometimes with a protective hood, and the rear sight was an aperture that was often minutely adjustable. This excellent aiming equipment identified a rifle as a specialized arm for precision shooting.

Finally, weights were usually attached to the muzzle to bring the balance of the piece far forward. Ordinarily these weights were separate, detachable pieces, so they frequently have failed to survive with their rifles. Nevertheless, they were very useful. With the palm rest acting as a fulcrum, the muzzle weight pulled down the fore end of the gun and caused the lower projection of the buttplate to push up against the underside of the shooter's arm. Awkward as this may sound, it afforded an unusually steady grip.

The best *Schuetzens* were custom-made, and their fine workmanship reflects the care that went into them. Dimensions such as the width and depth of the buttplate, the position of the palm rest and its distance from the barrel, as well as the weight and length of the barrel, had to be adjusted to fit the size and strength of the individual shooter. Thus, the *Schuetzen* rifle was a highly personal gun. A piece could handle well for the man who had it built, yet it might be awkward for someone else.

These were the principal characteristics of a *Schuetzen* rifle. Other details varied. A *Schuetzen* could be a muzzle-loader, a breechloader or a combination of both, known as a muzzle-breechloader. In the early nineteenth century, they were, of course, muzzle-loaders, usually percussion-cap, and this type remained popular to the end, in the second decade of the twentieth century. The muzzle-breechloaders became popular during the 1870s and 1880s; actually, these were true breechloaders, utilizing the standard actions of the day, such as the Ballard, Remington, or Winchester. For *Schuetzen* use, however, the breech was used only for loading the powder charge. The bullet was carefully patched, started into the bore through a protective false muzzle that was detachable and rammed home from the front end. Any type of bullet except a steel-jacketed slug was usually permitted, and either black or smokeless powder was allowed. At about the same time— during the third quarter of the nineteenth century—breechloaders using self-contained metallic ammunition also appeared at *Schuetzenfests*. They were perfectly legal, but the true enthusiast of that period handloaded his cartridges; he looked down on factory-made ammunition, preferring bullets that had been cast, swaged and seated by hand and powder charges that he had measured.

"Progress" was inevitable, however. First, breechloaders firing metallic cartridges, either handloaded or factory-made, became more and more common. Then, shortly after 1900, telescopic sights were allowed for many matches, and the old-

Remington No. 3 breechloading *Schuetzen*
rifle with modified rolling-block action, 1904-7.
Courtesy Remington Arms Company.

Winchester Model 1885 *Schuetzen*
rifle. Courtesy the
Winchester Gun Museum.

timer with his percussion-cap rifle and his muzzle-loading equipment soon became a curiosity. But the *Schuetzen* matches still maintained their identity by their strict offhand rules, their long ranges, and their traditional targets. Since interest among marksmen continued at a high peak, the *Schuetzenfest* gave every indication of becoming an enduring national institution. Then disaster struck. World War I broke out in Europe, and even before the United States became involved, anti-German feelings here ran high. In fact, there was a popular revulsion against all things German—among them the *Schuetzenfest*. National meets were abandoned. Local competitions gradually ceased, and with them, long-range offhand shooting disappeared as a major organized sport in America.

Chapter 35

Rifles at Creedmoor

In spite of the haze, there was a glare of light on the carefully cut turf. Heat mirages shimmered over the mounds of earth with the black and white targets erected in front of them. Thousands of spectators pressed against guard ropes, their eyes glued on two teams of men who aimed their rifles at targets an incredible 800, 900 and 1000 yards away. The date was September 26, 1874; the place was the new Creedmoor Range on Long Island, and America's first international long-range rifle match was well under way.

It was an important competition, and feeling ran high. The newspapers had whipped up enthusiasm with almost daily articles for months in advance, and now telegraphers stood ready to send word of the results across the country. The American riflemen were being challenged by the best marksmen of Europe.

In 1873, an Irish rifle team had won the celebrated Wimbledon competition with the best score ever compiled in that historic match. They were unquestionably the finest shots in the British Isles—and probably in the world—but they could not rest until they had tested the Americans. They sent a challenge addressed to the Riflemen of America, and had it printed in a New York newspaper.

This touched Americans in a sensitive area—their pride in

their reputation as a nation of crack shots. Unfortunately, it was a reputation based upon individual initiative, military exploits and local competitions. There had been no country-wide organization of target shooters until the National Rifle Association had been formed just three years earlier, and so far there had been no national competitions to select champions or pit the shooters of one region against another. Moreover, almost all of our match shooting had been at comparatively short ranges—600 yards or less. There had not even been a long-distance range in America until Creedmoor was built under the direction of the NRA in 1872, and there were still no American long-range target rifles.

But challenges are made to be accepted. Disadvantages simply have to be overcome. The spirit of the American marksmen would not let a chance like this pass. The challenge was accepted, and the Americans then set out to recruit a team, raise the prize money and obtain rifles. The Amateur Rifle Club was formed to make the arrangements. It promptly held competitions to select a team of eight men and to raise the funds needed to cover the £100 pledged by the Irish as a prize to the winning team. Then came the rifles.

Here the club found allies in two of America's foremost gunmaking firms, E. Remington & Sons and the Sharps Rifle Company. Both manufacturers promptly agreed not only to make the rifles for the American team but also to contribute substantially to the prize funds. Remington assigned the task of designing its new long-range rifle to Lewis L. Hepburn, the foreman of the company's mechanical shop and also a member of the American team. He built a rifle using the familiar Rem-

Remington No. 3 Improved Creedmoor rifle with Hepburn action. Courtesy Remington Arms Company.

ington rolling-block action. The other manufacturer produced one with the standard Sharps falling block. Both were graceful arms, with slightly tapering barrels, hooded front sights and adjustable Vernier and windgauge rear aperture sights. They were precision instruments, carefully machined in every part, and both of the rifles fired special .44-caliber cartridges with slightly hardened 550-grain bullets propelled by 90 grains of black powder. Completed rifles were delivered to the team in the spring of 1874, and the contestants practiced feverishly all through the summer. When September came they were ready.

On the appointed day, both teams assembled, the Irish in tweeds and deer-stalker hats or pith helmets, the Americans in business suits and bowlers or top hats. Six men from each team were selected to fire. The others were to remain on hand as substitutes. The United States team used three of the Sharps rifles and three Remingtons. The targets were the Wimbledon standard: rectangles measuring 12 feet wide by six feet high with a bull's-eye three feet square in an area six feet by six feet known as the "center," and the two remaining end strips three feet by six feet known as the "outer." A hit in the bull counted four points, in the center three, and in the outer two. Every contestant was to fire fifteen shots at each of the three distances—800, 900, and 1000 yards. At any of these ranges, a perfect individual score would be 60, and a perfect team score would therefore be 360. For the entire match a possible aggregate team score would add up to 1080 points.

At the very outset, things went well for the Americans. They scored 326 points at the 800-yard range, as compared

Early Sharps Creedmoor rifle. The original rifles for the 1874 match may have been of this model. Courtesy Archer L. Jackson.

to 317 for the Irish. It was too early to cheer, however, for the Americans were expected to do well at this relatively short range, which offered something like the kind of shooting they were used to. Sure enough, at 900 yards the Irish scored 312 to the Americans' 310, closing the gap by two points. They would have done even better except for an unfortunate accident. Their best shot, J. K. Milner, scored a bull's-eye on the wrong target! Some strange positions were permitted in this long-range shooting, and Milner customarily fired his rifle while lying half on his back and half on his side, with the butt in his armpit and the barrel held between his feet. In this position, his vision was restricted to the gap between his feet, and somehow as he lay down he lined himself up with the wrong mark. The shot counted for nothing. In the final round, the Irish again topped the Americans 302 to 298, but it was not enough. America won, 934 to 931. Had Milner not hit the wrong target, the Irish would have won by a single point. That was how close the contest was, and both sides could take satisfaction in some magnificent shooting.

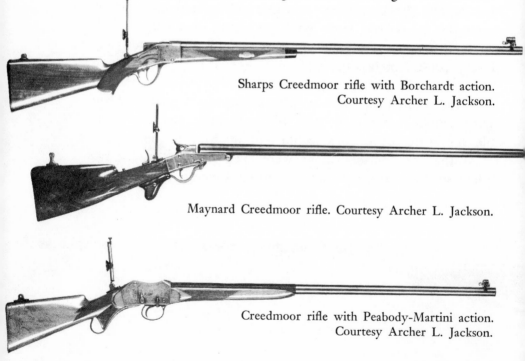

Sharps Creedmoor rifle with Borchardt action.
Courtesy Archer L. Jackson.

Maynard Creedmoor rifle. Courtesy Archer L. Jackson.

Creedmoor rifle with Peabody-Martini action.
Courtesy Archer L. Jackson.

The first Creedmoor match proved that Americans could compete at long range with the best marksmen in the world—and it also proved something else. It showed that breechloaders could shoot just as accurately as muzzle-loaders. The Irish team had used muzzle-loading rifles made by team member John Rigby of Dublin, and most conservative shooters agreed that only such arms offered the necessary accuracy for long-range marksmanship. Remington, Sharps, and the American team proved otherwise.

The match also fanned popular enthusiasm for long-range target shooting. Clubs and matches spread all over the country. Both Sharps and Remington added Creedmoor rifles to their regular lines, and these companies were joined by a host of other makers, including Ballard, Maynard, and Frank Wesson. A variety of actions was offered, but all of the rifles had to conform to National Rifle Association standards for long-range competition. They had to be single-shots, with barrels not longer than 34 inches, single triggers with not less than a three-pound pull and a total weight of not more than ten pounds. Bores were restricted to calibers from .40 to .45, and telescopic sights were forbidden. Because Creedmoor rifles were designed as high-quality precision arms, the workmanship throughout was usually fine. Stocks were often of Circassian walnut, and frequently there was engraved decoration on the action. A few rifles were specifically marked Creedmoor, and in such instances they generally represented the manufacturer's top-quality product. Lesser models of the same type were just classified as "Long Range" arms.

The Creedmoor rifle remained popular well after the turn of the century. But changing attitudes toward sport shooting brought a decline in long-range competition. The Creedmoor, like the *Schuetzen*, was doomed. With the advent of World War I, this special type of target match disappeared from the American scene, taking with it one of the finest single-shot precision shooting instruments ever developed on this side of the Atlantic.

Part VI

THE DUEL

Pair of flintlock duelers by William Moore of London, about 1815–20.
Courtesy Bluford W. Muir.

Chapter 36

Pistols for the Duel

Resting gracefully in their handsome case, a pair of dueling pistols command the immediate attention of all who see them, and very few arms enthusiasts are immune to their fascination. The viewer may be intrigued by both the fine quality and the precision workmanship of such pistols; he may be interested or puzzled by the variety of tools and accessories that surround them and by the fine wooden case with its separate compartments lined in felt or velvet. But all of these are secondary considerations. It is the primary purpose of these guns that captures the imagination and arouses a mixture of emotions in the onlooker. Beautiful as these pistols are, their obvious functionalism and efficiency leave no doubt that they are deadly tools, once used in an activity that the modern American cannot fully comprehend.

The duel has long since passed from the scene; the entire concept is repugnant to most people today. Even during its heyday, the practice was illegal in a great part of the country, but custom approved, and those citizens who had the time and the money purchased the best weapons available and practiced for the occasion when they might be called upon to give or receive a challenge.

The principle of the duel is perhaps as old as man himself; it dates from the time when primitive humans settled their quarrels by force, when might made right. Then, with the coming of the Middle Ages, a new concept appeared. Stemming from the deeply religious beliefs of the period was the idea that God would protect the innocent and would not permit him to be harmed by the guilty. From this arose trial by combat, the ancestor of the formal duel.

At first, duels were hand-to-hand encounters. Swords were the usual weapons, but other arms were also used—maces, axes, daggers, clubs, and sometimes combinations of weapons. In all of these conflicts the antagonists' physical strength and dexterity were most important. Then, shortly after 1650, firearms began to come into general use. England led the way in popularizing the new weapons for dueling.

In the late 1600s duels were relatively informal affairs. There was none of the ritual that marked the later *Code Duello*, and the guns used were not rigidly regulated. Since any firearm that was available might be pressed into service, the opponents did not even have to be armed alike. Long guns as well as pistols were used, and there is even one satirical cartoon of about that period depicting two combatants blazing away at each other with blunderbusses at close quarters while the ground around them is littered with an assortment of discarded weapons that have apparently proved ineffective.

As the years passed, the rules became stricter. By 1750, duels with the sword were rare; the pistol had almost completely taken over. And with the increasing likelihood that he might be called upon to defend his honor (and his life) with the firearm, the gentleman of that day devoted many hours to target practice. He also demanded pistols of high quality and efficiency.

Thus developed the true dueling pistol, made especially for combat between two men. These arms reached the peak of their perfection between 1770 and 1810. Because they were designed for such a specific and limited use, they had definite characteristics that enable today's collector to distinguish them from any other well-made pair of cased pistols of that particular period.

First of all, the dueling pistol had to be fast and accurate.

Often the rules of the duel precluded deliberate aiming; besides, the time factor was of primary importance. The man who fired the first shot had a tremendous advantage—provided he didn't waste his opportunity. For this reason, a superior dueling pistol will "point" almost automatically. A good test of such a pistol is to hold it down at your side, then suddenly raise it and point at a target. Hold it up long enough to check the aim with the sights, and if it is a real dueler, the aim should be true just as a result of pointing.

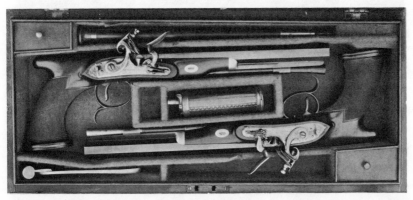

Saw-handled flint duelers by William Parker, London, about 1805–15. The bright mounts are unusual on dueling pistols. Courtesy Robert Abels.

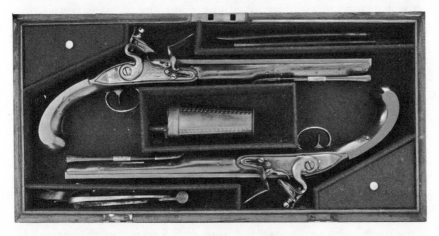

Early pair of flint duelers by Joyner of London, circa 1780. The heavy octagonal barrels on these pistols are a good indication of their purpose. Courtesy Robert Abels.

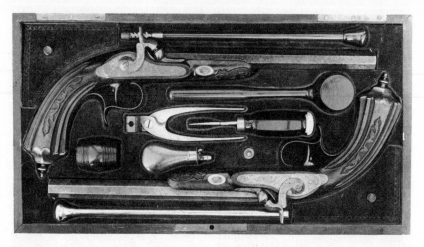

French percussion duelers, about 1830–40. In French cases the compartments are usually shaped exactly to fit the objects they hold. Courtesy Robert Abels.

The bore also had to be well made and finely polished to carry the ball straight to the target. French dueling pistols were usually rifled, but in deference to custom the great majority of the English variations were not. Some, however, had "blind" rifling which stopped a few inches short of the muzzle and gave the impression that the pistols were smoothbores. Rifled or smoothbored, a good pistol would shoot over the usual dueling distance of 20 paces without deviation. In fact, one English smoothbore of about 1790 vintage was tested not long ago, and it sent its ball into a man-sized target three times out of four at a range of 85 yards.

The outside of the barrels also received careful attention. Normally the barrel length was about 10 inches; the barrels were most often octagonal, and they were exceptionally heavy so that a nervous, jerky trigger pull would be less likely to affect the aim. To avoid glare, they were browned or blued. This desire to avoid any distraction carried over into the mountings as well. Silver or brass was seldom used; standard mounts were of iron or steel and they were browned or blued just like the barrels. The stocks were made without ornamentation or carving except for fine checkering on the grips. It was felt that any other decoration might be detrimental to a

French percussion duelers by F. Rochatte of Paris, circa 1850. Courtesy Bluford W. Muir.

sure and steady grip, or might distract the eye at a critical moment. The barrel tangs, lock plate, or trigger guard might be engraved, but this was the extent of decoration.

Finally, the mechanism of the pistol was refined and enormously speeded up. Special pans were designed for fast ignition and frizzens were made to operate against light springs so that they would open quickly and easily. Set triggers were provided with fine screw adjustments so that they could be adapted to the owner's requirements, giving him exactly the amount of pull he wanted.

When finished, these superb guns were cased in pairs with all of their accessories. The boxes were of walnut or mahogany, with their interiors divided into compartments and lined with felt or velvet. Here, too, there was no ostentation, just a simple but well-made case with a lock, handle, and possibly a plate for the owner's name or monogram. All essentials but no frills were included; on the field of honor, there is no need for trimmings.

With the advent of the percussion cap, formal duels became less frequent. Some percussion dueling pistols were made, primarily in Europe, but the majority of the true duelers were flintlocks. Not everyone could afford these expensive and specialized weapons. Those who could not used whatever guns were at hand—all sorts of pistols, pepperboxes, rifles and even shotguns. Other people patronized shops that rented dueling pistols. But to those who had the money, the possession of custom-made dueling pistols was a matter of great pride and satisfaction, as any collector who owns a pair today can testify.

Chapter 37

Choose Your Weapons

"Sweden is a piddling country," wrote the Earl of Arran in the *London Evening News*, and the irate Swedish ambassador challenged him to a duel. As the challenged party the Earl promptly chose the weapons: motorcars in the Hyde Park underpass. This was in 1962, and the air rang with comments that dueling in the "good old days" was never like this. Oh yes it was!

The formal ritual of the *Code Duello* supposedly set the standard to be followed on the field of honor. By about the middle of the eighteenth century, pistols had become the preferred weapon, and custom dictated that they were to be fired at a prescribed signal from a given distance such as 15 or 20 paces. Most gentlemen in England, on the Continent and in America abided by the rules; they even bought special matched pairs of pistols, specifically designed for dueling. But there were always some who refused to be bound by convention. A man's hatred for his opponent might be too vicious, or his shooting skill too limited or his imagination too great to be satisfied with the recommended practices. In some cases, standard dueling pistols simply might not be available when needed. Whatever the reasons, unusual and even bizarre duels were far more common than is generally supposed.

Sometimes the idea behind such procedures was actually

to avoid a duel by terrorizing the challenger or by insisting on weapons that would make him look ridiculous. Obviously, such "weapons" as motorcars would be beneath the dignity of an ambassador, and choosing them was the Earl of Arran's way of laughing off the challenge. The duel was, of course, never fought. In the past, similar maneuvers have sometimes avoided bloodshed, sometimes failed.

Abraham Lincoln tried these tactics when he suggested cow dung at five paces in response to a challenge from James Shields in 1842. Shields, who later became a distinguished Army officer and served senatorial terms for five different states, had been provoked by some statements about himself which appeared in a newspaper and were attributed to Lincoln. During the quarrel, Lincoln apparently made the suggestion about the cow dung in an effort to end the incident with a laugh. Shields, however, was in no laughing mood and the affair actually went as far as a final (and supposedly more serious) choice of weapons. Lincoln now selected broadswords, with the stipulation that the duelists were to stand on either side of a log and must not step over it. This would have given Lincoln a tremendous advantage because he had very long arms, while his challenger was a small man with a short reach.

Both men showed up at the field of combat, but their differences were settled without bloodshed. There was a mere verbal skirmish, which ended with friendly words and smiles. In fact, Lincoln afterward apologized to Shields, and they became friends.

Perhaps the cow-dung incident inspired "Fighting Bill" Bowman, a Kentucky preacher who became known shortly afterward for having whipped "The Bully of Grayson County." Each man was armed with a basket of potatoes, and it developed that the Reverend Mr. Bowman had a better throwing arm than his opponent.

As North-South tensions began to mount in the years before the Civil War, unusual tactics avoided more than one duel. When Congressman John Fox Potter of Wisconsin named

Bowie knives in a locked room, avoiding an actual fight was undoubtedly his intention. Roger Pryor of Virginia, his challenger and fellow Congressman, rejected the proposal as ungentlemanly. But such maneuvers didn't always cheat death.

In 1838, Representative William J. Graves of Kentucky forced a duel on Jonathan Cilley, Congressman from Maine. Being unfamiliar with pistols, Cilley chose rifles at a distance of 80 paces. The duelists were to hold the cocked rifles at their sides, raise them at the command "fire" and each get one shot off before the signaler could count to four. It was a tragic and disgraceful duel. The signaler had to give his count three times, and three shots were exchanged, Graves insisting each time that he had not had satisfaction because neither had been wounded. On the third exchange, Cilley was shot through the body and killed. Congress expelled Graves and censured both seconds (who were also Congressmen).

Other duels were fought with rifles, too. *Frank Leslie's Illustrated Newspaper* reported one that took place in Georgia in 1856. In this encounter, one of the duelists was apparently a crack shot who hoped to end the affair without seriously wounding his antagonist. At the first exchange, he nicked his opponent's left ear. This would have halted any duel except a fight to the death, since blood had been drawn, but the wounded man would not settle. He demanded another exchange. In this one, he got a bullet through the right ear while his shot again went wild. Only a completely enraged man would have insisted on another try; after all, a marksman such as his opponent could easily have ended the affair any time he chose. Nevertheless, the wounded man demanded a third shot. This time the opposing bullet went through his hat while he missed once again. Completely berserk and ignoring all rules, he rushed upon the marksman—who reluctantly knocked down the crazed attacker and beat his brains out with his rifle butt.

In a Texas duel, also in 1856, Dock Antrey and William Carson were armed with double-barreled shotguns and revolvers. They stationed themselves 120 paces apart and then began to advance. As they came closer, they emptied their shotguns at each other, threw them down and started firing their revolvers. Neither of them scored a hit until they had narrowed the range to about six or eight feet. Then Carson was shot through the heart.

Such bad marksmanship usually called for a different approach. If their hatred was strong enough, the opponents might stand close, with pistol muzzles overlapping—or even touching each other. In such instances, both men usually died. Still another arrangement was used by some duelists who lacked confidence in their skill or thought they could better their odds if actual aiming could be eliminated. One story of the early nineteenth century concerns an Englishman traveling on the Continent who was forced into a duel by a local nobleman. Hoping to avoid bloodshed, he stipulated that the encounter was to take place with pistols in a dark room of the challenger's ancestral home. After handing the principals their weapons and making sure there would be no light, the seconds apparently left the room while the antagonists stalked each other in the dark. Realizing too late he had made a dangerous mistake—the challenger had the advantage of familiarity with the surroundings—the Englishman waited as quietly as possible for him to fire. Finally, the flash and report of a shot relieved his anxiety. Having no real quarrel with his adversary and therefore not wishing to hurt him, the Englishman felt his way carefully along the wall until he came to the big, old-fashioned fireplace. Reaching in, he discharged his pistol up the chimney—only to be greeted by a dull thud as a body dropped to the hearth. His too cautious opponent had climbed up into the flue to hide.

Duels were fought with almost every weapon known. Swords, pistols, revolvers, rifles, shotguns, and knives were the most common, but there are records of duels with clubs, muskets at six paces, muskets with fixed bayonets, blunderbusses and pepperboxes. Combat took place on foot, on horseback, in the open, in locked rooms and in pre-dug graves. The award for the most spectacular and imaginative duel ever fought probably has to go to two Frenchmen named de Grandpré and le Pique. In the first decade of the nineteenth century, they quarreled (as might be expected) over a pretty woman, one Mademoiselle Tirevit of the Imperial Opera. She could not choose between them, so the two gallants decided to settle their claims to her favors by a duel. Since this was a very important matter, they determined that the encounter should be decisive and should be carried out in the grand manner. At their order, two identical aerial balloons were constructed, and on the day selected, the duelists, each with a second, clambered into their balloon baskets. Each combatant carried a blunderbuss. The idea was not to shoot at each other but at the balloons. At a signal, the ropes were cut. The balloons rose above the gardens of the Tuilleries in Paris. There was little or no wind, and they remained about 80 yards apart. When they had reached a height of about half a mile, an official gave the signal to fire. Somehow, le Pique missed completely. De Grandpré, however, scored a direct hit, and the wounded balloon plummeted to earth, killing both its passengers. De Grandpré triumphantly continued his ascent, and eventually landed some seven leagues from Paris. Mademoiselle Tirevit's decision had been made for her. Even motorcars in the Hyde Park underpass couldn't compare with imagination like that!

Part VII

FABULOUS
FOWLERS

Chapter 38

The Long, Long Fowling Piece

"The longer the range, the longer the barrel." So ran an ancient axiom for gun design. Gunsmiths and shooters learned very quickly that gunpowder exerts its force on a bullet only as long as the projectile remains within the barrel. The spurt of the flame from burning powder that sometimes followed a bullet out of the muzzle might be spectacular, but it indicated that the piece had been overloaded. It was a waste of good powder—unless the shooter was primarily interested in a fireworks display. From this knowledge, gun designers reasoned that if they made barrels longer, a bigger charge of powder could be burned efficiently. More force could be transmitted to the bullet, making it go further and hit harder.

They forgot to consider the countering effect of increased friction between the ball and the barrel, but still there was a germ of truth in the theory, since ignition was slow in early guns, and so was the powder's burning rate. This meant that a relatively great bore length was needed for propulsion to be most effective. The long-barrel idea influenced gun design for at least two centuries, and it gave birth to what most students consider the first truly specialized sporting gun—the long fowler.

The history of this interesting arm began in England shortly after 1600. People of almost all European countries had been firing charges of shot at birds and other small game long before then, but they had used almost any sort of gun that happened to be at hand. Even some large rifles had been loaded with "hayl shot," or bird shot, for the purpose. Until the seventeenth century, this had been an activity for the poorer classes who saw in such hunting an opportunity to add meat to their tables and at the same time protect their crops. For the gentry, only the larger—that is, "nobler"—beasts were considered worthy of hunting. When the upper classes did pot at birds or small creatures, it was looked upon as a form of target practice. Gradually, however, bird shooting became a sport in itself, and as interest among wealthy sportsmen increased, specialized guns were created. For field shooting, the usual light matchlock or wheel lock arquebus or slug gun could still be used without too much difficulty. For waterfowl, however, these arms left something to be desired in accuracy and range.

As duck hunting developed along the coasts of England, sportsmen began to take up positions in blinds near flyways and feeding areas. There they waited for flocks of birds to settle on the water or perhaps just to fly over. Frequently, the birds settled or flew by at some distance from the hunter in his fixed position, so he wanted a gun that would perform well at long range. And since it was his desire to bring home a large bag, he also wanted a smoothbore that would fire a big charge of shot—killing several birds at a time or at least increasing his chance of hitting the bird he was aiming at. Gunsmiths set to work to provide the hunter with just such an arm, and shortly after 1600 they produced the long fowler.

This was a huge firearm. In keeping with the ballistic theory about range and bore length, the barrel was sometimes as much as six feet long. This type of gun was heavily fortified at the breech so that a big charge of powder and shot could be used without bursting the piece. Calibers ranged from as small as .53 all the way up to .80 or, occasionally, a little larger, and the bores were usually very smooth and well polished. The combination of the careful boring and the long barrel pro-

duced an accurate arm as well as a powerful one. There may
have been some wheel locks among the first long fowlers,
but all of the surviving specimens that have been studied
utilized some form of flintlock ignition, which replaced the
wheel.

The earliest existing guns have dog locks, named for a little
dog catch that afforded a half-cock safety position on these
simple mechanisms. (The word "dog" is an old term for a
gripping or catching device.) Some long fowlers continued
to be made with dog locks until almost 1700. For a short
period between 1600 and about 1640, some had the so-called
English lock, a contemporary of the dog lock with a laterally
acting sear and a primitive half-cock notch in its internal
mechanism. After 1660 and for most of their history, however, long fowlers were made with true flintlock ignition.
Such hunting guns disappeared before the advent of percussion arms.

From England, the popularity of long fowlers spread to
other parts of the world. Some were made and used along the
coasts of the Low Countries and Denmark, but the biggest
area of production outside the British Isles seems to have been
America. Such arms began to reach these shores almost with
the first settlers. In 1621, Edward Winslow of Plymouth
wrote home to prospective Pilgrims advising them on the
things they would need in the New World. He included this
comment on guns: "Let your piece be long in the barrel and
fear not the weight of it, for most of our shooting is from
stands [blinds]." A colonist named John Thompson took this
advice, and the long fowler that he brought with him in 1622
still survives. So does another that belonged to John Forbes,
who settled in East Hartford (in what is now Connecticut).
When the settlers of the Massachusetts Bay Colony brought
their supplies in 1626, they included 10 long fowlers, six of
them with "musket bores" (about .75) 6½ feet long, the remaining four with "bastard musket bores," (.69) 5½ feet long.
Some of these guns utilized English locks; the later versions
were, of course, standard flintlocks.

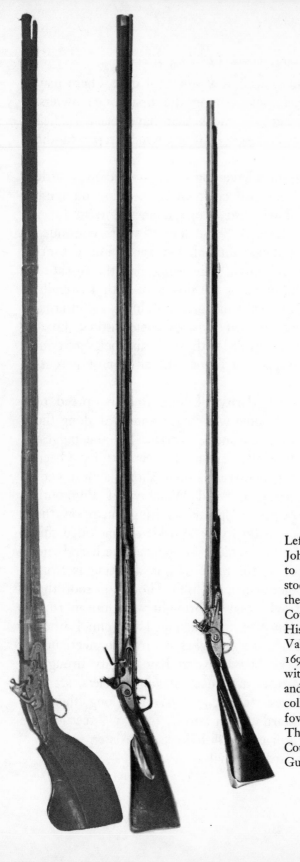

Left to right: Long fowler of John Thompson who came to Plymouth in 1622. The stock is probably American; the metal parts are English. Courtesy the Old Colony Historical Society. Hudson Valley long fowler, about 1690. It is seven feet long with a curly maple stock and Dutch barrel. Author's collection. American long fowler of the early 1700s. The barrel is 58 inches long. Courtesy the Winchester Gun Museum.

Although the early long fowlers were purely English, America soon began to develop its own style of designs. Along the southern shore of Cape Cod and down the coast of Connecticut, fowler stocks developed graceful drops similar to those seen on Kentucky rifles. Along the Hudson-Mohawk River flyway, the stocks became heavy and "fat-bellied," perhaps reflecting the Dutch influence. As a matter of fact, the barrels on these Hudson Valley guns were often imported from Holland even as late as 1690, and the brass hardware shows a strong Dutch or German flavor. The most common stock woods were curly maple and walnut, sometimes with excellent relief carving nearly comparable to the best on Kentucky rifles—although not as extensive and usually not as sharply defined.

As the eighteenth century wore on, the barrels tended to become somewhat shorter, perhaps only 4½ feet long, or even as short as four feet in some instances. English-made locks began to appear frequently, and even in the Hudson-Mohawk area the hardware again began to follow contemporary English design. Then, shortly after 1750, the long fowler disappeared almost completely. For those who wanted a huge fowling piece, punt guns now began to achieve prominence. These were cannon-sized smoothbores mounted on boats and designed to decimate a flock of sitting or just rising birds with a single shot. Aside from these arms, lighter, shorter, faster-handling guns came to dominate shore fowling.

By the mid-1700s, the long fowler was obsolete, but during its century and a half of existence, it became the very first of a host of specialized sporting arms that have been appearing ever since. It also had a military function: During the English Civil War, which took place in the middle of the seventeenth century, marksmen equipped with highly accurate long fowlers were employed to pick off enemy officers, much as Kentucky riflemen were used during the American Revolution more than a century later. The accuracy and long range of these pieces made them ideal for the purpose, and in America they were used in the same way to defend forts and garrisons against attacking Indians who thought they could remain out of range. The stock designs and carving on American specimens, and even the use of curly maple as stock wood, foreshadowed the development of the Kentucky rifle—which was reaching its peak just as the long fowler disappeared. It is no wonder that any modern collector fortunate enough to own an authentic long fowler considers it one of his most prized historic pieces.

Chapter 39

The Classic Double-Barrel

Consider the double-barreled shotgun. Most arms collectors pass it by quickly in their search for early Colt revolvers, Kentucky rifles, or other guns that seem to have more glamour. Yet few firearms have so long a history of continuous use, so wide a popularity among shooters, such great versatility or even such a wide range of quality—from the cheap "house gun" of the poor farmer to the gilded and carved plaything of the nobility.

The first guns designed especially to fire charges of small pellets were *single*-barreled, and their history goes back to the early years of the seventeenth century. (Shot pellets, known variously as swan shot, goose shot or hayl shot, had been used for hunting birds and small game for almost a hundred years before then, but all sorts of long guns had been used to fire them.) Soon specialization began, probably first in England. Very large guns such as long fowlers were developed for shooting at comparatively great range near flyways and feeding areas, and short, light pieces were manufactured for field use. Still, these were all *single*-barreled guns. *Double*-barreled pieces did not appear until the early eighteenth century, and even then they were uncommon.

These first double-barreled shotguns were flintlocks, and there was a good reason for their initial lack of popularity.

The ignition of the powder charge was slow, and it took a 40-inch barrel for the charge to burn completely and develop its full force; two barrels of that length made a gun very heavy and unwieldy. Then in 1787, Henry Nock, one of England's great gunsmiths, perfected a new breech that would transmit the flash from the priming pan to the charge in the barrel much more rapidly. He hollowed out a small chamber in the breechplug just behind the main charge in the barrel, from which it received a small amount of powder when the gun was loaded. The flash from the priming pan set off this small charge, which then blew a flame right up through the

Double-barreled flintlock shotguns by the great English maker Joe Manton, about 1800–10. Courtesy the Winchester Gun Museum.

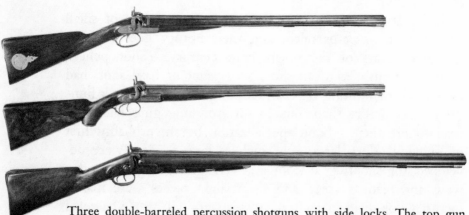

Three double-barreled percussion shotguns with side locks. The top gun has a cap box in the stock for percussion caps; the middle specimen is a high-quality piece with a fine walnut stock and nicely engraved lock. The bottom gun is good but plain, with light checkering and simple engraving. Most percussion double guns were imported from England. Courtesy the Winchester Gun Museum.

propellant. With this breech design, barrel lengths could be reduced to as little as 30 inches, and the resulting reduction of weight made the double gun practical.

This was just the beginning. In 1806, Joe Manton, another outstanding figure among English gunmakers, improved the side-by-side double gun still further by his invention of the elevated sighting rib, which increased the speed and accuracy of aiming.

After these two developments, the popularity of double guns grew by leaps and bounds, almost eclipsing the older single-barrel types completely. When the percussion ignition system was invented by the Reverend Alexander John Forsyth (himself an ardent shotgun man) it was quickly adapted in all its various phases to double guns. By 1830, most shotguns boasted the new percussion-cap ignition with standard side locks. Next came the back-action locks with the mainspring mounted behind the hammer instead of in front of it. This permitted a gun's forearm to be lightened and resulted in better balance. By 1850, these new locks were widely employed, but the older side locks continued in use as well. As late as 1884, some percussion shotguns were still being made with them.

Percussion shotguns were muzzle-loaders of the type many a man over forty can still remember seeing in his grandfather's attic. But breechloading shotguns were also available. In 1812 Johannes Samuel Pauly, of Paris, had invented a break-open breechloader firing a cartridge with a wrapped cardboard case and a soft brass head, the ancestor of all modern shotgun shells. Pauly's gun was delicate and it never became popular, but in 1835 a Frenchman named LeFaucheux brought forth a double-barreled shotgun utilizing a pin-fire cartridge. His gun's action broke open on an under-hinge and closed against a standing breech. A lever underneath the barrels released its catch. By the 1860s, improved versions of this action, handling center-fire cartridges, had appeared, and by the 1870s hammerless models with top-release levers and snap-closing latches were being offered for sale. The truly modern double-barreled shotgun had at last arrived on the scene. All that remained was the choke bore. This developed gradually, beginning in the 1700s, and finally reached its modern design shortly after 1850.

This, in capsule form, was the evolution of the double gun, but what of its use? Everyone knows that it was designed for hunting birds and small game, but the versatile firearm has done other things as well. Its function at weddings has become a part of American folklore. And loaded with buckshot, or single ball or slug, it has brought down deer and other large game.

Stagecoach guards of the Old West were quick to adopt it as the logical successor to the blunderbuss, and many a pioneer on the Oregon Trail stashed a shotgun behind the seat of his covered wagon. Not only would it add chance game to his food supply; it would also help to discourage attacking Indians or the ruthless white wagon jumpers. Both stagecoach guard and emigrant liked the way the shot spread out from the muzzle to compensate for poor aiming from a lurching wagon seat.

Shotguns also performed on the other side of such encounters. The notorious highwayman Black Bart used a double-barreled shotgun in every one of his twenty-eight successful stagecoach robberies. So impressive was its appearance that he never had to fire it. California outlaw Jim McKinney also fancied the shotgun—and he used it. There were six notches on the stock of the weapon he carried to his death.

There is a very long list of historical personages who recognized the versatility and the effectiveness of the double gun. Bloody Bill Anderson, the notorious guerrilla of the

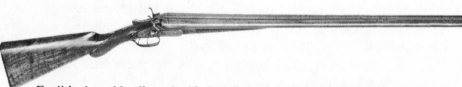

English breechloading double-barreled shotgun imported for sale by Winchester during the 1880s. Courtesy the Winchester Gun Museum.

Civil War era, was a shotgun man. So were many highly respectable Confederate cavalrymen. Doc Holliday, professional gambler and friend of the Earp brothers, habitually carried a cut-down double-barreled shotgun under his coat when he expected trouble. He killed Tom McLowery with it in the fight at the O K Corral. Wyatt Earp himself often reached for his shotgun when he expected real trouble, especially if the odds were against him. Almost every peace officer in the West did the same. When the fully armed lawman mounted up, he carried—in addition to side arms—a shotgun in front of his left leg to match the rifle at his right. The sawed-off scattergun of the 1920s and '30s was recognized as a classic gangster weapon, while even today police officers frequently use shotguns for certain situations.

Well before the turn of the century, repeating shotguns began to make their appearance. During the last fifty years, both repeaters and autoloading models have become increasingly popular, but they have never superseded the double gun among dedicated shooters. Collectors, too, should award the double-barreled shotgun the recognition its fascinating history deserves.

Chapter 40

Waterfowl Slaughter

The breeze from the east barely rippled the surface of the water, but it was bitterly cold. The two men lying prone in their narrow, flat-bottomed boat were chilled to the bone. For hours they had been paddling slowly, cautiously, over the surface of the water, stalking a "company" of ducks they intended to slaughter. If they were stealthy enough, they would be able to move within range—about 70 yards or perhaps a little less—without being detected. But the breeze had to be light; even a slight swell would make aiming difficult, if not impossible, and choppy water might easily swamp their shallow boat. Both men were well practiced in this technique of waterfowling, which was popular among sportsmen as well as professional market hunters in England and America during the late 1800s. A typical gunning team of this time, they had spent days waiting for the proper weather, stalking the birds, trying to get close enough for a good shot. They were tired, wet, cold, cramped and thoroughly uncomfortable, but at last the chances looked good. The ducks were feeding along a mud flat, easily within range now and unaware of the approaching danger.

The front man lay behind a huge gun that was mounted on the prow. He kicked the paddler and used hand signals to direct him to go steady and "set the boat to." There must be no noise. Then, with his finger on the trigger, he carefully aimed the gun, elevating its muzzle slightly. He gave a shrill whistle and the startled ducks sprang up in a cloud of whirring wings. Just as they cleared the mud, caught in their most vulnerable position, the big gun boomed. Its shot tore a path through the black mass, and birds dropped like hail on the mud flat below. Upright and paddling rapidly now, the hunters dashed to the flat and jumped out with their shoulder shotguns, or "cripple stoppers," to collect their bag. A good shot meant perhaps 20 birds, an excellent one could net forty, and with real luck a man might hope for even more. In those days, before the size of guns was regulated, there were records of a hundred or more birds brought down at one time. But this was many years ago. Such "sport" was outlawed in the United States in 1916. And in Great Britain, which was another stronghold of mass duck killing, the Protection of Wild Birds Act of 1954 limited the size of "punt guns" to 1 ¾ inches at the muzzle. While such oversized firearms are still used in England, they are becoming increasingly rare.

The punt gun was (and is) a gigantic smoothbore fowling piece fired from a small boat called a punt. This type of boat can be paddled or poled and will skim through shallow water or weed-choked marshes. It is awkward to do any paddling or poling while lying flat to avoid being spotted by the birds, but this is no great problem since the boat is meant to go slowly. The gun is pointed into a rising flock, not aimed at a single bird, and the usual result is butchery. Punt gunning was popular by the 1820s. Wildfowlers living along the English coast, especially in Hampshire and Sussex, developed crude techniques for stalking wigeon, teal, and other water birds from small boats and bringing them down with oversized shotguns. Then the celebrated sportsman Colonel Peter Hawker became interested, and he devised new equipment and procedures, and brought punt gunning to the attention of hunters.

Several types of boat have been used, though punts of one form or another have been most popular. Canoes and even light rowboats have been employed from time to time, especially in America. The principal requirements were shallow draft and a low silhouette, because the boats had to negotiate tidal flats as well as open rivers, and they had to be as inconspicuous as possible. The fully developed English one-man punt looked something like a kayak with a long, sharply pointed prow decked over to a cockpit barely roomy enough for the gunner to lie in. Larger versions provided for a two-man crew, one to shoot and one to paddle or pole. The stern was sometimes rounded and the bow had stanchions to support the gun.

The arms themselves came in an even greater variety than the boats. In the beginning, they were usually nothing more than huge versions of the typical single-barreled fowling piece of the nineteenth century, as long as the traditional long fowler but heavier and bigger in the bore. There were a few flintlocks at first, but most of the guns utilized percussion caps or some other sort of detonating primer. Since it was difficult to lead a target with such a huge gun, the shot had to catch the birds just as they were rising, and the relatively rapid ignition of the percussion system was an advantage.

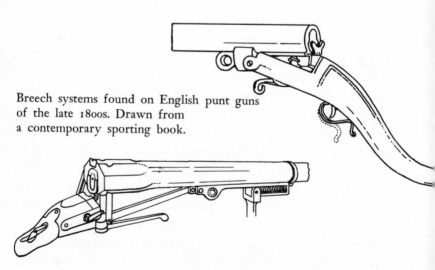

Breech systems found on English punt guns of the late 1800s. Drawn from a contemporary sporting book.

American punt gun with early English flintlock. Courtesy the Illinois State Museum.

These 30- to 50-pound smoothbores were rested on a simple forked support—or even fired from the shoulder! Old books on the subject mention the jarring and straining of the boat caused by the recoil, but apparently this did not stop a determined hunter. The early 50-pound firearms were small by punt-gun standards, however. The big ones had barrels seven to nine feet long, and they might weigh 70 to 120 pounds. Bores ranged from 1¼ inches to a full 2½ inches; they fired loads of as much as 2½ pounds of shot, propelled by five ounces of black powder. Most were single-barreled, but there were some double-barreled models as well.

Guns of such size could not be held manually; they had to be fixed to the boat or at least firmly supported by it. Some did not even have shoulder stocks but looked almost like Chinese matchlock guns with a rudimentary pistol grip to serve as a handhold for pointing the arm.

There were numerous devices for supporting these huge pieces. Some were fitted with swivels like oar locks that fit into a socket near the bow, while others were mounted in tight-fitting stanchions that prevented any movement of the arm and forced the shooters to do their aiming with the punt itself. Still other guns were supported in looser stanchions or forked rests and secured by ropes. This last system was the most popular and probably the most efficient. It is still used by punt gunners in England, even with the smaller guns now prescribed by law.

Muzzle-loading punt guns with fixed mounts were extremely difficult to reload "at sea." And the fact that some market hunting was done at night made the task even harder. Special tools were invented, and there were even "night cartridges" with a casing of silk (which burns very rapidly). But none of these innovations were completely satisfactory because the charge could not be rammed properly. Ignition was apt to be slow and the shot pattern unpredictable.

Percussion-cap punt gun. Courtesy Abercrombie & Fitch.

The obvious answer was the breechloader, and this type of gun quickly gained popularity among punt gunners. A host of different patterns were available—dropping breeches, screw breeches, break-open types and so on. Probably the most popular was the screw breech, especially among the wealthy sportsmen of the 1800s. In fact, Thomas Bland of London still makes a screw-breech punt gun in both a single- and double-barreled version. The double fires both barrels at once with a pull of a lanyard.

Market hunting is no longer a big industry, and as a so-called sport, punt gunning is fast dying out. Conservationists and field-shooting enthusiasts have long denounced it as murder. The declining number of game birds has strengthened their position. England is one of the few places where it still goes on, and even there its days are probably numbered.

Part VIII

SPECIALTY GUNS

Chapter 41

Signal Pistols

A pistol with a one-inch bore commands immediate respect. One with an inch-and-a-half bore astounds all beholders. The first time a man comes across a gun of this kind, he's likely to wonder whether handguns were ever made for hunting elephants. Then, noting the thin walls of the barrel, he might guess this type of side arm to be designed for firing shotshells. As a rule, only knowledgeable collectors discern the purpose of such guns at first sight. They're firearms—but not weapons. These big-barreled guns are signal pistols, made to shoot flares high into the air to indicate a location, transmit an order, call for help or sometimes even to send fairly complicated messages.

The idea of using fire for signaling goes back perhaps as far as the Stone Age. Torches were waved from hilltops as a means of communication in the ancient world, and even as late as the 1800s such primitive signaling methods were still being used.

By this time, however, there were much better devices than the simple torch. As early as the eighteenth century, Europeans—especially the French—had begun to experiment with modern techniques in pyrotechnics, the science of making fireworks and flares. Brilliant lights of various colors (depending on the chemicals and combustible powders used) were developed and perfected. Then came rockets. Actually Roger Bacon, the father of gunpowder in Europe, had made rockets of sorts as far back as 1250, but these new devices were vastly improved. Men like Sir William Congreve of England developed new and better directional controls. His principal concern was to make the rocket an effective weapon, and indeed it was employed in this way. But since the propellant powders burned brightly, and a pyrotechnic head could be used, it was also an effective nighttime signal. By 1850, its use for that purpose was widespread. This was the situation when the first flare pistols appeared, about a decade later. They were related to the earlier pyrotechnics and the rockets, but they were an exclusively American contribution. B. Franklin Coston began the breakthrough by developing a series of red, white and green lights that burned with great intensity and could be distinguished from far off. A signal code using twelve different combinations of these colored lights came next. Coston died before this was perfected, but his widow obtained a United States patent on April 5, 1859. The American Navy quickly became interested, and so did the Army, which appointed its first Signal Officer, Major Albert J. Myer, in June 1860.

Two official signal pistols were developed to fire the new Coston lights—or rather, to ignite them. In reality, these pistols were nothing more than torch handles with a built-in lighter. The flares burned right *in* the pistol barrels; they were not projected into the air. The first of the two guns appeared in 1861. It was made of brass, with a short tube to hold the flare, a long straight frame and a grip also formed of brass. A percussion cap, fired by a center hammer, ignited the light. Both Army and Navy markings are found on specimens of this model dated 1861. Some with Navy marks have been discovered with dates of manufacture as late as 1872, and the Navy used them until about 1879.

However, a second version, the distinctive Army signal pistol, appeared in 1862. It, too, was a percussion gun with a brass tube to hold the flare and a brass frame. Instead of being straight, the frame was sharply curved so that the Army pistol was much shorter than the Navy model. Also, the grips were made of wood instead of being a mere extension of the frame. Tradition has it that Major Myer, a former surgeon and the Army's first Signal Officer, designed this variation, but the exact extent of his connection with the pistol is unknown.

All surviving specimens of the Army signal pistol are dated 1862, indicating that there was only one year of manufacture, yet the model continued in use for almost two decades. The 1879 edition of Myer's *Manual of Signals* illustrates it as the current pattern but indicates that experiments with needle-fire ignition were being carried on in the search for a more up-to-date system. Both this gun and the earlier Navy model had drawbacks. The signaler had to hold such a pistol aloft until the light had burned out. For one thing, this limited the distance from which the light could be seen. For another, it illuminated the poor pistol holder, making him a fine target for any enemy within range.

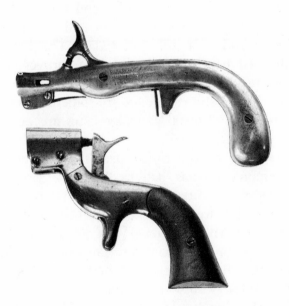

Above: First U.S. signal pistol, the so-called Navy Model of 1861. Below: U. S. Army signal pistol of 1862. Courtesy the West Point Museum.

Something better was needed if the signal pistol was ever to become really effective. In 1877 a thirty-year-old U. S. Navy lieutenant, Edward W. Very, produced it. He invented a series of colored lights and a system for firing them, using a cartridge pistol with self-contained flare ammunition to replace percussion ignition. His colors remained the same as Coston's, and he used both ball and star burning shapes. (As in fireworks displays, lights can be made to burn simply in a ball of fire or they can be constructed so that they will spray out in a shower, or starlike explosion.) The Very lights were placed in a cartridge closely resembling a modern shotgun shell. Generally, the body was made of cardboard and the head of brass. The propellant was black powder, usually from 25 to 50 grains. A wad separated this from the combustible charge that formed the lights, and the open end was normally sealed with paraffin. The burning powder lit a fuse leading to the payload; when fired, the lights would be hurled 50 feet into the air before they ignited. This was a tremendous improvement over the Coston lights and the Civil War pistols.

Very's system quickly won favor and was adopted all over the world. And it is still used today. The lights themselves have changed hardly at all, though improvements in manufacturing techniques have made the colors burn more intensely. Also, plastic cartridges are sometimes used instead of cardboard, and all-metal cartridge cases are occasionally employed.

The designs of the signal pistols, however, have varied widely among various nations over the last eighty years, though certain features have remained relatively constant. It is by these features that the informed collector promptly recognizes a signal pistol, or a Very pistol as it is often called. First, there is the bore diameter. The one-inch or 25-mm size has been the most popular, although there have been some models with bores up to 1½ inches. The next most noticeable feature is the thinness of the barrel walls. These were obviously not made to withstand high pressure or to resist expansion from heat, and accuracy was never considered. Since

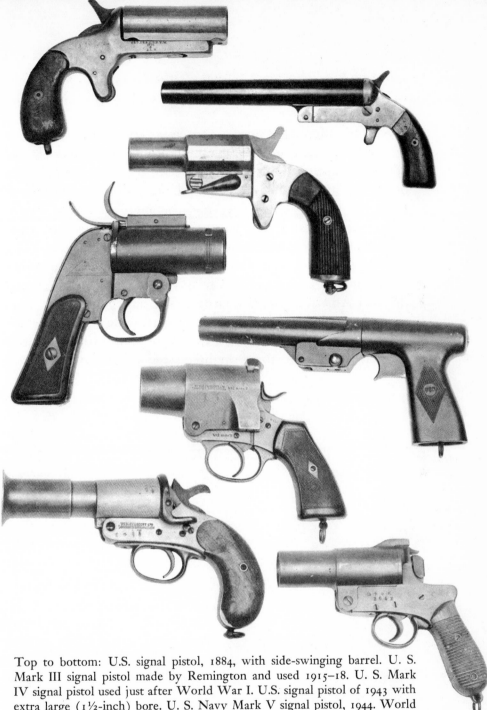

Top to bottom: U.S. signal pistol, 1884, with side-swinging barrel. U. S. Mark III signal pistol made by Remington and used 1915–18. U. S. Mark IV signal pistol used just after World War I. U.S. signal pistol of 1943 with extra large (1½-inch) bore. U. S. Navy Mark V signal pistol, 1944. World War I British Webley signal pistol with 1½-inch bore. British Webley & Scott signal pistol 1918. Japanese signal pistol used in World War II. All courtesy the Smithsonian Institution.

speed of fire is no more important than accuracy, the majority of flare guns are single-shot single-actions, and few double-actions exist.

As for differences among contemporary pistols, they may be made of brass, steel, or aluminum, and the barrel lengths vary, the most common being six inches. The action may break open, tip-up fashion, or the barrel may pivot to the left or right for loading—and there may be more than one barrel. The Germans and the Japanese had double-barreled cast-aluminum signal guns during World War II.

Whatever its design, the signal pistol is a colorful addition to any gun collection. The Civil War specimens rank among the real American martial rarities. But any gun of this type represents a link with the ancient past in the use of fire for signaling—and a major American contribution in bringing this signaling technique to its highest stage of perfection.

Chapter 42

Guns that Killed Silently

When an air rifle is mentioned, the average shooter thinks of a plaything such as the Daisy BB gun. It's a wonderful toy, but no one would call it a real weapon. Manufactured with a carefully limited muzzle velocity of some 300 feet per second, it will shoot fairly accurately up to 20 feet, and might even carry as far as 100 feet under proper conditions, but the trajectory at that range would defy accurate aiming. A shot from it is fatal only to small animals at very close range. Recent years have produced guns with special air-compressing pump-actions or CO_2 cartridges that fire little slugs at much higher velocities, and these can kill small animals or inflict injury if they should hit a man in a vulnerable spot. However, they are still short-range arms, used primarily for target training at 25-foot distances.

These are the modern air guns. But there was a time when the situation was far different. Air guns were effective and dangerous weapons, firing noiselessly and offering several shots with one loading. Soldiers were armed with them. Assassins and poachers selected them for their criminal purposes. Explorers Lewis and Clark carried an air gun on their famous cross-country expedition to the Pacific Coast in 1804–6. A German nobleman, Landgrave Louis VIII of Hesse, claimed he killed a 480-pound stag as well as a quantity of lesser game with one. Such guns were a force to be reckoned with. Many European localities banned them because of their association with crime, and there is an old but unconfirmed story that Napoleon was so concerned about air-gun sniping by Austrian marksmen that he ordered the execution of all enemy soldiers captured with such guns in their possession.

No one knows who first invented the air gun. The idea of using compressed air for propulsion is ancient, and one historian, Ctesibius of Alexandria, mentions a double catapult "gun" that probably worked on the compression principle as early as 250 B.C. These early inventions were apparently forgotten during the Dark Ages, however. It was not until the Renaissance revived an interest in the study of ancient writings that the idea of using air as a propellant for projectiles came back into prominence. By then, firearms were in common use. New designs were inevitable and true air guns in the modern sense quickly developed. The earliest surviving specimens date from the late 1500s.

Interestingly, these oldest air guns used the same general principle as the Daisy of today. A tight-fitting plunger in a cylinder behind the barrel compressed the air as a spring drove the plunger forward. This air pressure in turn drove the projectile, a lead ball. It was a simple system, and the force it developed was weak. A second type of air gun that appeared at about the same time was a little bit stronger. This arm had a hollow butt that held a set of spring-operated bellows to develop air pressure. Guns built on this system continued in use, especially in Germany, well into the nineteenth century.

Mid-eighteenth-century air gun with butt reservoir and dummy flintlock. The piece is European, possibly English in origin. Courtesy the Smithsonian Institution.

Most of them were breechloaders, the barrel tipping up to allow the insertion of the ball. They were fast-shooting guns, cheap to operate and accurate at short distances. They were almost noiseless, too, but still they were useful only for target practice or small-game hunting.

No gun that developed its air power by spring action at the moment of discharge could be made into a powerful weapon. A new principle was needed, and it soon appeared. Experimenters found that air could be compressed by a pump and stored in an air-tight magazine at far higher pressures than could be obtained from a single spring or bellows action. The earliest documented air gun with such a magazine was made by Marin le Bourgeoys of Lisieux, Normandy, between 1600 and 1610. It had a double-walled barrel with the space between the walls serving as a reservoir for the compressed air. Before setting out to shoot, the gunner pumped air into this chamber with a device closely resembling the modern bicycle-tire pump. A full supply of highly compressed air afforded power enough for perhaps as many as ten shots, a measured amount of the air being released by a valve each time the trigger was pulled. And these shots hit hard enough to kill a man. Le Bourgeoys recommended the use of wooden darts with iron points at the front and paper cones at the back to receive the air pressure. He felt these would be more efficient than lead balls, and darts were occasionally used in other air guns, but most designers preferred the standard lead projectiles. Later specimens frequently added magazines for their bullets, too, so that the guns were true repeaters.

German or Austrian air gun with butt reservoir, eighteenth century. Courtesy the Winchester Gun Museum.

Other varieties of compressed-air reservoirs followed. The most popular was a large hollow ball screwed to the barrel or a hollow butt stock. Both of these devices offered advantages over the double-walled barrel. They did not tend to make the gun so muzzle-heavy, and since they were separate features that could be screwed on and off, it was possible for a shooter to carry extra ready-charged reservoirs so that he could leave his pump at home and still enjoy an afternoon's shooting.

During the eighteenth and early nineteenth centuries, these were the most popular forms of the air gun. Most of them resembled the standard gunpowder firearms of the period, often with a dummy wheel, flint or percussion lock in the normal position. But there were other designs, including guns that resembled canes or walking sticks. Many theories have been advanced for this practice of camouflaging an air gun; most often, writers have cited the banning of such arms and the shooter's desire to conceal the fact that he was carrying a noiseless weapon, whatever his purpose. There was also the matter of tradition: If a man had a gun, he either wanted it to *look* like one—which explains the dummy locks—or he wanted to hide it.

There are a number of tales of air guns used for hunting, for assassination and for military purposes. A group of English conspirators who planned to assassinate Oliver Cromwell in about 1655 bought an air gun in Holland for the purpose.

Late eighteenth- or early nineteenth-century air gun with ball reservoir. Below is a typical pump for such a gun. Courtesy the Winchester Gun Museum.

The plan was dropped, but as one contemporary observed, this weapon was one "which shoots with wynde . . . a bullet at 150 paces, and that seven times one after another, with one charging with wynde. It makes no report . . . so 'tis difficult to discerne, whence the shot comes." All of which made it an ideal arm for the purpose of assassination. George III of England feared an attack on his life with an air gun. The celebrated English sportsman, Colonel Thomas Thornton, claimed he killed both wild boar and deer with one in 1802. Lewis and Clark seem to have used their air gun primarily to impress the Indians, many of whom were familiar with firearms but were amazed at a gun that could bring down game without making noise.

For military purposes, the only major use of air guns occurred in Austria. There an air rifle designated the Model 1780 was employed against Napoleon's troops. Invented by an Italian named Girardoni, it was a repeating weapon that fired a .50-caliber ball. Two-thousand strokes of a pump charged the gun's butt reservoir, which then produced a muzzle velocity of 975 feet per second. Of course, this initial velocity decreased as the air in the reservoir was depleted. The first ten shots were effective at 120 to 125 yards, the next ten at about 100 yards, and a few succeeding shots only at very close range.

It was this loss of power that undoubtedly prevented the air gun from becoming a more important military weapon. The

American Quackenbush air gun, Model No. 1, circa 1890. It was charged with a pump. Courtesy the Smithsonian Institution.

soldier constantly had to keep count of the number of shots he had fired from each magazine and adjust his target selection and his aiming to compensate for the decreased pressure. Some air guns had automatic counters that recorded the number of shots made, but the shooter still had to calculate distance and his trajectory carefully each time he pulled the trigger. As regular firearms became faster-operating, more powerful and more accurate at longer ranges, the air rifle's silence and speed of fire became less important, and such guns were relegated to sporting and target use only. During World War II, the OSS tried experiments with air guns for guerrilla and partisan work, where silence and stealth were again of extreme importance, but such arms were not used on any wide scale. The air rifle will probably never have another chance to play a role in military affairs, but there is every likelihood that it will long be with us as a fine short-range target gun and a wonderful toy for the youngster who can still find a hundred feet of open country and a tin can to plink at.

Chapter 43

Whaling Guns

Whales!—that word has always evoked the lure and mystery of the sea. Rulers of the watery kingdom, their tremendous thrashing caught the imagination of anyone who ever saw them in their element. There were killer whales, finbacks, bottlenoses, sperms, blues, bowheads, humpbacks—bigger than elephants, some of them, the biggest animals on the earth, yet hunted by daring men in small boats. Since the days of the Vikings and perhaps before that, men have pitted their courage and intelligence against these huge creatures. Whalers still pursue their ocean quarry today, of course, but modern equipment and techniques have done away with much of the romance and danger of hunting the biggest game in the world. Whaling is no longer considered a hazardous occupation.

A century ago, when New England whalers combed the seas, the test between whale and man was a highly personal affair. Crews in small boats rowed so close to their prey that a harpoon could be driven deep into the massive animal, holding him fast as he sought to break free or destroy his tormentors. This was the era of the famous "Nantucket sleighride"—the heaving, rolling course of a whaleboat plunging along at the end of a taut harpoon rope. If all went well, the whale finally tired, the crew rowed close again and a second lance was thrust into a vital spot for the kill. In these encounters, men might have the advantage of superior cunning, but a raging whale could swamp a boat or smash it apart with his tail.

Naturally the whalers tried in all sorts of ways to improve their techniques. With firearms, they could extend their harpooning range and improve the effectiveness of their killing weapons. They still had to lower small boats from the mother ship and row out to the whale, but they no longer had to approach so closely. Guns that fired harpoons first made their appearance in about 1731, in England, but they did not achieve wide and immediate popularity because the running line attached to the harpoon interfered with accuracy. Nevertheless, the manufacture of harpoon guns continued, and improvements in their shape and maneuverability brought them into greater use among whalers of many nations by about the middle of the nineteenth century. One of the best-known harpoon guns was produced by the famous London armsmaking firm of W. W. Greener. This gun was a heavy piece—weighing over 50 pounds—mounted on a swivel at the bow of a whaleboat. It had a short, thick wooden stock whose rear end was shaped almost like a pistol grip. The barrel had a bore of about 1¼ inches, and it was made of brass (though iron was later used) because Greener was afraid iron or steel might become brittle in the Arctic cold. Greener's gun, utilizing

Greener harpoon gun, dated 1853. The aiming guide is brass and the barrel is iron. Courtesy the Smithsonian Institution.

percussion-cap ignition, had an effective range of about 40 yards. This was a good deal farther than a man could hurl a harpoon, and every foot of distance made the operation less risky.

It must be remembered, however, that such a gun merely harpooned the whale—it didn't kill him outright. This aspect of the hunt now attracted the attention of whaling experts the world over. Among the numerous devices invented and tested, the American approach to the problem was the shoulder whaling gun. This was simply a huge version of the conventional shotgun of the period, designed to fire a lance. Arms of this type weighed between 18 and 23 pounds, and had smooth bores measuring from ⅞-inch to 1¼ inches in diameter. The butt stock was usually a thick metal skeleton, or frame, though a few were solid wood or hollow-cast metal.

Some of these ponderous shoulder whaling guns were muzzle-loaders, some were loaded at the breech. In the mid-nineteenth century, C. C. Brand of Norwich, Connecticut, designed one of the first successful types, a percussion-cap muzzle-loader utilizing a charge of three drams of black powder to fire a lance. With improvements in design made in 1852, iron and steel Brand guns continued in use for some thirty years.

Other American designers now began to bring out competitive guns. Ebenezer Pierce and Selmar Eggers, for example, patented an all-brass breechloader in 1876 and added refinements in 1884. It had a dropping breech, with the trigger guard acting as a lever, and it was chambered for a Winchester cartridge of about 8-gauge which propelled the lance. During the same period, Patrick Cunningham and Bernard Cogan produced another popular whaling gun, this one with a cast-iron stock and a steel barrel, and both types continued to be used during the early years of this century.

All of these whaling guns had one important feature in common. They fired lances with explosive charges in their heads, potent whale killers even at 20 or 30 yards. But despite their effectiveness and killing range, they also had one great drawback—recoil. Their kick was so heavy that many a gunner was knocked flat on his back when he pulled the trigger. Sometimes a man was slammed all the way from the bow to amidships, and there were reports of broken collarbones from the tremendous kick. Such a gun had to be tied to the boat or it might go overboard in the confusion following a shot. Firing a shoulder whaling gun was not only unpleasant but dangerous. There had to be a better arm.

American inventors developed another new device that accomplished the kill efficiently, and that was often used to catch and kill a whale in a single operation. Called the darting gun, it was a combination harpoon and self-firing gun. When a harpooner manually hurled this contrivance into his quarry, a rod-shaped trigger was pushed back by the impact of the harpoon burying itself in the whale; this automatically fired the gun attachment and sent the explosive lance head deep

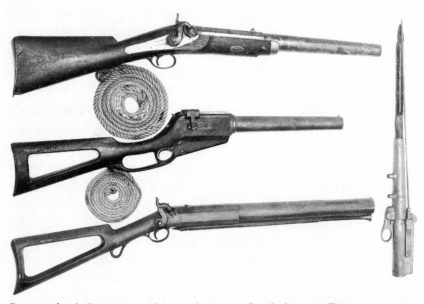

Group of whaling guns. Top to bottom: Grudschoss & Eggers percussion gun; cartridge model by Cunningham & Cogan; percussion gun by C. C. Brand; shown vertically at right is a darting gun with its bomb lance in position. Courtesy the Smithsonian Institution.

into the monster's vitals. This killed or disabled a whale almost instantly. The darting gun was an especially useful arm for hunting near ice shelves, because it killed the whale before he could dive under the ice and force the hunters to cut their line or be dragged under.

It is interesting to note that the same men who had designed the shoulder guns also devised the new darting guns. Pierce patented one in 1865, again using a brass barrel, and Cunningham and Cogan brought out an iron and brass one in 1875. These darting guns and others more or less like them were almost always breechloaders; some broke open like shotguns and some had screw breeches.

Many whalers carried both shoulder and darting guns aboard, favoring one or the other for a given species of whale or a particular set of shooting conditions. When not in use, the arms were hung above the bunks of the harpooners or boat steerers who used them and who were responsible for keeping them in perfect shooting condition at all times.

Other methods of conquering the whale were also tried. Two-grooved rifles, tested briefly during the 1860s, fired shells loaded with prussic acid, and whaling rockets were invented in 1883. But most whalers continued to use the conventional harpooning and killing guns for some years, and as long as they did, there was an element of danger in the hunting of whales.

Still, the purpose of whaling was obviously profit, not sport, and it was inevitable that a more efficient weapon would be developed and would put an end to the industry's adventurous aspects. It was the Foyn bomb-harpoon gun that brought whaling into the modern era. Invented by a Norwegian named Svend Foyn in 1865, this was a three-inch-bored swivel gun that fired a harpoon with an explosive head. It was sometimes mounted on the deck of the mother ship instead of a small "killer boat."

Like the darting gun, it harpooned and killed the whale in a single procedure. But the Foyn gun did it from a distance, safely and quickly, and virtually gave whale hunting the atmosphere of an assembly line. By the 1870s or '80s, it was a standard tool of Norwegian whalers, and soon after the turn of the century it came into almost universal use. Now there was no need to get close to the mighty monarchs of the sea until they were dead, and whaling was no longer an adventure. It was just another industry.

Chapter 44

Howdah Pistols

How big is big enough? In connection with bore sizes, gun designers have asked themselves this question for centuries. So have the men whose lives depend on firearms. Always, the answer has been vague in terms of millimeters or fractions of an inch—but definite in terms of effect: it must be big enough so that the bullet will drop any adversary the shooter is apt to face. A small caliber may be sufficient to stop a small animal or even to discourage a civilized man who understands the danger of being shot. But big game is another matter; so are uncivilized humans, especially if they are hypnotized by drugs or by religious or political fanaticism. In order to stop either a wild beast or a savage, a gun has to have enough shocking power to knock him down and keep him down, without counting on psychological assistance from knowledge or fear.

Many of today's powerful handguns can easily—and instantly—stop an attack, but in the era of black powder the problem was much more difficult to solve. The English found an answer in the *howdah* pistol—an arm primarily designed for sporting use. American military men found out the hard way that they would have done well to emulate the British. The United States Army encountered an almost unstoppable foe during the Philippine Insurrection at the turn of the century, and the lack of a powerful enough gun almost caused disaster.

Beginning in 1892, Ordnance had started to replace the old single-action .45 revolvers with Colt double-action .38s. These were fast-firing weapons, but they failed against the Philippine Moros, who were bound by oath to win their way to the Mohammedan heaven by chopping down as many unbelievers as possible. The Moros, or *juramentados,* could not be stopped by the 150-grain bullet that the .38 threw. A heavier pistol was needed, and the American campaigners sent back a hurried plea for the old .45s. Quickly reissued, the big revolvers with their 230-grain slugs did the job.

The Philippine Insurrection was the most dramatic—and possibly the only—instance when Americans had to face a foe who could not be stopped with regulation handguns in close combat. Even the American Indians had not been given to such frenzied suicide tactics. In dealing with large, dangerous game, including the ferocious grizzly, our experience had been similarly limited, because such animals were usually dispatched with a rifle. In the task of designing extra-powerful pistols, Americans could have taken a lesson from the English.

Their experiences in Africa and India with both wild animals and frenzied natives prompted them to develop a number of very powerful handguns specifically designed to meet emergencies. As far back as the flintlock era, some English single-shot pistols had been made with bores of .75-caliber, the same as the standard musket of that period and firing almost the same powder charge. These guns could be used for

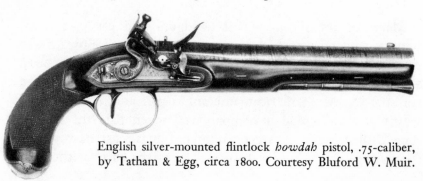

English silver-mounted flintlock *howdah* pistol, .75-caliber, by Tatham & Egg, circa 1800. Courtesy Bluford W. Muir.

military operations or as "support" arms when hunting elephants, lions, or tigers. Actually, this sporting use was probably the principal one for most of these arms; they were commonly called *howdah* pistols, because tiger hunters often carried one or a pair in the *howdah*—a large riding seat or covered pavilion on the back of an elephant. If the shooter only wounded one of the great cats with his long smoothbore, the enraged beast might charge before he could reload, so a ready pistol was useful.

A big pistol weighed less than a shoulder arm, yet it could be equally effective at close range, and it could be aimed and fired faster. Even if the shot did not kill, a well placed ball from one of these monster pistols would disable the animal and stop the charge. The popularity of single-barreled "big-game pistols" of this kind reached its height about the middle of the 1800s and carried well toward the end of the century. Collectors can recognize these guns by their bore sizes (usually .70 or larger), by their heavily reinforced breeches and by the quality of their workmanship, which was normally very high—suitable for a sportsman who could afford to go half-way around the world to hunt. Mid-century types were percussion guns; later ones were break-open cartridge models. Most were smoothbores, but some were rifled.

In the 1870s, double-barreled *howdah* pistols became favorites among big-game hunters. One of the most widely used models was manufactured by Wilkinson & Son of London, and similar but less popular ones were turned out by Horsley and other makers. These were side-by-side handguns with external hammers and back-action locks. The barrels were rifled, and they were chambered as a rule for the standard .577 Snider rifle cartridge. They were powerful arms, packing all the force of a rifle in their short length and offering two fast shots to the hunter in distress. Military men also liked these ponderous pistols, which were used in the Sudan against the fanatic Dervishes.

British soldiers in Africa had become disenchanted with their .450 service revolvers, just as the Americans in the Phil-

ippines lost faith in their light .38s. The British military revolvers were bigger than the American service gun, and they
fired a rounded slug with considerable stopping power. Still,
they were not hefty enough to halt the frenzied Dervishes.
Moreover, desert sand frequently caused jams.

The embattled Redcoats therefore turned to the .577 Wilkinson double-barreled pistols and to another group of repeating two- and four-barreled side arms. Interestingly enough,

Left: English *howdah* pistol in .722-caliber by Westley Richards, about
1835–50. Courtesy Jac Weller. Right: Double-barreled breechloading *howdah* pistol by Wilkinson & Son of London. It fired a .577 Snider rifle
cartridge. Courtesy Jac Weller.

Lancaster four-barreled repeating pistol, .455-caliber. Courtesy the Smithsonian Institution.

these latter repeaters were patented in 1881 in the name of Charles Lancaster—even though that gentleman had been dead since 1878. The firm he had founded, however, was still in business, and this probably accounts for his seemingly posthumous contribution. His pistols boasted an enclosed movable hammer or striker that fired each barrel in turn. They were rugged guns that would not jam or become unusable even when dropped in the sand or left out in the rain. Some of them were chambered for the Government .455 cartridge, which had a bullet velocity of 970 feet per second when 75 feet from the muzzle. This was real power, far greater than the same cartridge produced in a revolver, because there was no escape of gas between the cylinder and barrel. What's more, they could be loaded with shot cartridges for hunting when the circumstances of war permitted. They were ideal weapons for campaigns in wild regions, and their popularity for this purpose was unsurpassed in the 1880s and early 1890s.

British soldiers and sportsmen had already been through many decades of experience with large-caliber pistols before the United States Army encountered the *juramentados*. Ironically, the American campaign came at almost the last possible moment for such a crisis: smokeless powder had already been invented. It was this new propellant that ended the days of the huge-bored pistol. Smokeless charges could develop so much more power than the old black powder that a bullet of only .38-caliber could stop a ferocious beast, or the wildest human.

Chapter 45

To Down a Mammoth

Show the average man an outsized shoulder arm of any sort, and he is apt to comment admiringly that it is a "real elephant gun." The truth is that some modern big-game hunters have successfully used calibers as small as .275 for elephants, but the association of a large bore size with the greatest of four-footed beasts is firmly fixed in the public mind. Historically speaking, there is a good basis for this association. There is also much support for using the term elephant gun rather than elephant rifle, because the arms used on these mammoths were often smoothbores.

Little is known of the earliest theories about hunting elephants with firearms. The Portuguese who visited the African coast and reached India early in the 1500s undoubtedly encountered the great animals and attempted to shoot them with their arquebuses, or primitive muskets. Later explorers probably tried their hands at the hazardous and difficult sport too, but no definite advice or recommendation survives from these hunters. There is surprisingly little information even in writings from as late as the eighteenth century, when several European nations were firmly established in both Africa and India with permanent colonies as well as frontier outposts.

It was inevitable that the elephant would soon attract large numbers of determined hunters, sportsmen seeking a new challenge as well as professionals eager to meet the demand for ivory. An Indian elephant may stand nine feet at the shoulder; the African variety is even bigger, often 11 feet at the shoulder and weighing as much as five tons. A single African tusk may supply nearly 200 pounds of ivory . . . if the huge and dangerous beast can be killed.

For this kind of shooting, hunters found that very powerful guns were needed, and by the early 1800s a definite school of thought had developed in this connection, particularly among the English. Experienced hunters advocated firearms that were specifically designed for use on the gigantic animals. These muzzle-loaders had four-, six-, or eight-gauge smooth or rifled bores, though some sportsmen might accept a 10-gauge as adequate. (The size was usually stated in a gauge designation, but in terms of caliber, such arms would range from .77 to slightly more than 1.00, or an inch.) They were double-barreled in order to provide a fast second shot and also to add extra weight to help compensate for the recoil. The barrels were heavily fortified at the breech to withstand the pressures generated by a charge of 10 or sometimes 12 drams of black powder pushing a round ball that might weigh from two to four ounces, depending on the gauge.

Most of the experts agreed that these were the proper characteristics of a good elephant arm, though even then there were some advocates of smaller bores. The one aspect of design that really divided opinion was the matter of rifles versus smoothbores. One school of thought championed the rifle, citing its greater accuracy. An apparently larger group, however, advocated the smoothbore. They pointed out that the heavy powder charges commonly used often caused the bullet to strip itself on the rifling and blast straight down the bore without acquiring a stabilizing spin.

To make rifling effective, the bullet had to fit very tightly or a reduced charge had to be used. And in either case, there would be a great loss in velocity—and consequently in the energy or striking power of the bullet. A smoothbore, on the other hand, offered reduced friction and therefore greater velocity and energy for stopping a charging elephant in its tracks. In a case like this, extremely precise shooting was less important than power, and at the normal hunting ranges of 50 or 60 yards, a smoothbore's accuracy was sufficient. Moreover, a smoothbore muzzle-loader could be readied to fire much faster than a rifle with its tight-fitting ball.

Because of their great size, big-game rifles of the muzzle-loading period are easy to recognize. No other rifles except some military wall pieces, or rampart guns, were made in such large calibers—and the wall pieces were normally much longer and heavier, obviously not designed to be fired from the shoulder. In the smoothbore category, however, identification is more difficult because similar guns were occasionally used for fowling, especially in the eight- and 10-gauge sizes. In such instances, the principal clues to look for are the extra-strong breeches that were designed to withstand heavy gas pressures, plus the shorter barrel lengths of big-game arms.

The second half of the nineteenth century witnessed further refinements in the design of elephant guns. The cartridge breechloader became predominant, and specialists in London such as W. W. Greener, Evans, Purdey and Holland & Holland turned out beautifully made arms of this type for the big-game hunter. These guns usually broke open like the modern double-barreled shotgun, employing either a top lever release or a lever that pivoted below the trigger guard. Four-bores became somewhat less common, while the 10-gauge size increased in popularity with the advent of hardened bullets. The six-gauge disappeared almost entirely. Previously, typical elephant guns had been straight-stocked, but now there was almost always a pistol grip.

Single-barreled smoothbore elephant gun. It is a four-gauge percussion arm. Courtesy Jac Weller.

Eight-bore breechloading double elephant gun by Stephen Grant & Sons of London. Below: Detail of the Grant elephant gun, showing fine workmanship and the 3½-inch cartridge. Courtesy Bluford W. Muir.

The Grant elephant gun broken down and packed in its carrying case. Courtesy Bluford W. Muir.

W. W. Greener described his eight-bore model of the 1870s and 1880s as having 24-inch barrels and weighing between 13 and 16 pounds, depending primarily upon the fortification of the breech and the stock dimensions. According to their manufacturer, such guns would handle a charge of 10 drams of powder "with perfect ease to the shooter" and would withstand even 12 drams if necessary. Greener's eight-bore models were designed to fire a brass-cased cartridge with a spherical slug. His four-bores, weighing 19 to 21 pounds, utilized powder charges of 12 or 14 drams. Again, the maker claimed that the recoil from such a charge was not excessive, "a steady push only being felt," adding also that "An Indian writer states that on a certain occasion one of these rifles with 12 drams of powder went off both barrels together, and that he did not notice the recoil." Modern shooters who have fired such arms can only wonder what the "Indian writer" was thinking about at the time, for experiments show that the recoil from a single shot can move an experienced 200-pound shooter back two steps.

Until late in the nineteenth century, the argument over rifling continued. The use of the cartridge arm eliminated the factor of loading speed, but there remained the question of velocity and energy. The hardened cylindro-conoidal, or bullet-shaped, projectiles that were now employed in rifles offered an advantage in penetration, but many conservative sportsmen believed that only a round ball at high velocity could be counted on to drop a charging elephant. In this situation, most makers apparently catered to the whim of each sportsman who ordered an arm, offering either a rifle or a

Eight-gauge double elephant rifle made by Evans of London in 1912 and proved with smokeless powder. Courtesy Jac Weller.

smoothbore. Then, late in the 1880s, there came a compromise that ended the debate once and for all: By choking the bore for the last few inches and rifling only this section, all of the best features of both systems seemed obtainable. Stability and accuracy could be imparted to bullet-shaped projectiles without the loss of velocity suffered with full rifling. Holland & Holland called this system Paradox rifling, but this was merely one of several trade names for the technique. Other makers referred to it as Explora, Cosmos, Euoplia or whatever took their fancy. Before 1900, this barrel design had spread widely.

By that time, however, the days of the big-bore elephant gun were numbered. The advocates of small-bore rifles had become more and more numerous. The Boers, as a matter of fact, had been shooting African elephants for some time with standard .45- and .303-caliber Martini-Henry rifles.

Still, the traditionalists died hard. Some big-bore rifles were actually manufactured for the new smokeless powder, including an eight-bore rifle by Evans of London which is known to have been ordered and made for a hunter as late as 1912. Even on the day it was made, however, such an arm was an anachronism, a dinosaur among the much lighter rifles that had taken over the field. The era of the big elephant gun was over. Only the popular impression remained.

Chapter 46

Upside-Down Guns

Underhammer guns look wrong by any standard. A hammer projecting down from the underside of the barrel, directly in front of the trigger guard, seems fundamentally out of place. The normal first reaction to such guns is that the barrel has somehow been put on upside down. Far from it. For some 200 years, certain guns have been made this way deliberately, and for a number of very good reasons. No one knows who first tried the experiment of putting the hammer beneath the barrel, but the earliest underhammers that have been found so far are flintlocks, dating back to the early 1700s. Both pistols and long guns have survived, some of them made in Europe and some in America.

Looking at them today, it seems almost impossible that these strange arms could have worked—but they did. The priming powder was, of course, held in the pan (upside down, beneath the barrel) as long as the pan's lid was closed; but when the flint in the jaws of the cock struck the frizzen to produce sparks, it also automatically opened the pan cover and let the powder fall out. The sparks thus ignited this falling powder, which actually burned upwards—amazing though this may seem—the flame passing through the touchhole and setting off the main charge inside the barrel.

It all seems an incredible combination of luck and split-second timing, yet modern tests reveal that such arms when properly handled seldom misfire. Still, the gun buyers of the eighteenth century must have had some mental reservations about the system, for the small number of such arms made would seem to indicate a lack of confidence by the public.

It was the invention of the percussion cap that brought the underhammer (or "understriker") gun to its greatest period of prominence. Some understrikers were made for pellet priming, it is true, but the primer pills had to be held in the touchholes with some sort of paste, and this was an inconvenience. A percussion cap, on the other hand, could be placed firmly on a nipple, and it would stay there whether it was facing up or down. Gravity was of little importance. The upside-down percussion-cap gun could function easily, and it flourished.

From about 1835 until 1860, a wide variety of underhammer guns appeared in Europe and America. There were single-shot pistols, pepperboxes and true revolvers, single- and double-barreled rifles and shotguns, and even such oddities as turret- and harmonica-magazine guns.

Most common of all were the single-shot pistols of plain workmanship produced in the northeastern United States. Collectors call them bootleg pistols today, partly because their silhouette somewhat resembles a boot, partly because they were of a convenient shape for carrying in a boot top.

These were extremely simple pistols, and consequently they were cheap. The trigger could engage the hammer directly, thus eliminating the need for a sear and sear spring, and the simplest of mainsprings could drive the hammer. There was almost nothing to the mechanism. Practically any gunsmith or even a good blacksmith could make such a pistol all by himself. Many did, in fact, and this accounts for the great number of these guns, all different and all unmarked by any maker's name, that are continually encountered. Regular manufacturers made them, too, however, and their products are well marked. A few were finely finished, and some even boasted a decorative inlay or two, but most were plain or even rough. This was a pistol for the common man . . . the farmer, the stage driver and the mule skinner. It fit their pocket books, their boots and their needs, and they made it popular in a diversity of dimensions. Calibers ranged from very small to shotgun size; barrel lengths ran all the way from three or four inches for pocket or boot models to 18 to 20 inches for a gun meant to be stashed on a wagon. These longer ones, in fact, are often called buggy rifles, especially those equipped with a detachable shoulder stock.

Even the U. S. Ordnance Department and other government war offices showed interest in underhammers. During the Civil War, the United States purchased 900 bolt-action underhammer rifles of a kind invented by Lieutenant Colonel J. Durrell Greene, and perhaps another 2000 of these rifles were made by Greene with the hope of private sales. England, France, Denmark, and Norway also tested underhammer arms, and all but England actually adopted them, at least for limited use.

Why? This is the almost universal question. Conventional arms were well established so why should there be this pursuit of the strange? There were a number of reasons. In the percussion system, a hammer under the barrel lessened the

Top: Underhammer pistol, .31-caliber, with silver mounts made by M. D. & A. G. Lull, Woodstock, Vermont. Bottom: Silver-mounted .41-caliber underhammer pistol by E. Chamberlain of Southbridge, Massachusetts. Courtesy Herschel C. Logan.

danger of flying particles of metal from the exploding caps; these had been known to get into a shooter's eyes, and if such a hazard could be eliminated, it would be helpful. There was the simplicity of construction mentioned above, holding out hope for cheaper manufacturing costs. The streamlined silhouette of a pistol designed with every protuberance—grips, trigger and guard, and hammer—on one side of the gun made it easier to carry in boot, belt or pocket (and faster to draw as well). Finally, removing the firing mechanism from the side or top permitted a clear, unobstructed view for sighting the piece. And there would be no flash and explosion toward the rear that might cause a shooter to flinch.

These were the benefits the designers of underhammers sought. As long as guns with external ignition systems were fired, such advantages were recognized as valid. Even today, many of the finest precision muzzle-loading bench rifles are still being made with the hammer underneath. The silhouette may look strange, but the telescopic sight can be mounted without obstruction, and the marksman can ignore flying fragments of percussion caps with the same sense of complete safety that made his predecessors more than a century ago bless the upside-down design of the underhammer gun.

Top: Cochran turret pistol with underhammer and unusual metal stock. Courtesy the Winchester Gun Museum. Bottom: Classic bootleg underhammer pistol, .28-caliber, made by a Cherokee Indian blacksmith in 1843. Courtesy the Smithsonian Institution.

Chapter 47

A Hail of Lead

Looking down the business end of a pistol pointed in one's direction is an uncomfortable experience, to say the least. But imagine what it would be like if that pistol had ten barrels—all of which might go off at once—and possibly a long, dagger-like bayonet as well. This was the pepperbox pistol, and a burglar of the 1830s or '40s had to take a chance on finding himself in just such a ticklish situation with all those barrels beneath his nose and an irate householder on the other end.

In theory, the pepperbox was a series of barrels clustered around a central axis in such a way that they could be revolved and fired in turn as each passed under the hammer. These pistols usually had four to six barrels, but a few were made with three and at least one specimen had eighteen! The idea was not new. The same principle had governed gunmaking for almost two hundred years before the first really successful pepperboxes were developed in the middle 1830s, and long after they dropped from sight the system was utilized by the Gatling gun and the modern Vulcan, a high-rate-of-fire machine gun recently adopted by the armed forces.

The development that made the pepperbox practical was the invention of the percussion cap. In the old snaphaunce and flintlock pepperboxes, each barrel had to have its separate steel or battery to strike the spark. Loose powder for priming was also a problem, for it was apt to fall out or run into the barrel and mix with the main charge, leaving only an empty pan when the spark fell from the steel. With the simple little percussion cap, which exploded when struck, each barrel merely needed its own nipple to receive the cap with a tight enough fit to hold it in place even when the barrel was upside down on the underside of the cluster.

In the earliest pepperboxes it was necessary to revolve the barrels by hand between shots, but this drawback was soon remedied. On April 13, 1836, the brothers Benjamin and Barton Darling of Shrewsbury, Massachusetts, obtained the first American patent for a pepperbox; their gun featured automatic revolving of the barrels when the hammer was cocked. Once again, this was not a new idea. Patents had been granted in Sweden and England for similar devices many years before, and just a month earlier Samuel Colt had claimed it as his own in his new "revolving pistol." A greater step forward came the next year when Ethan Allen of Grafton, Massachusetts, invented a double-action pepperbox in which a single pull on the trigger revolved the barrels, cocked and then fired the gun. All this was done in one motion, making the Allen pepperbox the fastest-firing arm of its day.

Here was the very gun that people had been waiting for—a weapon for personal defense that could be carried in a pocket or handbag and could fire more than once. The frightened shopkeeper or homeowner no longer had to make his first shot count or find himself unarmed; by giving him several chances, this new gun made him feel much safer. Sales skyrocketed. Shopkeepers and homeowners were joined by the Forty-niners, who found the pepperbox a handy companion on the long trek across the continent as well as excellent protection against claim jumpers and would-be gold thieves. Less savory characters also joined the ranks of pepperbox enthusiasts: gamblers, dance-hall girls, and the like. Some pepperboxes were even employed by the Army, and their use is recorded in a fight with the Cheyennes as late as 1857.

Of all its uses, however, the one that most appealed to the

storyteller's fancy was the duel. According to one fanciful version that keeps cropping up, the duelists' seconds would load only one barrel of each gun and spin the cluster so that nobody knew the exact position of the barrel containing the charge. The principals would then face each other, pulling the triggers in a race to see who could reach the "live" barrel first—a nineteenth-century version of Russian roulette. Despite the tales of duels fought by this method, not a single instance has ever been substantiated. In fact, only one duel with pepperboxes has been documented to this day—and this took place between two "ladies!" They met in Buffalo, New York, with Allen pepperboxes, but the authorities arrested both of them before the duel could get under way.

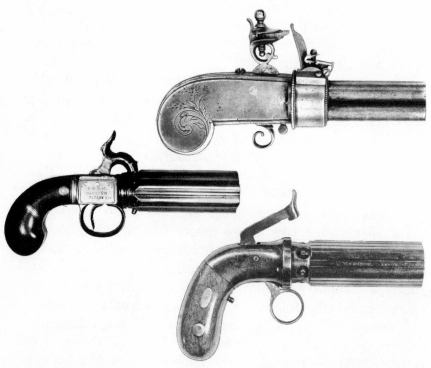

Top to bottom: Swiss eighteenth-century flintlock pepperbox with hand-turned barrels and all metal stock. Courtesy Robert Abels. Darlings' pepperbox, made under the first American patent for such a firearm. Courtesy Frank R. Horner. Patent model of the Allen pepperbox, the first American double-action type. Courtesy the Smithsonian Institution.

In addition to Allen and the Darlings, there were several other American makers plus a great many in England and on the Continent. None of their guns, however, came close to equaling the popularity of the Allen in the U.S. market, despite such European variations as large numbers of barrels, dagger bayonets, belt hooks for easy carrying and differences in size.

Along with their good qualities, all pepperboxes had serious defects. Worst of all was their inaccuracy. The hammer was right in the gunner's line of sight. The heavy trigger pull and —on the double-action models—the revolving of the barrels also prevented aiming. Mark Twain, who was well acquainted with the pepperbox from his days in the gold camps of the

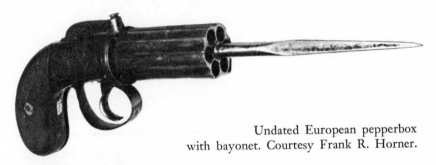

Undated European pepperbox with bayonet. Courtesy Frank R. Horner.

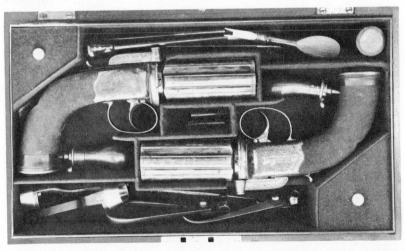

Cased English pepperboxes by Westley Richards. Courtesy Robert Abels.

West and on the river steamers, makes several humorous comments on the Allen and its shortcomings. On the subject of accuracy, he tells of a stagecoach passenger who attempted to demonstrate the effectiveness of his pepperbox by shooting out of the coach window. "He aimed at the trunk of a live oak," wrote Twain, "but fetched the nigh mule!"

Twain also noted another defect of the pepperbox. This was the tendency for the flash from the explosion of one charge to spread over the other barrels and set off some or all of them simultaneously, which gave the shooter a serious shock and sprayed the landscape with a hail of bullets. In Twain's version, a storyteller, upset because his tale of shooting a tree-climbing buffalo with his pepperbox had been hooted at, complained: "I would have shot the long gangly lubber they called Hank if I could have done it without crippling six or seven other people—but of course I couldn't, the old Allen's so confounded comprehensive."

When one adds to these drawbacks the fact that the number of barrels made the gun muzzle-heavy and difficult to carry if the caliber was large, it is obvious why the pepperbox succumbed to the revolver when that weapon was finally perfected. Still, it was not until the 1850s that the changeover took place, and during its years of popularity the pepperbox embellished a colorful era in American history.

Chapter 48

Rocket Guns

SCIENCE-FICTION GUN COMES TRUE, proclaimed the headlines. "Revolutionary," "unique" and similar adjectives have been used by many experts who examined the recently invented MBA Gyrojet pistol. Introduced in the summer of 1965, this arm is designed to fire miniature rocket projectiles. No other handgun has ever before used self-propelled ammunition, so the MBA development is certainly a breakthrough in every sense of the word. It is actually a hand-held rocket launcher; in fact, its handsome presentation case contains a medal stamped with a picture of Robert Goddard—the father of modern rocketry.

From the historian's point of view, however, the Gyrojet pistol is less a revolutionary arm than the end result of a long process of evolution. Hand-held rocket launchers were used almost three hundred years ago in Europe, and even earlier in China. Some have been mere signal devices; some have been dangerous and wildly inaccurate, and some have been very effective weapons. None have been handguns, though, and none have fired a projectile as small as the Gyrojet missile—which is made in a 13-mm handgun version that closely corresponds to a .45 cartridge.

The earliest military rockets were probably used for signaling. They were simply fireworks that arched up into the air and burned with a bright light. As such, they were useful in sending messages, coordinating attacks, and the like. They were often fired without a launcher of any kind, much in the manner of modern skyrockets. Sometimes, however, these missiles were used as incendiary weapons or as devices to frighten horses or green troops. To perform these functions, the rocketeers needed to control the rocket's flight with greater accuracy than they could obtain simply by thrusting a stick at its rear end into the ground and lighting a fuse. At such times, they used rocket launchers. Often, the aiming and firing devices were stands or troughs, but some were designed to be held by hand. One of these early launching guns still survives. It is a Danish specimen made in 1686 with a short, thin-walled barrel, a bore diameter of about 3¼ inches, a chunky, full-length wooden stock—and a conventional flintlock for igniting the rocket. The shape of the stock indicates that the piece was designed to be fired from the shoulder. Yet no shield was provided to guard against the flash of the rocket as it left the muzzle—which was only a trifle more than 17 inches from the shooter's nose. It is a good guess that the Danish launcher was an unpopular device, not often used.

More efficient military rockets with specialized warheads did not appear for more than a century after this earliest surviving launcher was made. Then an Englishman named Sir William Congreve perfected missiles with incendiary, explosive and shrapnel heads. Heavy British models were fired into Boulogne in 1806 and Copenhagen in 1807.

Danish rocket launcher dated 1686. Courtesy the Tøjhusmuseet, Copenhagen.

During the War of 1812, British rockets scattered American militiamen at Bladensburg, outside Washington, but failed to daunt the defenders of Fort McHenry or to defeat Andrew Jackson at New Orleans. (It is worth noting that Francis Scott Key wrote our National Anthem while watching the British bombardment of Fort McHenry at Baltimore on the night of September 13–14, 1814, and his line about "the rockets' red glare" refers to self-propelled missiles.) Most of these projectiles were heavy artillery rockets, fired from a trough or stand just as some of the earliest ones had been launched, and they were wildly inaccurate.

Still, they were effective in many cases, and British Ordnance officers were anxious to get rockets into the hands of the infantry as well as the artillery. They also wanted to improve the missiles' accuracy, so they set about experimenting with one-man hand-held launchers that would give the rockets better guidance during the takeoff. Between 1810 and 1820, the British produced a number of different launchers. A series of them can be seen at the Tower of London, and others survive in private collections.

There were two principal designs. One type was mounted on a pike staff; the other employed a shoulder stock like the usual musket of the period. The pike models had a copper or steel tube for the rocket, and the lower end of the pike staff terminated in a point that the shooter could stick into the ground to steady his aim. A few had bayonets attached to the launching tube for hand-to-hand combat in emergencies. Ignition of the rocket was obtained with a standard flintlock firing mechanism of the same type used on the muskets and carbines of the period, but the trigger was usually mounted on the side, two feet to the rear of the lock to protect the rocketeer from the flash. It was connected to the lock by a rod.

The musket-type rocket launchers were designed to be held against the shoulder and fired like a conventional flintlock.

English rocket launcher mounted on pike staff. Courtesy Herbert G. Ratner, Jr.

Some had the trigger set well back behind the lock in the manner of the pike launchers, while on others it was placed in the normal musket position. Some surviving examples have flash shields, and it is possible that they all had them at one time since this protection would seem almost indispensable to safe firing from the shoulder.

The end of the War of 1812 and the Napoleonic Wars brought the usual economizing in military affairs, and the experiments with hand-held rocket launchers suffered the typi-

The first U.S. bazooka, 1942. Courtesy the West Point Museum.

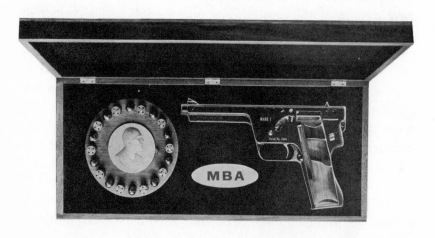

MBA Gyrojet pistol in presentation case, with medal commemorating rocketry pioneer Robert Goddard; 13-mm projectiles, viewed from nose and base, surround the medal. Courtesy MB Associates.

cal fate of new weapons ideas when peace is first restored: they were abandoned completely. The older, heavy rockets continued in use off and on during the Crimean War, and Americans used them in the Mexican and Civil Wars, but the lack of accuracy inherent in such missiles prevented real success and popularity for almost another century.

It was World War II that revived combat rocketry—including our own artillery and even rocket machine guns used experimentally by Japan. The breakthrough came in 1942. In that year, the United States Ordnance Department succeeded where others had failed and developed a marvelously simple, hand-held rocket launcher. Nicknamed the "bazooka," it fired a projectile with a 2.36-inch diameter, and it startled the world with its efficiency and effectiveness. The bazooka was light, it was accurate, and it struck with stupefying force. It knocked out tanks and machine-gun nests with ease, giving the foot soldier the equivalent of portable, short-range artillery. The hand-held launcher had come of age, though it remained somewhat unwieldly—55 inches in length and weighing more than 14 pounds. The step from the bazooka to the single-hand Gyrojet pistol was a giant stride indeed, but historically speaking, the origin of this unique arm clearly goes back almost three hundred years.

Military-style prototype of MBA Gyrojet carbine, shown with rocket ammunition. Courtesy MB Associates.

Part IX

GUNS IN
THE EAST

Group of three Indian matchlock guns. The left specimen has an Afghan stock; the other two have more typical stocks, similar to the Persian style but thinner. Courtesy the Winchester Gun Museum.

Chapter 49

Variety in India

"East is East, and West is West, and never the twain shall meet . . ." Every schoolboy knows Rudyard Kipling's famous commentary upon the contrast between the Occident and the Orient. The two differed in almost all phases of life and culture, including firearms. But when the Western collector decides to go in for Oriental firearms, he has a rare chance for fun at a low cost. Take, for example, the guns of Kipling's India and the immediately neighboring areas.

Firearms have a long history in that vast sub-continent. There was even a time when students thought that gunpowder might have been invented in India, and there were legends about ancient guns, made of bamboo or hollowed from rocks, that hurled fire arrows and other projectiles. In recent years such stories have been proved to be false. Historians now realize that guns probably came to India by an overland route from Turkey and Persia through Afghanistan and what is now Pakistan. The exact time of their introduction is unknown, but firearms must have been made in India before 1500; early Portuguese explorers mention seeing them there during the opening years of the sixteenth century. Contact with the Europeans brought more and different firearms to India, but their effect was small. The native population clung to the original Near Eastern types. And they continued to cling to them for some four hundred more years.

Throughout the vast territory that stretches from Afghanistan to the tip of the Indian peninsula, there were many stylistic variations that immediately indicated the specific area in which a gun was made, but there was one feature that remained the same for all. This was the firing mechanism. The guns were invariably matchlocks with a simple sear-lever lock and a match holder, or serpentine, that fell forward—away from the shooter instead of toward him in the usual European fashion. The trigger was a simple blade under the stock. When this trigger was pressed, the serpentine moved forward and down, bringing the lighted match into contact with the priming powder in the pan. When the trigger was released, a spring forced the serpentine back to its normal position.

All the working parts were enclosed in a slot cut into the stock so that only the extremities of the action—the trigger and the forward end of the serpentine—protruded. As in European matchlocks, the priming pan was forged as part of the barrel. Sometimes there was a single hinged pan cover, sometimes just a snap-on lid.

There was never a trigger guard. During the nineteenth century, when English flintlock parts became available in the East, a few Indian guns were made with these firing systems, and standard trigger guards were added. Flintlocks were imported, however; they were seldom if ever made in India, and the matchlock remained the standard ignition system for all native-made firearms until the modernization of the area in the present century.

This basic and simple Indian matchlock was applied to a great variety of guns. In Afghanistan, for instance, there was the *jezail*. This long weapon—often measuring from five to seven feet—was characterized by a narrow, gracefully curved stock, oval in cross section. Sometimes the bore was rifled, and many a gun of this kind was fitted with an A-shape bipod for the muzzle of its heavy barrel. In the state of Sind (in what is now Pakistan) the guns were slightly shorter and lighter, and the narrow, curved stock flared out to form a wide vertical butt. When the British entered Sind in the 1840s, they found the natives using guns with stocks of this shape, and they promptly began to call them Afghan stocks because the area was then ruled by Afghanistan. The name has survived to the present day, even though the form is seldom found in Afghanistan, where the *jezail* is standard.

In India itself, the most popular gun designs were closer to the original Turkish and Persian forms. The stocks were straight and angular, with only a very slight drop to the butt. There was, however, a sharp step-down behind the barrel tang. In the north, these butts were pentagonal in cross section like those of the Near East, but they were not as thick as the Persian and Turkish prototypes. Farther down the peninsula, the stocks became rounded in cross section; and finally in the area of the Coorgs, along the southwest coast, they became thin and flat while still retaining the same general outline. The Coorgs favored a very unusual stock design, with the narrow butt tapering back, then turning forward again to form a hook. It could only have been used for holding against the cheek like the early European wheel locks of the type called *tschinkes*, with their small pointed stocks. In all of these forms, the barrel was held to the stock by wrappings of rawhide, wire or silver bands. It might be smoothbored or occasionally rifled, and sometimes it was actually square instead of round—apparently because the gunmaker thought a square projectile would be more devastating than a conventional ball.

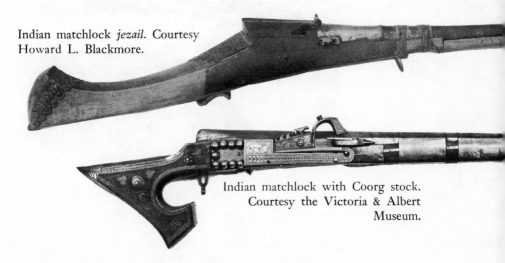

Indian matchlock *jezail*. Courtesy
Howard L. Blackmore.

Indian matchlock with Coorg stock.
Courtesy the Victoria & Albert
Museum.

The single-shot matchlock, in one or another of these forms, was the typical Indian gun, but there were some unusual firearms, too. One was the matchlock revolver. Strange as it may seem, these peculiar specimens seem to have worked. They were shoulder arms, not handguns, and they had straight stocks that swelled out to form a round section of the same diameter as the cylinder. This section held the lock and served as a flash shield. The cylinder itself was long and designed to be turned by hand, each chamber boasting its own priming pan complete with a sliding cover. Cylinder capacity varied; a gun might hold three shots, or five or seven or whatever number the native designer fancied. The barrel was normally quite short, but the big cylinder made this type of gun an impressive-looking weapon even if it never became popular.

Another unusual sort of firearm was occasionally built when an Indian gunsmith managed to get his hands on a European barrel. Given this sort of luck, he frequently copied a Western stock design with some fidelity—but managed to adapt its shape to fit the local form of matchlock. Finally, of course, there are the short flintlock blunderbusses with cheap, soft-iron barrels and huge flaring bells. While they may look like

Detail of Indian matchlock revolving long gun. Courtesy Howard L. Blackmore.

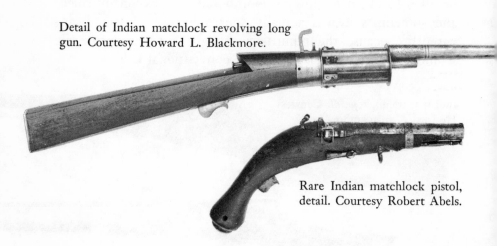

Rare Indian matchlock pistol, detail. Courtesy Robert Abels.

antiques, these are a late development, still being made for the tourist trade, and they hardly deserve notice with the fine native designs.

As with the products of almost any other area of the world, the quality of Indian firearms varied greatly. Some were simple, crude instruments for hunting and warfare, made for the common people. Others were magnificent works of art, fashioned for the nobility. Indian ironwork reached a highly developed stage hundreds of years ago, and some Indian firearms that were made as far back as the seventeenth century boast Damascus barrels of a quality that has never been surpassed. Beautiful decoration with silver, gold and precious or semiprecious stones also enhanced the finest specimens made for the great rulers. Yet, because so few people are aware of these firearms, their cost is not usually high. The collector who decides to gather a group of these Indian arms has an opportunity to obtain handsome and colorful guns at a lower price than he can find in almost any other type of gun collecting. Best of all, he sometimes has the chance to choose between a round and a square bore. What other field can offer him that opportunity?

Chapter 50

The Typhoon Brought Guns

Typhoons repeatedly bring torrential rains, high winds, shipwreck, and destruction to Japan. One of them also brought firearms. According to Japanese tradition, a Chinese trading junk bearing three Portuguese adventurers was blown off its course in 1542, and finally landed at one of the southern Japanese islands. The very name of this little island, Tanegashima, came to mean "firearm" to the Japanese because of the deep impression made on them by the invention the strangers brought.

Portugal was noted for its explorers and merchants. They had discovered a route around the tip of Africa to India and on to China, where they had established an active trade. But no Europeans had ever visited Japan until the typhoon brought this storm-tossed trio to Tanegashima. The guns carried by these men (whose names have been lost to history) were smoothbore matchlocks.

By the mid-sixteenth century, such firearms were well known in Europe, but these particular ones were a very unusual form of matchlock. Most European guns of this sort employed a pivoted arm called a serpentine, with a clamp on the end to hold the match. When the trigger was pulled, this serpentine moved down toward the priming pan. The movement was controlled by finger pressure on the trigger. As soon as this pressure was released, a spring raised the serpentine up out of the way. The guns brought to Japan, however, were snapping matchlocks, a variation that became popular for a short time in the early 1500s in a few places. In these snapping locks, the serpentine was "cocked" by pulling it back against a spring. When the trigger was pressed, the serpentine was released, and the spring hurled it down toward the pan; it remained down until the gun was cocked once again. This sort of lock had two major disadvantages: It was more complicated to make than the standard type, and the sudden movement of the match striking hard against the priming powder and the pan sometimes extinguished the glowing coal that was supposed to ignite the powder. For these reasons, the snapping matchlock did not long remain popular in Europe. The coincidence of the typhoon, however, by bringing it to Japan, introduced it to the Orient and gave it an added life span of over three hundred years.

The sodden voyagers had hardly struggled ashore before their guns became the talk of the island. The Portuguese were well aware of the awe that a shooting demonstration could awaken in an uninitiated audience, and they quickly exploited it. One Japanese eyewitness described the scene:

". . . they carried with them one article . . . which was about two or three feet in length, straight, heavy, and hollow. One end, however, was closed, and near it there was a small hole through which fire was to be lighted. The article was used in the following way: Some mysterious medicine was put into it, with a small piece of lead, and when someone lit the medicine through that hole, the lead piece was discharged and hit everything. When it was discharged, light like lightning was seen and noise like thunder was heard, so the bystanders . . . closed their ears with their hands."

It must have been a magnificent and impressive performance, and the Japanese naturally coveted the spectacular "article" which could make such a noise and "hit everything." For an exorbitant price, the Portuguese eventually agreed to let the local shogun, or feudal lord, have two of their precious firearms, but then the happy potentate found he could not make them shoot. He still needed powder and ball. It took more negotiating, of course, before the traders would show him how this was made. Finally, however, an agreement was reached, and the enthusiastic ruler practiced until observers said he could "nearly hit" a target at almost 100 paces.

The one thing that the Portuguese refused to teach the islanders was the method of making guns. With their skill as craftsmen and copyists, though, the Japanese set out to devise their own system, and they promptly succeeded except for the problem of closing the breech end. There are several legends about how they tried to solve this puzzle. One story involves a lonely Portuguese and the charms of a Japanese maiden; another maintains that the Japanese craftsmen promised to become Christians if the Europeans would reveal their manufacturing secrets. In any event, the Orientals learned a trick that seems to have involved inserting an iron rod into a heated breech so that the contraction of the hot metal as it cooled made a tight seal. And an unknown Japanese craftsman, working independently, is supposed to have found another solution by inventing a breech plug with a screw thread. While this story can't be authenticated, all surviving Japanese matchlocks have threaded breech plugs, although the Japanese generally avoided screws elsewhere. They used pins and pin-and-key fasteners for almost all gun work.

Such technicalities were the only areas in which the Japanese craftsmen failed, however. When it came to barrel forging and decoration, they were unsurpassed. They forged their gun barrels like their sword blades, with countless layers of iron and steel, built up like the skin of an onion. So strong were these barrels that seventeenth-century examples have been found that were converted to bolt-action arms firing modern cartridges. Few European barrels of comparable age could stand such a test. Decoration, too, was brought to an exceptionally high level, with exquisite chiseling, engraving and inlaying. Gun barrels at first had a straight taper or slight flare at the muzzle. Then, after about 1800, flared muzzle moldings similar to those on cannon were added.

Japanese shooters aimed and fired the matchlock as they had been taught by the sixteenth-century Europeans, who held the stock against the cheek, not braced against the chest or shoulder in the later European fashion. The entire weight of the gun was supported by the shooter's hands.

The sights were rectangular blocks of metal fastened atop the barrel, and the front sight was similar to the European blade type. The rear had an open aiming groove, and sometimes an additional cut in the top of the block, crossing this groove at a right angle. There might also be a shallow circular depression in the top of the block, or a hole through its sides. These extra features appear to have no functional purpose, unless they were attempts to reduce glare.

A few Japanese guns have been found with a third sight between the front and rear—and sometimes these third sights are out of line! It is believed that guns with such sights were made primarily as household ornaments during the two and a half centuries known as Japan's "Time of Peace," and were fired so rarely that gunsmiths apparently ignored practical considerations.

Firearms came to Japan at a turbulent era in its history. It was known as the "Time of War," and the demand for firearms was great, as fights among the local rulers went on almost incessantly. In 1600 the "Time of Peace" began, and for more than 250 years there was no fighting in the islands. Gun

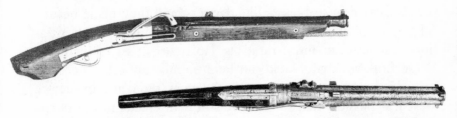

Left to right: Short Japanese gun with 13¼-inch barrel. It could be held in one hand if necessary. Courtesy the Winchester Gun Museum. Japanese .40-caliber revolving gun. The cluster of three barrels is rotated by hand. Courtesy the Smithsonian Institution. Japanese long gun with seventeenth-century barrel and eighteenth-century stock. Courtesy the Winchester Gun Museum.

ownership was generally restricted to warriors and the nobility, who apparently used their arms for hunting but not at all for combat.

Most guns became show pieces, kept in racks to impress visitors. Thus the art of decoration flourished, but there were few attempts to improve the mechanism or speed the process of loading and firing. The matchlock remained the standard ignition system until the mid-nineteenth century although the Japanese were familiar with the flintlock mechanism and used it for tinder lighters.

Most of these matchlocks were single-shots, although multi-barreled, hand-rotated matchlock revolvers were also made. Since guns of this type have been found in India, it is possible that a knowledge of their design spread from the Asian mainland. However, hand-turned revolvers were made in Europe as early as the 1500s; therefore, it is virtually certain they were introduced to Japan by European traders. Only a few of these multi-barreled revolving arms were turned out. Until late in the nineteenth century, the single-barreled design remained standard, and such refinements as rifling were unknown in Japan.

This was the firearms situation as Commodore Matthew C. Perry found it in 1853. Only after he opened the island kingdom to foreign commerce and introduced firearms of all sorts —from Elgin cutlass pistols to Colt revolvers—did changes come about. The Japanese began to manufacture percussion pistols carried in scabbards like daggers, and they made beautiful copies of percussion Colts. After 1871, arms modernization became even more rapid as Japan began to emulate the West. Still, the matchlock gun held popular appeal. There are records of such arms being made as late as 1896, and in remote areas it is possible that some were still being made in the twentieth century. For over 350 years the Japanese had clung to the typhoon's gift.

Part X

AMMUNITION AND EQUIPMENT

Chapter 51

Gunpowder

The origin of gunpowder is shrouded in mystery. No one knows who invented it or even the general area of the world in which it was discovered. There have been claims and counterclaims for China, India, Arabia, and Europe as the place of the historic event. Real men such as Friar Roger Bacon of England and Albertus Magnus of Germany have been cited as possible inventors, along with entirely mythical personages such as the legendary Black Berthold or Berthold Schwartz.

Only one fact is reasonably certain: the first definite description of true gunpowder that survives was written by Roger Bacon in about 1248. Bacon hid his formula in an anagram because he thought the substance was too dangerous for general publication, but scholars have solved his code. His disguised description proves that he knew about gunpowder and realized that it would explode with a thunderous noise if it were confined in a parchment wrapping. But this does not mean that Bacon necessarily invented the compound. He was a student of the chemistry of his time, and he read widely in Greek and Arabic texts. Many students think he found the gunpowder formula in one of these, since he makes no claim for its discovery. And it is interesting to note that Albertus Magnus, a German scholar who also read widely, gave the same formula as Bacon a very short time later—apparently without being aware of Bacon's description.

Thus there is no doubt that gunpowder was known in Europe in the middle 1200s. Some claim that the Chinese had invented it many years before, and that it reached Bacon and Magnus via the Arabs who served as a liaison between the civilizations of the East and West. The only trouble with this theory is that there is no proof. The Chinese did have incendiary weapons at an early date, but the formulas they have passed down would not *explode*. Interestingly enough, the oldest formula for true gunpowder that can be found in Chinese writings dates from exactly the same period as those in Europe. Perhaps the Orientals did invent the fearful substance and sent knowledge of it to Europe via the Arabs; or perhaps the Europeans discovered it and brought the knowledge to China via Arabia. Or it may be that the Arabian scholars made the earthshaking breakthrough and passed the information along in both directions at once. The answer will probably never be known.

Whoever invented it, the earliest gunpowder was a simple mixture of charcoal, sulphur, and saltpeter. Saltpeter was the key ingredient, for it provided the necessary oxygen that permitted the sulphur and charcoal to burn rapidly in a confined space. Without it, there could be no explosion. At first, the formulas for gunpowder ran about seven parts of saltpeter to five of charcoal and five of sulphur. Since this made a weak powder, huge quantities were needed to fire a gun with any force. By 1400, the formula had been improved so that it was often 22 (saltpeter): 4 (charcoal): 5 (sulphur)—and by the eighteenth century it was usually 75:15:10, which is essentially what black powder is today.

At first, the three ingredients were simply ground to a fine powder and stirred together. This resulted in a dust-like substance that collectors call "meal powder." It had many drawbacks. For one thing, kegs of this powder gave off a highly explosive dust when they were moved about. For another, the three ingredients had different specific gravities, and after the powder had stayed in a keg for a length of time the elements tended to separate according to their weights. Finally, meal powder attracted moisture. It would form lumps when rammed into a gun, and sometimes it got so wet it wouldn't burn at all.

The solution to these problems was "corned," or grained, gunpowder, which was developed as early as the 1400s. It was produced by moistening the mixed ingredients with alcohol, then pressing the compound through a sieve to form little grains. When these grains dried, the mixture was solidly held together; there was no longer so much danger from explosive dust, and the fear of dampness was greatly decreased. As an extra bonus, the new corned powder burned faster and generated more power than the primitive meal. Black-powder grains are now sometimes glazed with black lead, but otherwise no major changes have been made in its composition in the last five hundred years.

Once it was perfected, black powder proved to be a good dependable propellant. As long as the purity and proportion of the ingredients were kept constant, the power was relatively uniform and it did not deteriorate with age. Still, it was far from perfect. One drawback was that burning powder released great quantities of thick, white smoke. Whole battlefields might be obscured after a few volleys, and there was no chance whatever of firing from a hidden position. As soon as a gun was shot, telltale smoke marked the shooter's location for all to see. Also, black powder left a gummy residue in gun barrels each time it was fired. After a number of shots, the accumulated deposit could make it difficult to seat a bullet, and the bore had to be cleaned as soon as the shooting was over, no matter how tired the hunter or soldier might be. The gummy deposit attracted moisture, which converted the sulphur residue to sulphuric acid that quickly ate pits into the metal of the bore. Some marksmen who prized their guns highly would clean them after each shot, but most gunners waited until the end of the firing session. Even that seemed too troublesome to many a weary shooter.

Relief from both the smoke and residue problems came with the invention of smokeless powder. As early as the 1600s, chemists had experimented with smokeless explosives, but they were too violent and unpredictable to be adopted for firing guns. Then, in 1846, three chemists working separately —Sobrero in Italy, Schönbein in Switzerland, and Böttger in Germany—all discovered nitroglycerine and nitrocellulose, or guncotton. These were promising explosives, and many men worked on improving them for possible use in firearms. In 1886, a French chemist named Vielle produced the first workable smokeless powder. He mixed guncotton with ether and alcohol, rolled it into sheets, cut it up into grains and flakes and let it dry. France adopted his new powder for her military arms that very year, and other nations soon followed suit. By 1900, almost all countries had converted to the new propellant. The smoke of battle had disappeared and the modern era of shooting had begun.

Chapter 52

How Bullets Evolved

Man's search for a better firearm has been paralleled throughout history by his quest for a better projectile to fire in it. It may never be possible to learn what kind of projectiles were fired in the very first small arms; they could well have been stone balls similar to those used for early cannon. By about 1375, however, there definitely were metal bullets, for an English document of that period lists "twelve iron ladles for casting lead pellets and ten brass molds for making them." With these early balls, the history of the metal bullet can be said to have begun.

Right from the start, there was much experimentation. Designers were by no means certain what shape these "pellets" should assume. Spheres were used, of course, but there was no handicap to the imagination in those heady days when the gun was new. Some experimenters tried arrows. Such missiles had worked well with bows for years and it was assumed they might do just as well for the new projectile throwers. As it turned out, they didn't, but darts and arrows were used in firearms for more than two hundred years. Other shapes were tried as well—diamonds, cones, barrel-shapes, and rods as well as balls. In all of this testing, the ball led the field in popularity, but it was almost 1600 before the other more imaginative designs were scrapped.

There was also the question of what metal to use. Lead very quickly appeared; in fact, it was perhaps the first substance to be used after stone. But theorists were not satisfied that it was best until considerable debate and trial proved it to be. Iron was tested at the beginning. So were bronze, brass, tin, and even silver and gold. Iron and steel balls remained popular as armor-piercing projectiles for a number of years. In France, such bullets came to be known as *stuardes*. The term originated because a Scot named Stuart killed a French hero with a ball that was believed to be of steel. At the Battle of Saint-Denis in 1567, Stuart shot the Constable of France, Anne de Montmorency (a man despite his name); the ball pierced Montmorency's armor and passed through his kidneys, but despite his mortal wound, the seventy-four-year-old Constable whirled and struck his assailant so hard with the pommel of his sword that he broke the Scotsman's jaw.

Some philosophers advanced the theory that the metal used for the bullet should be determined by the "quality" of the proposed target. With this in mind, a French warrior who set out against the Emperor Charles V took along half a dozen gold bullets for his arquebus. And the idea has persisted, although sometimes the metal of the bullet has been determined by the target, sometimes by the shooter. In modern fiction, for example, the Emperor Jones was supposed to be vulnerable only to a silver bullet, while the Lone Ranger customarily used bullets of the same metal.

Gradually, however, lead replaced all the other materials. It had a low melting point, so it could be cast easily in portable hand molds. At the same time, it had a sufficiently high specific gravity to give it good ballistic qualities. It was also readily available. By 1600, when the ball had replaced other projectile shapes, lead was in almost universal use, and for more than two hundred years it had no serious competition from other metals.

Then came the elongated bullet. Experiments with such projectiles for use in rifles began in England and France toward the end of the 1700s. The spin imparted by the rifling kept such missiles from tumbling, and the pointed nose reduced air resistance. This streamlining, combined with smaller diameter and realignment of the projectile's weight, made it travel farther and strike harder than the standard round balls. The main difficulty—as long as guns remained muzzle-loaders—was to design an elongated bullet that could be dropped down the barrel easily but still fit tightly enough to take the rifling. Some experimenters tested loose-fitting bullets with lugs designed to enter the grooves. Sir Joseph Whitworth of England developed a rifle with a hexagonal bore and he shaped his bullets to match it. Various French designers experimented with projectiles that could be dropped loosely down the barrel and then hammered with the ramrod so that they flattened out to fit tightly. (Unfortunately, this also distorted their shape so that they lost both velocity and accuracy.)

Real success for elongated muzzle-loading projectiles came with the hollow-based bullet. British, French, and American gun experts all worked to develop such a bullet, and most Americans know the finished version by the name minié ball after French Captain Claude Etienne Minié, one of the several men who perfected it. In its final form, this was a cylindro-conoidal projectile with a hollow base. It was small enough in relation to the bore so that it would slide in easily; then, when the gun was fired, gas from the burning powder pushed into the bullet's hollow base and expanded its thin walls so that they fit tightly into the rifling. Early versions of this bullet had utilized plugs of iron or wood which were driven forward upon firing to expand the projectile, but it was soon found that the gas alone was sufficient to cause expansion. With the minié ball, a rifle could be loaded as quickly as a smoothbore, and the advantages of the elongated bullet could be obtained as well. Fired from the guns of both the Union and Confederacy, it became the deadliest killer of the American Civil War.

Just at the moment when the minié ball brought the muzzle-loading military rifle to its highest development, the breech-loader shunted it into obsolescence. This changed the requirements for a bullet and opened new possibilities. Since

breechloading arms could be made with a chamber slightly
larger than the bore diameter, tight-fitting bullets could be
loaded with ease, and there was no longer any need for types
that expanded within the barrel. Elongated projectiles became
standard. Some of them were pointed to increase their velocity
and penetration. Others were flattened or even hollowed at
the tip so that they would expand upon impact and destroy
more tissue. Hollow-points were soon outlawed for warfare,
but they continue in use today as game-getters. Long, slender and sharply pointed bullets were developed for military
purposes in Germany in about 1898. The United States

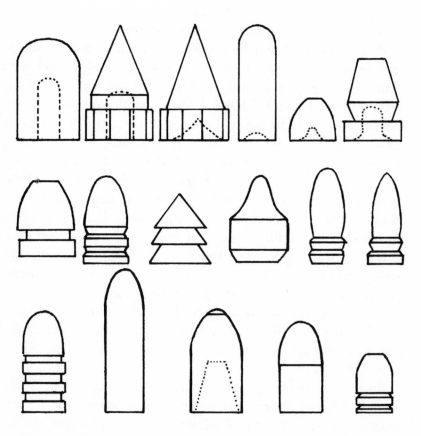

Group of rifle-bullet designs from the mid-1800s.

adopted them for its .30-caliber Model 1903 Springfield, and they quickly became popular for martial weapons throughout the Western world.

During this period of evolution, the typical bullet had been a simple mass of lead. Smokeless powder changed that. Introduced in the 1880s, the new propellant was so much more powerful than black powder that the gas it released eroded lead bullets before they left the bore and made them inaccurate. To prevent this, jackets of harder metals were added. Steel was tested and so was brass before the modern copper-zinc alloys were found to be the most successful combinations.

Ammunition from the Revolutionary War, including a complete paper cartridge (lower left), .75-caliber bullets, bullet mold, gun flint, and small mound of black powder. Author's collection.

Today the shooter has a wide choice of designs and materials. There are blunt, soft bullets for great shocking power, and long, sharply pointed projectiles with tapered bases for high velocity and long range. Hard jackets afford heat protection and aid penetration. There are armor-piercing bullets, tracers, observing and incendiary types, and various combinations of these designs. Even the wildest dreamer of the early experimental years could never have imagined the diversity and versatility made possible by modern technological advances.

Chapter 53

Cartridges

A modern cartridge can easily be taken for granted. Putting a bullet and a charge of powder into a package ready for instant use seems like an obvious idea. Yet firearms had been in use for more than a century before shooters thought of measuring and wrapping the powder charge in advance, and it was a long journey from these first crude cartridges—which did not include the projectile or primer—to the self-contained metal-cased loads of today. The story of ammunition development offers an interesting supplement to the history of firearms, for cartridges enabled even early guns to shoot faster; improvements in the ammunition made the breechloader practical and, finally, sturdy cartridge cases made true magazine arms possible.

The very first paper cartridges probably appeared in about 1500. The Italian genius Leonardo da Vinci mentions that they were being used by mounted soldiers a few years after that date, and he was apparently just reporting a fact, not suggesting something new. These ancient cartridges were merely charges of powder wrapped in paper. For convenience in loading, a horseman bit off one end of the paper package, poured a little of the powder into the priming pan of his gun and dumped the rest down the barrel. He followed this with a ball from his pouch (or possibly from his mouth if he was in battle), and then rammed the paper wrapping of the cartridge down on top of the ball so that it served as a wad.

Obviously, digging a bullet out of a pouch took time. Spitting one into the barrel from a supply in the mouth was faster, but that practice had inconveniences that might become downright unpleasant. In battle, a sneeze could be disastrous. It was readily apparent that if the bullet could be included in the same unit with the powder, it would be much more convenient, and ingenious men all over Europe set out to find a way to do just that. By the late sixteenth century, a few cartridges were being made with a flanged bullet that could be tied to the front end of the powder package. Unfortunately, such bullets did not shoot well because of their odd shape, so they never became widely popular. A century later, designers were still trying to tie the ball to the outside of the packet, sometimes by means of the projectile's casting sprue. But even this small protuberance affected accuracy. Actually, the solution was simple—all they had to do was wrap the ball securely *inside* the packet, but it was about 1700 before anyone thought of that.

Meanwhile, the use of the powder cartridge had spread widely. Throughout most of the 1500s and the early 1600s it remained a device meant for cavalrymen who had to load while on horseback. Then, in the seventeenth century, the great soldier-king Gustavus Adolphus of Sweden is said to have ordered cartridges for his infantry. Other leaders did the same, and within a century the use of the paper cartridge had become almost universal for military purposes. It continued to be standard for over a hundred years. Percussion-cap arms replaced flintlocks in the nineteenth century but, except for minor differences in wrapping techniques, the paper cartridge remained the same.

Despite the speed and convenience that it offered, such a cartridge had a number of serious drawbacks. It was fragile; a sharp blow or too much jostling, and it was apt to break open and spill out its contents. Also, as long as the soldier had to bite off the end of the cartridge, it was necessary for him to

have at least two teeth opposite each in the front of his mouth
—and this remained a criterion for Army physical tests until
the paper cartridge was abandoned. Most important of all, this
kind of load lacked a primer. The spark had to be produced
by flint striking steel or by a percussion cap seated separately
on a nipple.

To overcome the fragility of paper, other wrappings were
tried. Inventors substituted cardboard, linen, "goldbeaters'
skin" (a membrane from the large intestine of an ox, commonly used in goldbeating), collodion, metal foils, rubber
and finally full metal cases. Successful cartridges were made
with casings from every one of these materials and from
others as well.

Meanwhile, some inventors turned their attention to the
problem of adding a primer to the cartridge. One of the first
men to succeed was Johannes Samuel Pauly, a Swiss gunsmith
living in Paris. In 1812, Pauly patented a cartridge that was
truly world-shaking in its implications. Not only did it include
its own primer, it was also the first center-fire cartridge. This
tremendously important ammunition package boasted a brass
head with a small depression in its center that Pauly called a
bassinet, or pan. This held a small pellet of detonating compound. Actually, the priming was still kept outside the cartridge, but there was a little hole in the pan which transmitted the flash to the charge inside. Some Pauly cartridges
were made with brass heads and cardboard bodies, like modern
shotgun shells, while others were entirely metallic.

The outside primer of Pauly's cartridge was a weakness.
The compound could fall out of the pan and be lost, or the
little hole in the base might become stopped up. Therefore,
the search for a better cartridge continued, and some wonderfully ingenious types were developed. Some early metal-
cased versions were equipped with nipples for caps, just like
percussion firearms. Pin-fire cartridges featured a primer shaped
like the standard percussion cap but placed inside the case
with a pin above it that protruded through the case wall.
When this pin was struck by the hammer, it drove down

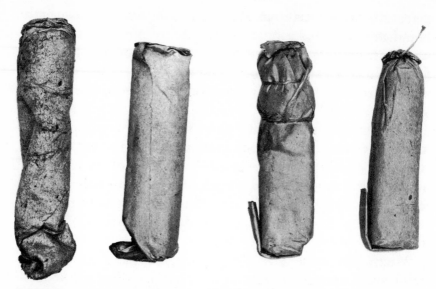

Four paper-wrapped cartridges, left to right: British eighteenth-century cartridge tied at the top; French pasted type of the American Revolution; combination buck-and-ball cartridge used by U.S. troops in the 1830s and '40s; minié-ball cartridge of the Civil War. Author's collection.

Six early metal-cased cartridges. The first three, from left, are primerless and have holes in their bases to let in the flash from a standard percussion cap. Left to right: Billinghurst & Requa machine-gun cartridge; Burnside; Maynard; French pin-fire; early French rim-fire cartridge for a Perrin revolver; fully developed rim-fire cartridge for the Spencer repeater. Author's collection.

against the primer and exploded it. Pin-fires worked well, but they were fragile and subject to accidental discharge from any blow that struck the pin. A student of Pauly's, Johann Niko- laus von Dreyse, invented a cartridge with the primer up front, in the base of the bullet, so that a long sharp firing pin had to pass all the way through the powder charge to strike it and set it off. This long firing pin gave the famous "needle gun" its name. It, too, had drawbacks, since the slender pin was apt to bend or break.

Some cartridges consisted of just a bullet holding a combina- tion primer-propellant charge in a hollow base. The Ameri- can Volcanic repeating arms, immediate ancestors of the Henry and Winchester rifles, used such cartridges, but the loads were too weak to be really successful. Still, it was the use of such a combination primer-propellant charge that led the way to the efficient modern cartridge. A Frenchman named Flobert patented a cartridge in 1849 which was essen- tially a standard percussion cap with a bullet stuck in the open end. The detonating compound generated sufficient force to hurl the bullet a short distance. It was useful primarily for indoor target practice, but from this step it was only a natural advance to add a charge of powder between the primer and the bullet.

The Americans Horace Smith and Daniel B. Wesson did this in the mid-1850s but did not patent their cartridge until 1860, by which time they were already using it in the first of their famous line of revolvers. Smith & Wesson cartridges were rim-fires, but at almost the same time another American, G. W. Morse, developed a center-fire. Hiram Berdan, the famous sharpshooter of the Civil War, improved the priming system in 1866, and Colonel Edward M. Boxer of the British Royal Laboratory developed a different but equally good priming system at about the same time. Berdan's type of wide-capped primer was difficult to remove in order to reload the cartridge, while Boxer's could easily be taken out and replaced. Since reloading has always been important in the United States, an interesting switch took place which soon saw the English

Boxer primer become almost universal in this country while the American Berdan type is the most common form in Great Britain.

It has been nearly a hundred years since Berdan and Boxer perfected the primers for metal-cased cartridges. There have been a few minor improvements in the types of metal used for cases in the intervening years; bullets have changed shape, and of course the propellant charge has advanced from black to smokeless powder. But there has been no basic change in the concept or function of the case and primer. In one form or another, the cartridge has been with us so long that it seems natural—something to be taken for granted.

Chapter 54

The Bullet Mold

The local sporting-goods dealer, with his abundant supply of all sorts and sizes of cartridges, was undreamed of as recently as a century ago. Of course, powder had to be bought, since it was beyond the ability of the average individual to manufacture it, but a merchant or trader had to carry only two or three grades to take care of the needs of almost any gun. Shot could also be supplied easily, because it was adaptable to many different bore sizes. Individual bullets, however, presented quite a problem. These had to fit a gun with some precision, and there were so many different calibers that few shopkeepers even considered stocking them ready-made.

Fortunately, though, bullets were easy for a shooter to make himself. All he had to do was to buy the necessary lead and cast his own projectiles in a mold that was either supplied by the gunsmith who produced the firearm—or sold by a professional mold maker and guaranteed to be exactly the right size. For more than four centuries, such molds were an essential part of almost every shooter's equipment.

The first bullet molds appeared at almost the same time as the first portable hand firearms. Such guns are believed to have been developed about 1350. Surviving references to bullet molds date back to 1373, and there is no indication that they were brand new devices even then. Probably these were "gang molds," designed to cast a number of bullets at once. A few molds for casting lead "pilgrim's tokens" (medals carried by religious pilgrims) have survived from this period, and all of them have a number of cavities that could be filled with one pouring. The earliest surviving bullet molds were made almost two centuries later than those token molds—dating from the late 1500s—and they, too, are gang molds.

The experienced collector can quickly recognize one of these very ancient bullet molds. Typical specimens have thin leaves of iron or brass into which the casting cavities have been cut. Usually there are two to four big holes for making single bullets, plus a number of little holes for casting small shot. Often, in addition to the usual spherical balls, there is a wide variety of other forms—cones, pyramids, barrel shapes, and the like—which are almost never found in molds that were produced after the beginning of the seventeenth century. Some of these early molds had only two leaves; others had many. The handles were always metal, sometimes forged or cast in a fixed position and sometimes hinged, or pivoted.

The thin metal leaves of these very early bullet molds were a design weakness. They tended to bend or warp so that they did not fit tightly, and a lot of melted lead would therefore run right through the mold. This wasted material, and it also left much work to be done in trimming up the castings. In addition, the leaves broke easily. As the years passed, these leaves were made thicker and thicker. Still, archaeologists digging in American Colonial sites find a sizable number of mold fragments in their excavations, indicating that breakage remained a problem.

It was not until the beginning of the eighteenth century that really solid leaves became standard. At the same time, wooden handles became fashionable, and the whole design of bullet molds changed. These early-eighteenth-century molds were almost always brass and were made in a small and a large size. The smaller type had four holes of varying calibers, so that a purchaser needed only one mold to cast bullets for his musket, plus a sporting gun and one or two pistols; the most common sizes cast bullets for a .75-caliber musket, a .69 musket or fowling piece, a .65 pistol or fowling piece and a .60 pistol. The larger molds offered cavities in three or four of these calibers, plus rows of smaller holes for two sizes of buckshot. The wooden handles were attached to two short tangs, projecting from the free ends of the leaves.

These were personal molds, designed for individual use. There were also large military gang molds of brass and iron that could cast up to 20 musket balls simultaneously. In these instances, of course, the cavities were all of the same size.

Toward the end of the 1500s, another pattern of mold had also developed, and this one remained popular as long as individual casting devices continued in use. This was the scissors-type mold. Usually it cast just one projectile at a time, though specimens exist that cast two or even three. The earliest of these tools were forged around an iron or steel ball of the proper size to make a cavity of the desired caliber. Later examples (from the 1700s on) were forged solid, and the cavity was then made with a "cherry bit"—a drill that was designed

Multi-leaved sixteenth-century brass mold for casting four large balls and a variety of shot. Author's collection.

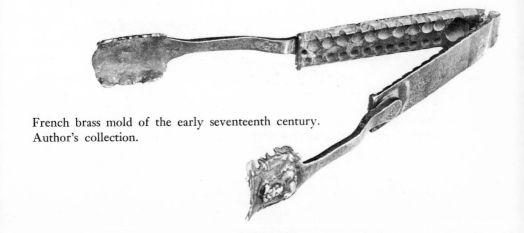

French brass mold of the early seventeenth century. Author's collection.

to cut a spherical shape. These drilled molds were found in cased sets of dueling and coach pistols, and were carried by frontier riflemen, Indian traders, mountain men and Eastern farmers. They remained in use as long as muzzle-loading rifles were used. In nineteenth-century examples, the number of balls to the pound of lead is frequently stamped on one of the handles as an indication of bore size, like standard gauge designations. And some very rare military specimens are marked

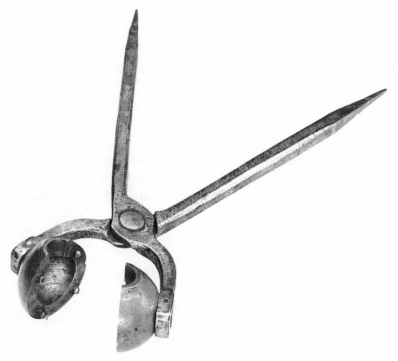

Scissors-type mold for a swivel gun of the seventeenth century. Author's collection.

American brass mold of the mid-eighteenth century for casting four different sizes of ball plus two sizes of buckshot. Author's collection.

"Hall's Rifle"—meaning that they cast .526-caliber bullets for these service weapons.

Like many other mechanical devices, the bullet mold grew more complex and varied in form just as it was becoming obsolete. Each of the host of percussion revolvers that followed in the wake of Sam Colt's invention had its own special mold. These were usually leaved molds, pivoted at the forward end, but, unlike the earlier types, they cast only one or

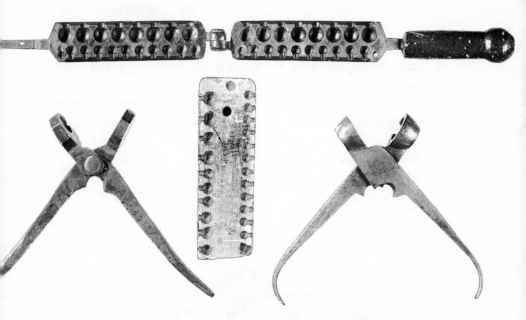

Group of bullet molds, including: (top) two halves of a soapstone mold; open eighteenth-century brass mold for casting buck and ball with one original wooden handle still in place; two iron scissors-type molds with sprue cutters of the early 1800s; half of a soapstone mold for casting graduated sizes of ball and a row of buckshot. Courtesy the Smithsonian Institution.

two bullets, often one conical and one round. Normally, there was also a sliding "sprue cutter" for removing the surplus metal at the point of casting, and sometimes these molds were combined with screwdrivers, wrenches, drifts, or other tools. When bullets with hollow bases appeared, more complicated molds were necessary to produce the new form. Then came the era of the metal-cased cartridge, and the days of the bullet mold were over except for handloaders. Paradoxically, better molds are available for these enthusiasts, now that such devices are no longer vital, than were ever made when the casting of a bullet might mean the difference between life and death to a shooter.

Today, antique molds offer the discriminating collector a fascinating field of study. They come in an almost infinite variety. In addition to the metal types described above, there were also more primitive—sometimes crude—soapstone versions; these were used alongside the sophisticated models ever since the beginning. The connoisseur can build a collection of these simple artifacts, paralleling the history of shooting and illustrating many of the advances in technology during the last four hundred years. Best of all, bullet molds are still relatively inexpensive, and they are readily available from antique-arms dealers and fellow collectors. The man who knows the subject can often find a real rarity at a very low price.

Mold for casting hollow-based bullet, late 1800s. Courtesy the Smithsonian Institution.

Chapter 55

Gadget Fever

Shooters love gadgets. Beginners, especially, like to rig themselves out with devices that might come in handy for every sort of emergency or that might give them a special advantage under the most wildly improbable circumstances. They gain stature in their own eyes through the quantity and complexity of their gear. The expert, on the other hand, recognizes the need for some accessories, but he carries as few as possible. While he is just as intrigued with the clever gadget as the amateur, he often puts it aside—reluctantly perhaps—in favor of efficiency. It has always been that way.

Take the matter of tools, for instance. By the early sixteenth century, when firearms had developed into fairly complex machines, a need arose for basic tools in case of a malfunction of some sort. Matchlocks were too simple to require such devices, but the wheel lock was a mechanic's delight. It produced its spark by bringing a piece of iron pyrite into contact with a rough-edged wheel much in the fashion of a modern "flint" cigarette lighter. Obviously, a wrench was needed to wind the wheel. Also, since iron pyrite is a comparatively soft mineral, the piece in the lock had to be adjusted frequently and a new one had to be substituted when it wore down; a wrench or screwdriver was therefore needed to operate the vise holding the pyrite. A screwdriver was also useful for adjustments elsewhere in this complicated mechanism, and gunsmiths were quick to design a combination implement that had a socket wrench (or spanner) at one end for winding the wheel and a screwdriver at the opposite end. This was the basic tool.

Almost every wheel lock shooter owned one. But the gadgeteers were not satisfied. Soon, more elaborate spanners with two, three or four screwdriver blades of varying sizes appeared. Vent picks to keep the touchhole clear were sometimes added. So were spring vises to clamp and remove springs in the lock. And some combination tools even included adjustable powder measures for pouring out exact loads according to the power desired or the range of the expected shot.

Once in a while, a hammer was also added for good measure, perhaps for shaping a piece of pyrite or for driving out a barrel

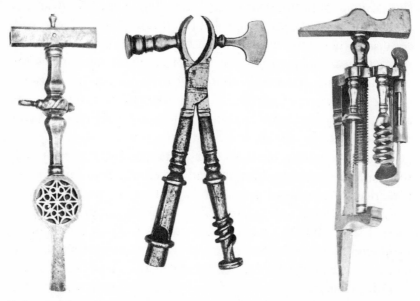

Left to right: Combination wheel lock spanner and screwdriver, seventeenth century. German huntsman's pocket tool, combining pliers, flint knapper, worm and dog whistle, late seventeenth or early eighteenth century. Combination tool with vent pick, spring vise, hammer, worm, bullet screw and screwdriver, made in the late 1600s or early 1700s. Courtesy Howard L. Blackmore.

pin. Sometimes all of these tools were combined in one magnificent gadget; sometimes they were divided into two tools, with the spanner and screwdriver on one and the hammer-spring clamp, vent pick and additional screwdrivers on another. With such a set, the most avid gadgeteer must have been completely happy. The complexity of these contrivances would especially tickle the fancy (and the ego) of a tyro to whom firearms were a novelty.

When flint arms appeared in the sixteenth century, the actual firing mechanism was simplified, yet almost all the tools remained. The spanner was no longer necessary, but the others could still be used. Though flint was harder than pyrite, it still became dull after many firings. When it did, a new flint had to be added or, if none was available, the old one had to be sharpened by chipping away near its edge. A hammer was therefore as useful as ever. So was a screwdriver for loosening the flint vise of the cock. (If the jaw screw of the flint vise was pierced instead of slotted, then a bar was needed instead of a screwdriver to loosen it.) Vent picks were still useful, and so were spring clamps.

By this time (the late seventeenth century), the military began to take an interest in combination gun tools. Commanders frowned on a soldier taking his own gun apart—this was a task reserved for an official armorer—but they recognized that every man who used a gun did have a need for changing or sharpening flints and tightening screws. Thus, most armies began to issue combination tools to the troops. The British soldiers who fought in the American Revolution, for instance, carried little devices made up of three screwdriver blades radiating out from a common center, and they also carried vent picks.

Timothy Pickering, the Quartermaster General of the Continental Army, suggested that soldiers should carry a little tool he had invented—combining a hammer, a screwdriver and a vent pick in one handy instrument, shaped somewhat like a hammer head. George Washington was greatly impressed with Pickering's ideas, but there is no evidence that his new gadget was ever actually used. American tools patterned after the British type remained standard as long as flintlock muskets were used, sometimes with one or more of the screwdriver heads modified to form a turning bar for a pierced-jaw screw, a vent pick, or possibly a carrier for a "gun worm." A worm was a device that could be attached to a ramrod for use in removing a load from the barrel. It resembled a corkscrew with two intertwining spirals and two points.

Private sportsmen were not often satisfied with these relatively simple tools. They were more intrigued by fancy gadgets that combined all these devices with pincers, whistles for calling dogs, cleaning implements, and all manner of other useful items. Accessories for gunsmiths and regimental armorers were something else again. These professional craftsmen began to outdo the amateur shooters in their love of ingenious contraptions—but for different reasons. Their portable tool kits, or sets, contained everything imaginable. Sometimes these sets included as many as a dozen pieces—each with one or more special uses—that hooked, screwed, or dovetailed into each other so that they could be picked up and carried as a unit. Quite possibly all of the gimmicks were useful, but in any event they testified to the skill and ingenuity of their owner.

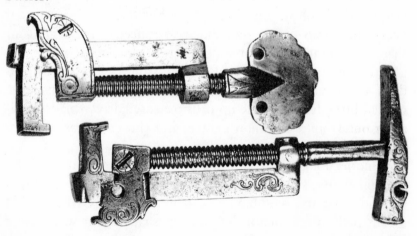

Two Spanish eighteenth-century spring vises for a miquelet lock. The specimen with the hammer is dated 1775. Courtesy James D. Lavin.

Timothy Pickering's design for a musket tool for the Continental Army. The letters *a* and *b* indicate screwdriver heads, *c* is a vent pick, *d* is a hammer.

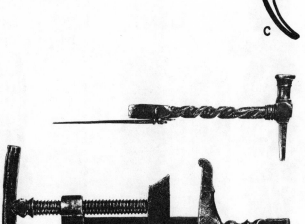

Two combination tools. The top one, probably German, dates from the seventeenth century and combines a hammer, two screwdrivers, and a vent pick. The lower specimen is Spanish and combines a hammer head shaped like an *eslabón* fire striker, a screwdriver and a spring vise. Courtesy J. P. Junot.

Spring vise and combination nipple wrench and screwdrivers for the U. S. Model 1855 rifled musket. Author's collection.

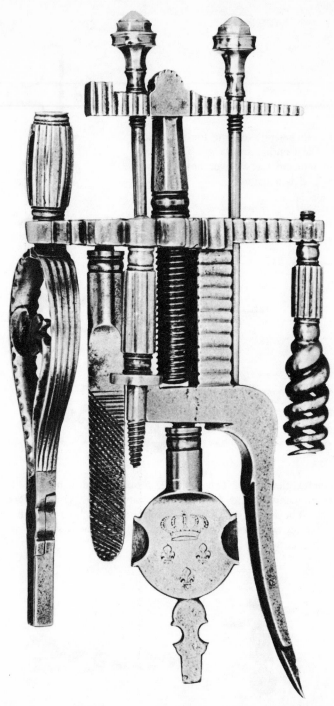

French regimental armorer's tool set, circa 1820. Courtesy Howard L. Blackmore.

In Spain there was an entirely different sort of tool called an *eslabón*. It was generally T-shaped, with the cross-bar serving as a hammer and the end of the vertical element providing a screwdriver. A vent pick was usually pivoted someplace on the instrument, and the top bar was normally serrated along its upper surface for use in striking a light with a flint.

With the advent of percussion arms, the need for a vent pick disappeared, but now the shooter might want to remove a mashed or badly fouled nipple. Therefore, a nipple wrench was added to the typical combination tool; the screwdriver remained, while the hammer disappeared with the vent pick. And dog whistles again appeared on a number of examples.

No matter when they were made, these little gadgets offer a wonderful field for the collector. Because so few people recognize them for what they are, the usual selling price for good combination tools has remained relatively low. Yet they offer a fine variety that differs with the type of arm for which they were designed. Some are relatively simple, others are highly complex and beautifully decorated, but all reflect a real ingenuity, since the ancient designer tried to combine as many functions as possible into one small instrument.

Special Collectors' Appendix

A
GUIDE TO
RESTORING
ANTIQUE ARMS

A Guide to Restoring Antique Arms

One old gun may be worth $100, while another specimen of the same model is worth two or three times that much—though the history of both pieces is exactly the same. The difference lies in their condition. In every phase of firearms collecting, a gun that appears "factory-new" or "as issued" is worth much more than the same model as a rusted relic. Between these two extremes are various stages of condition ranging from fair to excellent, or fine, and each step represents an increase in the monetary value of the arm. It is impossible to restore to fine shape a gun that is pitted by rust, but skillful cleaning and repair can do a great deal to improve it; in addition, careful maintenance can prevent an arm that's well preserved from sliding down the scale of desirability and value. Every owner of antique arms should understand the basic techniques of gun care and restoration. With them he can not only protect—or even enhance—his investment, but as an important bonus, he will learn a great deal about his guns and derive much extra pleasure from them.

Before describing the methods of restoration and preservation, I must stress that a single how-to treatise can't make you an expert in the wood- and metalwork that are occasionally needed to salvage a rare antique from the scrap pile. As a matter of fact, in some cases it is necessary to turn the piece over to a professional specialist—and in a few instances the gun won't be worth the effort and expense of trying to save it. The replacement of missing or broken parts will not always enhance an antique's value and in any event should be left to an expert. However, it is possible to offer some guidelines and hints, gained from many years of restoration work, which will enable any collector to maintain his guns properly. With experience, you will find that the proper techniques become easier and easier to apply, so if you have a gun that's worth very little or is in extremely poor condition, you'll be wise to use it as a "learning" piece. But regardless of what arm you want to work on, here are the procedures to follow:

Let's suppose that you have just acquired an antique firearm. It was a "steal" in a junk shop and is dirty and battered but seems worth the effort of cleaning and restoration. The first thing to do is to look it over carefully and learn as much as you can about it. Make sure you understand the action and are familiar with the parts. It might be a good idea to compare it with similar arms or study a reference work to determine what the original finish was like on all elements and what the gun looked like when new. With this information firmly in mind, thoroughly inspect your gun. First the wood: Are there any small round holes in it—evidence that it has been attacked by powder-post beetles, or "worms" as they are often called by collectors? If so, tap the wood sharply and see if a fine yellow dust falls out of the holes. This is a sign of continued activity, meaning that the voracious little creatures are eating away inside. Are there dents, scratches and breaks in the wood? Now the metal: Does any original finish remain on it? If it does, can it be saved or is it so far gone that it will have to be ignored? This is an important decision, because rebluing or rebrowning will lessen the value of an antique. Your work with the metal finish will therefore be limited to protecting what's already there or sacrificing it for the sake of other restorative operations. Once you've decided exactly what work is needed, you're ready to proceed.

Now, take the gun apart. Remember that a firearm is a

complex instrument, made of many parts and several materials. The techniques used to improve one sort of material will often harm another, so disassembly is a must. Also, both cleaning and preservative operations can be carried out much more efficiently if you can reach all sides of each part. Take the piece apart slowly and carefully. Loosen "frozen" screws with penetrating oil or kerosene; don't attempt to force them. Make sure you have the proper tools for the job. Most of them are the standard types that can be obtained at any hardware store —screwdrivers of appropriate sizes, a light hammer and a pair of pliers, etc.

In working on the locks of muzzle-loading arms, however, it is almost essential to have one specialized tool called a spring vise. Dealers in old guns frequently have these for sale, and they are extremely useful. Sometimes small C-clamps can be pressed into service for removing mainsprings, but a spring vise is much more efficient and with it there is less risk of snapping the spring.

(Most of the other tools and materials I'm going to mention in connection with various restorative procedures can be obtained from local suppliers—paint and hardware stores and even the supermarket. They include such items as detergent, kerosene, metal polishes, solvents, emery paper, steel wool, etc. In one or two instances, a product may be difficult to obtain locally and I will therefore give the address of the manufacturer. If no such address is given, you can buy the product in the nearest store that handles such articles.)

Once the gun has been taken apart, clean the accumulated dirt and old preservatives off the metal parts. Warm water with a little mild detergent in it is usually effective in getting off any form of dirt. Oils and grease will respond to a bath in kerosene or Stoddard's Solvent, while varnish will require a paint remover and hand scraping. Lacquer will normally come off easily with acetone or Stoddard's Solvent.

While the metal parts are soaking, you can begin work on the wood. If you've found evidence of active beetles, this is the very first problem to be attacked, for it is amazing how fast these creatures can completely ruin a gun stock (before moving on to your floors and furniture). If there are only a few holes, they can be approached individually with a syringe full of DDT or chlordane. Repeat this treatment, putting a shot in each hole at two-day intervals for a week, and you should clear up the infestation, but give the stock the tapping test again a month or so later just to be sure. If the wood is riddled with holes so that it is impractical to inject an insecticide into each one, the whole stock may be thoroughly soaked with the common poisoned denatured alcohol of the type sold at most filling stations. It is harmless to wood finish—except for shellac, which is rendered soft and gummy by this solution. If there is any doubt, test the alcohol on a small and inconspicuous place and check the results. After the piece has dried, it will have a white coat over its entire surface, formed by the poison in the alcohol. This can be removed by rubbing with an alcohol-soaked cloth, followed by a polishing with a clean, soft rag. If the wood is coated with shellac, you will have to consult a professional, who will have other suitable insecticides on hand.

Dents and many scars in a battered stock may be removed by moistening the area, covering it with a wet cloth and holding a steam iron about an inch above it. The heat and moisture will work wonders in swelling the crushed and bruised fibers back to their original shape. Be careful, because if you press the iron directly to the cloth or wood, you may leave a scorch mark.

The appearance of most stocks can be improved by treating them with a mixture of equal parts of boiled linseed oil, vinegar, and turpentine. This liquid is painted on, allowed to remain for a few minutes, and then wiped off with a soft cloth. For a finer appearance, this process should be repeated several times. Some military stocks were originally finished with linseed oil alone, and these can be vastly improved by further treatments of boiled linseed oil without the vinegar and turpentine. Never use raw linseed oil, for it will not dry properly and will leave a gummy residue. Most of the dirt found on old gunstocks will be automatically removed during these processes. More stubborn patches or paint spots can be cleaned off with fine steel wool or by gentle scraping with a knife blade while the wood is wet with oil.

One of the frequent blemishes on a gun stock is caused by the cleaning of metal parts without removing them from the stock. The chemicals and abrasives used may take off the wood's finish and leave light-colored areas. These discolorations can normally be restored to their proper hue by the use of oil paints mixed with linseed oil. This combination is rubbed on the light area and allowed to soak in, then rubbed off. These oil colors are the same as those used by artists and can be purchased in small tubes at art-supply stores. A good selection of colors to have on hand would be browns and reds such as raw umber, burnt umber, carmine, and burnt sienna. For walnut stocks, burnt umber will usually match the color of the rest of the wood. Mahogany and cherry will require some red.

This is all that should normally be done to the stock of an antique firearm. Complete refinishing reduces the arm's value, and unless you are a skilled cabinetmaker, the repair of broken stocks and the inletting of wood to replace damaged or missing pieces will be too much for you. Such jobs should be left to professionals.

With the stock work finished or well on the way, it is time to return to the metal parts—which should now be completely cleaned of dirt and old preservatives. Most of these parts will be iron or steel—ferrous metals that pose problems in cleaning and maintenance. These metals will rust, as every collector knows, and rust is highly destructive. Once this process of oxidation has begun, all active rust should be removed or it is apt to continue underneath any protective coat that may be applied. The black stains known generally as "inactive rust" can be stabilized and left without further injury to the gun; this stabilization can be accomplished by heat and a coat of lacquer, wax or silicone preparation, as described below.

There are two common ways to remove rust from metal— a chemical process or a mechanical one. In recent years, the chemical method has become more and more popular because it offers a saving in labor. A number of different commerical rust removers are on the market with various trade names, but most of them are based upon hydrochloric acid, phosphoric acid or ammonium citrate. While they are all effective rust removers, they also etch the metal slightly, despite claims to the contrary; if parts are left immersed too long, this etching can become severe enough to ruin a piece. These commercial rust removers are also injurious to springs and should not be used on them.

The slight etching of the metal results in a dull lead color on pieces cleaned with chemicals. This can normally be polished off with abrasives, but the same abrasive effort will go a long way toward cleaning the piece mechanically, without the use of any chemical. It will also result in a far finer finish than can be obtained with a chemical cleaner, and will eliminate one of the great hazards of chemical cleaning—the destruction of the original blued or browned finishes. Most blued or browned surfaces are produced by artificial oxidation of the metal. This oxidation is a form of controlled rust, and any chemical rust remover quickly takes off this finish as well as the rust you want to remove. A number of professional preservators who restore antique guns use rust removers because of the amount of work they must do. They are skilled in the use of these chemicals and they know that they are sacrificing some quality in order to turn out the necessary quantity of work. The collector who is interested only in putting his own pieces into as fine condition as possible, however, would be well advised to leave all such chemical cleaners alone.

If you decide in favor of mechanical cleaning, you have a number of methods and materials to choose from. The most important rule to remember is to go slowly and to avoid too coarse or too powerful an abrasive. Harsh overcleaning can ruin a specimen just as surely as the ravages of time, and it takes many hours of patient work to eliminate deep scratches caused by too coarse an abrasive and/or too much power in applying it. Generally speaking, it is well to do all such cleaning by hand. Leave the motor-driven buffer and wire wheel to experts; these devices can take off too much metal.

For cleaning and brightening iron that isn't blued or browned, there are a number of good abrasives on the market. The one you choose will depend on your personal preference. Some preservators like to use steel wool, which can be obtained in a number of grades of coarseness. Others prefer fine emery paper in various grades—depending on whether it's to be used for a first, rough cleaning or for finer polishing. Personally, I use Wetordry TRI-M-ITE abrasive paper, made by the Minnesota Mining and Manufacturing Company and available at hardware stores. It comes in a number of "grits," with numerical designations; 320 will suffice for very rough work, 400 for average and 600 for fine, fine finishing. After completing the rubbing with the 600 grit, the worn-out pieces of the paper may be dipped in water and used again for a final polishing.

If you have a blued or browned surface that you wish to retain, the cleaning process is more delicate. The pieces should be soaked thoroughly in kerosene to soften the rust, and then scoured gently with fine steel wool. Bluing and browning are remarkably tough coatings, and it is surprising how much will be left underneath a surface rust. Instead of using steel wool for an all-over cleaning, some preservators prefer to work only on the rust spots themselves, scraping these places with a razor blade or strip of brass. This is a slightly tricky operation, however, and you must be very careful not to scratch the surfaces near the rust spots.

Some old gun barrels were browned with a lacquer instead of an oxidized coating. These will not rust unless the lacquer coat has been scratched or otherwise damaged. With such a gun, you must work on the individual places where such injury has occurred, while protecting the remaining lacquer as carefully as possible. Needless to say, such original lacquer browning should not be subjected to any solvents in attempting to remove dirt and old grease before cleaning. Even a soaking in water should be avoided because moisture might penetrate under portions of the coat that has slightly loosened, thereby producing rust.

The inside of a bore can usually be cleaned by running ordinary oiled rags or patches through it. If this doesn't do the job, you can use a wire brush and one of the commercial penetrating oils that are made for such work.

Once the iron parts of your gun have been cleaned to your satisfaction, the next step is to apply a preservative that will keep them from rusting in the future. In the old days, the standard procedure was to apply a coat of oil, and this works quite well. When applied to the metal, the oil quickly penetrates pits and crevices and offers good protection. It also provides lubrication for moving parts. But oil has drawbacks as well. For one thing, a protective oil coating is apt to come off when it is handled, leaving an area of the iron unprotected. Also, oil tends to collect dust and thereby dull the finish of the gun in a few weeks' time.

Despite these drawbacks, oil still has its place in caring for firearms. Generally speaking, oil or grease should always be used for the insides of locks or actions when moving parts are involved, and for the bore, where the other types of preservative are not so efficient. Any sort of oil that will adhere well will serve for this task. The best are the new synthetic-diester types, which outperform all of the older sperm or petroleum oils. Most of these new synthetics are sold only in large commercial quantities, but there is one called Anderol, manufactured by the Lehigh Chemical Company, Chestertown, Maryland, that is merchandised in small quantities specifically for gun care.

For outside surfaces there are several other kinds of preservatives to choose from, including lacquers, waxes and silicones, singly or in combination. Before applying any of these, however, it is essential that the metal surface be absolutely clean. Otherwise, the coatings will not adhere properly. Wipe the metal carefully with a cloth, or perhaps even with Stoddard's Solvent if there is no original lacquer surface that might be harmed. And wear cotton gloves on your hands while you are doing it. Even a fingerprint will lessen the effectiveness of the protective coating.

If you decide to use a lacquer, there are a number of good ones available at paint and hardware stores. Those manufactured by the Stoner-Mudge Company of Pittsburgh are excellent, for instance. So is Krylon, which can be otained in most hardware and drug stores. Krylon has the added advantage of coming in a pressure can, ready to spray on the clean metal. If you decide to try another brand, however, be sure to buy a lacquer preparation and not a varnish. Varnish will not adhere tightly to metal, it is not waterproof and will not remain clear and transparent as lacquer will. The chief drawbacks to using lacquer are the difficulty in obtaining a good even coat, without skips or ripples, and the ease with which the coat can be injured by scratching or chipping. Such damaged spots are often very hard to notice—until rust begins to form on them.

Waxes are far more durable than lacquers, and they are at least as effective if not more so. There are many good brands on the market; just be sure to read the label and pick one with a good carnauba base rather than a synthetic, which may have some acid or water in it. Simoniz has been a standard for many years, and it is excellent except for very rough surfaces where it is apt to remain an opaque white in pits and crevices that cannot be reached with the polishing cloth. For such rough surfaces, a purer carnauba wax should be used; good ones are the Esquire and Griffin transparent paste shoe polishes. Be careful not to use just any neutral shoe polish, however, since some contain tannic acid, which may be good for leather but is not recommended for iron. Sears, Roebuck markets automobile wax made of carnauba and silicone, and this is also an excellent product for iron preservation.

All of the products mentioned above are paste waxes. These generally give the best results. There are, however, some preservatives currently on the market that consist of a wax in a volatile solvent. These are sprayed on the metal, and in a short time the solvent evaporates and leaves a waxy coat behind. All such products that have been tested so far, however, have left a fairly soft coating. This is efficient as a rust preventive, but it has a tendency to collect dust and dirt.

A final useful product for preserving iron or steel surfaces is silicone. Cloths impregnated with silicone can be purchased in most sporting-goods stores. They are very effective, but the coating they leave is not as permanent as a wax finish. It must be renewed at regular intervals for absolute safety.

Once the iron has been taken care of, it is time to look after the other metals often found on old guns. Normally these include brass or bronze, pewter, silver, gold and possibly a little platinum. All of them are soft and will scratch very easily. Handle them gently and use mild abrasives for cleaning. For brass, bronze and pewter, a mixture of precipitated chalk and ammonia is very effective. You can mix this yourself or buy it under trade names such as Noxon. Other brass polishes are also effective and harmless, provided they are not too harsh and do not contain any chlorides such as are often included in cleaners designed for kitchen and bathroom use. Silver is softer still, and polishes such as Noxon are too harsh. Goddard's Non-Mercurial Plate Powder is an excellent silver polish. So is Silverbath. A new liquid product, Hagerty Tarnish Preventive, manufactured by W. J. Hagerty & Sons, South Bend, Indiana, is also excellent and contains a tarnish inhibitor that is reasonably effective.

The only really certain tarnish preventive for brass, pewter and silver is lacquer. None of the so-called anti-tarnish waxes have proved successful in the long run. Learning to apply lacquer either by brush or from a spray can requires practice. When it is done properly, the coating is invisible, and it offers real protection for many months. Once again, make sure the surface is absolutely clean before applying the lacquer—and do it immediately after you have finished polishing the piece. Dulling and tarnishing set in very quickly.

Gold and platinum do not tarnish. All that is necessary is to remove any dirt that has accumulated on them. Often, you can simply use warm water and a neutral detergent. If the coating is troublesome, a 10 percent solution of household ammonia in water will normally clean it off. No protective coat need be applied.

All of these suggestions have been for antique arms in relatively good condition. With the growing popularity of mine-detector exploring for relics, an increasing number of collectors own badly damaged arms that they are interested in preserving. As a rule, these can never be restored even to fair condition; they must be treated as historic relics rather than handsome collectors' items. The main thing is to remove all dirt and loose rust and to stabilize them so that they do not continue to deteriorate. Museums achieve this with elaborate electrolytic treatments that are not practical for the private collector. The best thing to do is to remove the dirt and loose rust scales by hand. Tapping gently with a light hammer will take off much of the scaly crust. Follow this with a stiff bristle brush, and clean out crevices with a metal pick. Excellent picks can be made by having dental tools ground down; the broken ones that your family dentist throws away almost every month are fine for use on old iron. When you have worked the surface down to a stable level, warm the piece by putting it in an oven or on a radiator or stove top. Then melt some wax (preferably ceresin, but beeswax will do) in the top of a double boiler. Use a low flame to avoid accidental fires, and never use paraffin because of its low flash point.

When the wax is melted, brush it on the warm metal with a soft paint brush and let it thoroughly impregnate the rust. This will prevent further rusting and will also give the relic a pleasing, uniformly dark finish. Small guns may be attached to wires and immersed directly in the melted wax. This is really the best way of applying the wax, and museums prepare long tanks so that they can dip entire shoulder arms, stocks and all.

Dozens of techniques and materials can be employed to restore and care for antique firearms, and I have included only the most generally useful methods and products. Many refinements can only be learned by experience, but there are two books that can be of great help to the collector who wants to go into the subject deeply. One of these is *Antique Firearms, Their Care, Repair & Restoration,* by Ronald Lister, Crown Publishers, New York, New York. This gives excellent instructions for taking most muzzle-loading arms apart, for assembling tools and for making a great many minor repairs, but it almost completely ignores cleaning methods and preservatives. For those who want to understand all the basic chemistry and physics for the conservation of all sorts of materials, the standard reference used by all professionals is H. J. Plenderleith's *The Conservation of Antiquities and Works of Art,* Oxford University Press, New York, New York.

I hope that these tips will encourage some readers to delve more deeply into the study of restoring and preserving old firearms—but the main purpose of each suggestion has been to guide the average owner who wants to keep his guns looking as handsome as possible and prevent them from diminishing in value. By following these suggestions, you will be able to turn many a second-rate antique gun into a real delight.

Index

Adams and Kerr revolvers, 63, 65
Afghanistan, 278, 379, 380–81
Africa, 252, 253–54, 256–61
Aiming (accuracy), 10–11, 43–53 *passim*, 116, 117–18, 127–30, 190, 223, 269–70, 287 (*see also* Sharpshooters and sharpshooting; Target contests; specific kinds and makes of firearms); crossbows, 5, 6; dueling, 202–3
Air guns, 24, 239–44
Alamo, Texas, 105, 123
Albertus Magnus, 291, 292
Algonkian Indians, 96
Allen, Cyrus Ballard, 125, 126
Allen (Ethan) pepperboxes, 267, 268–70
Allin, Erskine S., 53, 145–49
Amateur Rifle Club, 194
American Committee of Safety muskets, 42
American Revolution. *See* Revolutionary War
American rifle, 115–18. *See also* Kentucky rifle
Americans. *See* United States and the Americans
Ames, Nathan Peabody, 125
Ammunition, 291–94, 295–300, 301–6, 307–12 (*see also* Bullets; Cartridges; Gunpowder; specific kinds and makes of weapons); breechloading, 32–37, 147, 191; Civil War, 49, 50–53, 55–56, 78–81; explosive, 78–81; hunting, 215, 216, 221; Indian

wars, 147; molds, 307–12; Revolutionary War, 42–44, 299, 303; rocket, 271–75
Anderol, 330
Anderson, "Bloody" Bill, 224
Anderson, General Patton, 72
Angular bayonets, 91, 92, 93
Anne, Queen of England, 98
Ansbach, Germany, 46
Antique firearms: bullet molds, 312; restoration and care, 323–34
Antique Firearms, Their Care, Repair & Restoration (Lister), 334
Antrey, Dock, 209–10
Apache Indians, 171, 174
Appomattox, 82
Arabia and the Arabs, 291, 292
Arizona, 171, 174
Armor, 58, 296, 300
Armstrong, Major, 132
Army, U. S., 53, 117, 266, 267 (*see also* Military, the; Ordnance Department, U. S.; specific individuals, inventions, locations, units, wars, weapons); bayonets, 89 (*see also* Bayonets); gun tools, 315–17; Indians and (*see* Indians and Indian wars); machine guns, 20–21, 266, 304; in Philippines, 251–55; revolvers, 60–66, 69–72, 83, 138–39, 151, 153 (*see also* specific kinds and makes); rifles, 53, 117, 142–43, 145–49 (*see also* specific kinds and makes);